Falvey's Guide to
Fishing Long Island

By Kevin Falvey

Published by Schiffer Publishing Ltd.
Falvey's Guide to Fishing Long Island was originally published by Geared Up Publications, LLC. in 2009.

Library of Congress Control Number: 2012938141

ISBN: 978-0-9787278-2-6
Printed in the United States of America

Schiffer Books are available at special discounts for bulk purchases for sales promotions or premiums. Special editions, including personalized covers, corporate imprints, and excerpts can be created in large quantities for special needs. For more information contact the publisher:

Published by Schiffer Publishing Ltd.
4880 Lower Valley Road
Atglen, PA 19310
Phone: (610) 593-1777; Fax: (610) 593-2002
E-mail: Info@schifferbooks.com

For the largest selection of fine reference books on this and related subjects, please visit our website at **www.schifferbooks.com**
We are always looking for people to write books on new and related subjects. If you have an idea for a book, please contact us at proposals@schifferbooks.com

This book may be purchased from the publisher.
Please try your bookstore first.
You may write for a free catalog.

In Europe, Schiffer books are distributed by
Bushwood Books
6 Marksbury Ave.
Kew Gardens
Surrey TW9 4JF England
Phone: 44 (0) 20 8392 8585; Fax: 44 (0) 20 8392 9876
E-mail: info@bushwoodbooks.co.uk
Website: www.bushwoodbooks.co.uk

"We are all apprentices in a craft where no one becomes a master."

—Ernest Hemmingway, In a letter.

"They're waiting there for me. Running deep."

—Joan Baez, "Fishing."

"I am, Sir, a brother of the Angle."

—Izaak Walton, "The Complete Angler."

"Fisherman: A jerk at the end of a line waiting for a jerk at the end of a line."

--Anonymous

THIS BOOK IS DEDICATED TO CHARLES FALVEY.

If there's fish in heaven, Dad, "Catch 'em up big."

Foreword

Long Island's waters are blessed with a diversity of marine life. Even we, who spend lots of time on the water, may not fully appreciate this. It has always been so, though, some species, once regularly sought by sport fishermen, are currently not as numerous as they once were. I say currently, because I have an abiding belief in the replenishing power of the ocean's vastness. In just my short life, I've witnessed declines and rebounds of several fish. Most notably are the striped bass, the weakfish and the fluke. Sure these may have been helped by the management measures. But despite the efforts of politicians and scientific experts, we cannot discount history. Records and recounts going back to the age of the Vikings tell of decades of

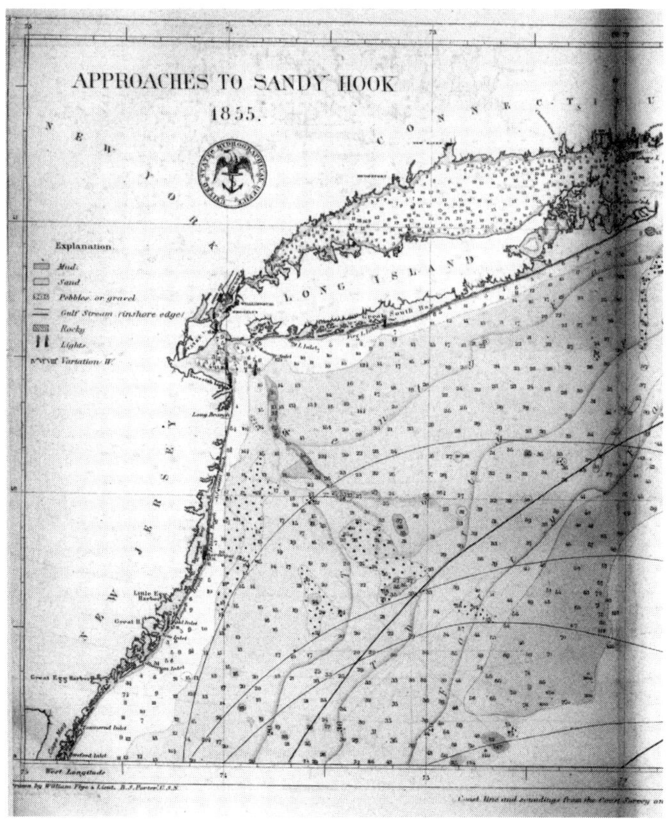

feast, followed by those of famine, as certain species inexplicably waned, and then, just as suddenly, became abundant once more. Records from Europe, Asia and the Mediterranean, records even older than those relating to this continent, say the same thing. Nature does nothing uselessly.

Still, many species that I caught inshore in 1960's and 1970's, are not numerous enough to pursue with regularity today. Cod can be caught in the deep ocean, but fishing them in 60 or 80 feet outside our inlets isn't really viable. The same holds for whiting, which I can remember catching from the winter surf at Rockaway as a kid, under the tutelage of my grandfather. This "frost fishing" is no longer a deal that will pay-off. The same can be said of blowfish and kingfish. It is the dearth of these fish inshore, and at the time of this writing, that led me to leave them out of this book. Do not make the mistake of leaving them out of your consciousness. They will come back. You read it here first.

A lot of folks helped with this book, and in a variety of ways. The fishing charts are courtesy of Maptech, thanks to Martin Fox. I used Chart Navigator Pro software running on a PC to generate the custom images herein.

Many of the images, including the neat, sepia-toned line drawings, and all underwater photography, are courtesy of NOAA's Historical Fisheries Library and the collection of the Northeast Fisheries Science Center at Woods Hole, Massachussets. Special thanks to Brenda Figueri at Woods Hole. These images are our tax dollars at work, so enjoy them. Ditto New York State DEC and New York Sea Grant, for the Fishing Access Map and Launch Ramp Locator provided for your convenience in the back of the book.

Most of the "grin and grab" fishing shots I photographed myself. But really they are courtesy of my many good friends, too numerous to list, who put up with my shutter-buggery, often during a hot bite. To you all a collective "Thanks."

Special Thanks, alphabetically, to: Hank Altenkirch, Capt. Tred Barta (*Makiara,* Shinnecock), Bill "Saltweed" Bennett, Bob Bossung, Capt. Elly Brown (*Do Stay*, Jupiter, FL); the late Charles Falvey, the late Pat Heany, Sr., Capt. Tim Hermus (*M & M Charters*, Westhampton, NY), Capt. Scott Horowitz (*Lady Pamela*, Shinnecock, NY), the late Capt. Martin Landy (*Indulgence*, Shinnecock, NY), Peter Mulligan; Capt. Capt. David Parsons (*Hakuna Matata*, Miami, Fl.), Capt. John Raguso (*MarCeeJay*,

Babylon, NY), The crew of the Party Boat, Capt Al (when it was berthed in Freeport), the crew of the old party boat Capt. Hall (Freeport, New York), The crew of the long-gone livery, Bills Boats (Port Washington, NY), The 1980's crew of Scotty's Fishing Station, Pt. Lookout, NY. All of you helped me, in ways beyond description, to better pursue my passion for fish, boats, and the sea.

There's lots of biological information presented. An understanding of the ocean, and its inhabitants, (as much as they can be understood, anyway), is as much a part of fishing as anything. The bulk of this information comes from personal experience. But, despite a lifetime on the water, I remain an amateur naturalist. To make sure it was right, Bigelow and Schroeder's "Fishes of the Gulf of Maine" was a constant companion, as was, "The First Year in the Life of Estuarine Fishes in the Middle Atlantic Bight," by Kenneth W. Able. I also spoke with divers, commercial fisherman, and other sport fishermen to confirm my "gut and observation." Thanks all.

Those I need to thank most for writing this book are those dearest to me—my daughters Keira and Margaret.

TABLE OF CONTENTS

Introduction

The impetus for this book came from a recurring experience. Upon returning to the dock, I'm frequently asked by those who don't have the luxury of fishing as much as I do: "Where did you catch them?" Always "where?" Few ever ask "why." It is the better question.

To consistently catch fish, you have to think like a fish (and fish a lot). Learn its habits, determine its needs, and observe the natural conditions in which it feeds. A spot that produces on incoming water and a west wind may be void of life on falling water and a south breeze, or incoming and an east wind. Or perhaps the outgoing water is too warm, making the fish too sluggish to chase a drifted bait, but more than willing to respond to one placed and worked right in front of their nose. Or maybe the fish are there, but conditions prevent presenting your bait properly. It might pay to leave a "honey-hole" and try elsewhere where bait presentation isn't impeded. Tried and true does work. But flexibility, an absorptive mind-set, and the ability to see how two spots, miles apart, might provide identical feeding conditions under different environmental conditions, are the qualities I strive for when fishing. It is a process. And I try to learn something new every time I go out.

So, while I packed this book with "how-to" and "where-to" information, the text and charts are not absolute. I know the spots are good—I've fished each one of them. But you gotta know why, so you can figure out when, and finally, where. No book can teach that. You gotta get on the water and do it. I hope only to illuminate a path, shown to me by others: Consider what that fish needs and wants, with every plan you make, with every knot you tie, and with every bait you dunk. For me, doing so is as exciting as having a fish bend the rod, pull some drag, or beat a tattoo onto the deck with its tail.

East Quogue, New York
2008

CHAPTER 1

Winter Flounder

(Pseudopleuronectes americanus)

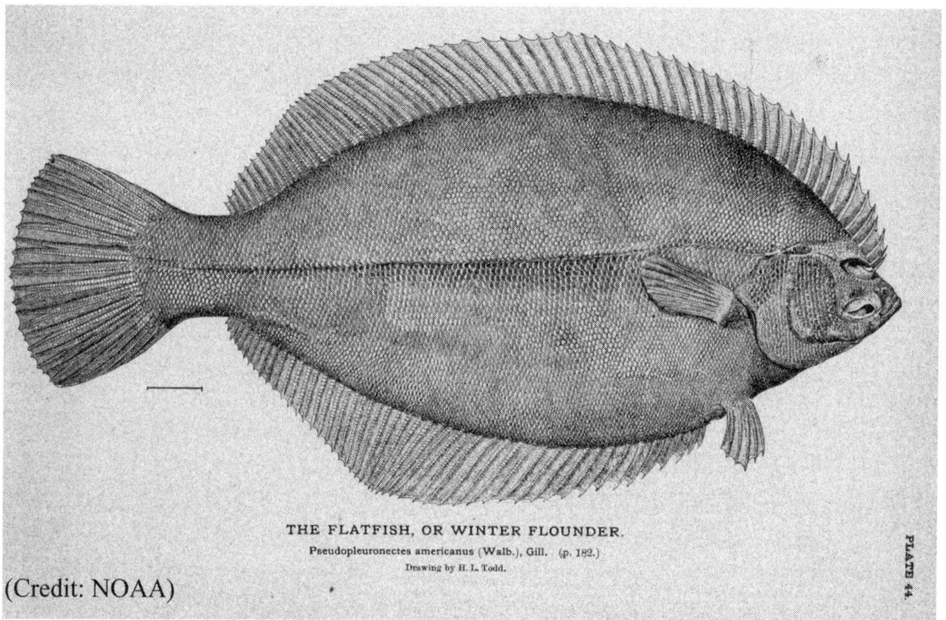

(Credit: NOAA)

Flounder represent much more than their small size and diminutive fighting ability suggests. They are the fish that everybody eats, so bringing home a bucketful makes family and friends cheer. They make great bait for other, harder fighting species, like weakfish, and especially striped bass. They are sought after by anglers of every ilk, from shore fisherman to those with gold-plater convertible fishing boats. And though not nearly as plentiful now as they were when I started fishing in the 1960's, their numbers have rebounded in this new millennium to a point that, with some effort and hopefully the help of this book, you can once again expect a respectable catch. Modern catch limits don't allow us to fill a skiff to the gunwales with flatties anyhow.

But the flounder's most endearing attribute is that it's the fish that gets the ball rolling every year. Yes, the mackerel arrive at about the same time. But the vast schools of those feisty mini-tunas have become unreliable in recent springs. So it is the flounder, a.k.a, flattie, or black back, that gets anglers blowing the dust off tackle, uncovering the boats, and, if they're savvy, hunting around for sources of fresh bait and chum. Once we're flounder fishing, we're fishing again, looking forward to a new season and a multitude of species that'll keep us busy 'til at least Thanksgiving. The flounder, then, represents more than an angling challenge, some tasty fillets, and a reason to be on the water. He is hope and catching him is an affirmation of faith.

TAXONOMY AND BIOLOGY

Winter flounder lie on their side. They start out life as juvenile fish looking like most other fishes, with a relatively long, conical body and with an eye on each side of the head. But they quickly become flatfish, the eye moving over to the left side, and begin to swim right-side-down, before they are even an inch long. These little "postage stamp" flounder are often caught in killifish traps, and, occasionally on hook and line. The flounder's mouth is small, with puffy lips, and a row of tiny teeth on the blind side. The eye side of the mouth is usually toothless. To differentiate from yellowtail flounder,

A winter flounder on the prowl…is she headed for your bait?
(Credit: NOAA)

another species that frequents Long Island waters, check the lateral line. That's the dark strip along the side that the flounder, like most fishes, uses to pick up vibrations in the water to indicate the presence of food or danger. On winter flounder, the lateral line is nearly straight. Yellowtail flounder have a curved lateral line. Don't be confused if you see a yellow tinge on the caudal peduncle—the stem of the tail—and think you've caught a yellowtail flounder because I've caught plenty of blackbacks showing some yellow. Check that lateral line. Compared to witch flounder, another less numerous Long Island species, winter flounder lack mucous pits on their head. Windowpane are a common by-catch while flounder fishing, and are easily distinguished from winter flounder by their transparency—hence the name—and by their shape: winter flounder are oblong and window pane are nearly as wide as they are long.

Winter flounder have some ability to change color to match the bottom conditions in which they are currently living, though not as much as other locally caught flatfish, such as fluke. Still, fish caught over mud bottoms tend to be darker and fish caught over sandy bottom tend to be lighter. This is not a hard and fast rule, however. For instance, I can remember skiff fishing with my dad at Oak Beach as a kid and literally mauling the fish, doubleheaders flying over the rail. Some of those fish were black, some were light tan, and this over a piece of bottom no larger than the length of the 14-foot tin boat we were anchored in. Mostly, the winter flounder will be a mottled grey brown, with more mottling showing in fish under a pound than in their larger brethren. On occasion you might catch a double-sided flounder, either white both sides or dark both sides. I've never been so lucky. But I have caught fish with white patches on the eye side and dark patches on the bottom side plenty of times.

The New York State record winter flounder weighed seven pounds, three and a half ounces and was caught in the near-shore Atlantic Ocean in 1997. Winter flounder larger than this have been captured by commercial fisherman offshore, particularly to the East, on Georges Bank, where five pound, two foot flounder don't raise eyebrows. So your first tip to use in catching flounder is: Do not to restrict yourself to the tried-and true flounder grounds; i.e., shallow, protected, bays and harbors. Expanded discussion of deepwater flounder fishing follows later in this chapter. Mostly though, you can expect to catch fish ranging in size from postage stamps up to about three pounds, with most fish falling in the one pound range.

Flounder can tolerate water temperatures down to about 30-degrees. Long Island waters temperatures rarely dip that low. Though the bays and harbors often freeze over, bottom temperatures remain somewhat warmer. (The opposite, ironically, of what happens in the warmer months, where surface temps are typically warmer than those on the bottom). Additionally, flounder are unique in that they have the ability to secrete anti-freeze protein (AFP) both into their blood and through their skin, providing protection, and thus the ability to move and feed, as the water chills. So you shouldn't be shy about flounder fishing if the snow flies. In fact I remember a great March day of flounder-pounding in Hempstead Harbor, near Bar Beach, during blinding snow squalls in a leaky wooden skiff rented from the now long-gone Bill's Boats. Of course, regulations at the time of this writing don't allow flounder fishing that early in the year anymore. But should the rules change, or should we have an especially cold April, remember AFP and the flounder's amazing ability to operate in the cold.

On the hot side, 70-degrees is about the hottest water flounder can tolerate. In fact a study conducted by divers in Great South Bay showed that flounder remained active in water temps, measured at the bottom, of 72-degrees. When the temp rose to 73-degrees, the fish in the study buried themselves in the bottom, where the temps were a few degrees cooler. This research bears out my personal experience of catching flounder for use as striper bait (before the size limit crested the 12" mark) in Shinnecock Bay. My log shows that I recorded surface temps as high as 70-degrees one particularly hot June while "making bait" by way of catching flounder. So don't let a spring hot spell ruin your hopes for a day of floundering. Ideal water temperature for actively feeding flounder is about 50-degrees, remembering that's its generally going to be a bit warmer on the bottom in the very early season and a bit cooler on the bottom as we get into May and June. The winter flounder's preferred inshore habitat is a sand/mud bottom and so much the better if there's some eel grass growing. As you may already know, this type of habitat is also likely to support hard clams, snails, and other life upon which the flounder feed. The edges of mussel beds are also typical habitat, though beds in which the mussels are so thick as to create a carpeted bottom tend not to produce as much. This is probably a result of how the winter flounder feeds and stalks its prey. Biologists tell us that flounder bury themselves into the bottom, protuberant eyes raised on stalks and rotating independently, looking for food. A thick, solid mussel bottom doesn't make for good burying. However, a bed in which baymen have been harvesting mussels, and in so doing leaving clusters, or "islands" of mussels between patches of bare bottom, is a prime spot to look for Mr. Winter Flounder. Mussel spat, the larval stage of the bivalve's life, is a prime food.

I'm not saying you won't catch flounder over hard sand, pebbly or even rocky bottom. You will. In fact the larger fish, those over three pounds, tend to move offshore and/or to deeper water where harder bottom predominates.

So what does a flounder eat? Even the biggest flounder has a tiny mouth, an important point to remember when baiting a hook. The aforementioned shellfish spat ranks high on the list. They also tear off the protruding siphons of clams. Filter feeders, clams have two siphons, one protruding from either side of the shell. They suck in water with one siphon, filter the food out it, and eject the water out the other. Tiny crabs, squids and seaworms also comprise their diet. Notable is the fact that they eat flounder eggs, which are often yellow in color. This suggests why using corn for chum can be very effective, and has been widely practiced over the years. Flounder don't cruise for prey. Instead, they tend to set up shop in one area, buried in the sand, and with their protuberant eyes rotating independently. When food is sighted, they lunge for it. If after a time no food is spotted, they move three or four feet, according the research, re-bury themselves and start looking again. That's probably why moving around, making several "drops," until you find fish, is often productive. Re-anchoring just a few yards away can really make your day. Expect to pull anchor and re-set a lot if you want to catch blackbacks.

Like all fish, flounder will use structure and current to their advantage. A hole, or the down-current side of a bar or hump, is a good spot to look for them, as bait tumbling over the edge is both disoriented and slowed down in the resulting eddy. Another likely spot is a flat at the edge of the main strength of the current. Eddies at the edge of current keep food moving by, but at a slower rate, so it's easier for flounder to catch its dinner. And, of course, you'll find them over fertile shellfish beds as described above, due to the abundance of food in one spot. Checking your charts, being aware or how the water flows, and paying attention to where baymen are working will all reap big dividends for you if you want to catch flounder. Most importantly, to catch flounder, or any fish, is to remember that they are wild animals, just like lions on the Serengeti or eagles in the Rocky Mountains. And like lions and eagles, flounder must practice conservation of energy.

They cannot expend more energy catching food than the total energy they'll derive from eating that food once they catch it. In the wild, animals and fish always use the environment to best advantage.

TACKLE AND RIGGING

Fiesty though they may be, flounder are small fish. Most that you catch will weigh less than two pounds. Tackle should be sized accordingly. My favorite flounder stick is a 5'6" graphite baitcasting rod with a trigger handle, and a fast action. The tip is sensitive, indicating the subtle change in weight that is sometimes the only indication that a flounder has bit. But it's not so soft as to collapse under the weight of up to three ounces of lead. (Even when you don't need that much weight to hold bottom, a big sinker lets you pound the bottom by jigging the rod, more successfully) The stiff backbone makes it easier to lift and swing a flounder over the rail and into your pail. The trigger grip is a personal preference, but I find it more comfortable when I'm holding a rod for a whole tide, especially if the flounder like a jigged bait (more on this to follow). To this rod, custom made by Altenkirch, as are all my rods, I mount a conventional reel loaded with 15-pound test mono. You can fish this setup from a skiff over a Jamaica Bay flat to the deeper waters of Long Island Sound and it will serve you equally well.

I never leave the dock without at least two rods. For flounder pounding, my alternate stick is a 6-foot spinning rod, fast action, graphite, to which I mount a light spinning reel loaded with 10-pound mono. This allows the flounder to give a sporty account of itself. It also makes it easier for me to prospect around the boat, casting out and s-l-o-w-l-y retrieving my baited hooks, looking for fish that either aren't directly below, or are there and just aren't interested for reasons of their own. Plus, on some days the fish prefer a moving bait. You can drop this down to the tiniest ultralight spinning outfit if you like, say a four pound class trout outfit. Personally, I don't like going that light. For one thing, you're bound to snag weed, polyps, the mussel bed, eel grass or whatever during the course of the day. The gossamer stuff just breaks off when this happens, whereas when you have a little beef—but not to much—you can free a snag without breaking off and having to re-tie. Plus, tying knots in spider silk is for eyes younger than mine.

Terminal tackle is the tried and true tandem rig. You can make the rig from scratch, but I buy the components pre-tied and just do the final assembly. It consists of a pair of number 6 hooks, I prefer sproats over the old Chestertown style, on foot-long 20 pound leaders each with a yellow corn bead. The leaders come pre-tied with loops at their ends. To make the tandem rig, bend one leader in half, and insert it through the tied loop of the other leader. Now take the hook of that second leader and pass it (don't forget the corn bead!) through the loop formed by the bend in the first leader. Pull tight, them make an overhand knot with the second leader right at the point where the two leaders are now connected to prevent the "catspaw" from slipping. (Catspaw means running the entire loop knot through the eye of the sinker or swivel and then bringing the hardware back through the loop.) You now have a single leader with a loop at the top from and from which two hooks splay outwards. Connect this to your line using a three-way swivel with a sinker snap. Simply take the loop at the head of the leader and pass it through one eye of the three-way. Now pass both hooks, again including those corn beads, through the leader loop and pull tight, catspawing it in place. I use an Improved Clinch knot to connect the other eye of the three-way to my running line. You can use a Uniknot, a Palomar, whatever. Most times, though, I use the Improved Clinch for connecting terminal tackle. It serves me well. Finally, attach a sinker of appropriate weight to hold bottom—plus a little more for more effective pounding.

You can dress up your terminal rigging in several ways. In fact, I like to start out with one rig "decorated" one way, and another rig bedecked differently. This allows me to see if the fish have a preference for one rig over the other, which often they will, on any given day and even during different stages of the tide. I usually fish two rods while floundering, holding one in each hand. Sometimes I'll even dead-stick a third, placing it in a rod holder, the reel in free spool and the clicker on. (A fourth hook, tied to the chum pot, though not sporting, has also put fish in the boat for me. I'm a meat fisherman when it comes to flounder and not shy about it.) So even when fishing solo, I can present a variety of rigs to see what the fish like. If you're fishing with buddies, setup one guy one way, one guy another, and yourself a third. If a pattern emerges, switch everyone over to what's catching. So what are these variations in rigging?

Well, you can paint your sinkers. My log books show that yellow works best, though red has had its days as well. The tackle purveyors now offer a variety of rubbery coatings that you can simply dip your sinkers into and achieve a bright, durable coating. These work well. Of course, I've been painting sinkers since before the advent of such high tech chemistry and have found leftover house paint to work just fine.

Another variation is a substitute for the corn bead. Instead, try using a small yellow, pink, or red plastic grubtail slid up the shank of your hook. Ditto for tiny squid skirts in the same colors. Just make sure these artificials are far enough from the point and bend of the hooks so that they don't interfere with baiting the hooks. Glow sticks are another alternative. Small inch-long glow sticks in yellow, red or green can be attached to your leader with a small piece of fish tank tubing. Get some tubing the same diameter as the glow sticks. Slide this on the leaders before tying them in tandem. The glow sticks can be force-slid into the tubing to hold them in place. Neat, simple and no knots.

All of these, and in any combination, have been proven to work. Again, remember that the scientists say flounder sometimes eat their own eggs, and eggs of other fish. Often, fish eggs are yellow, pink and green. So there you are. Just don't forget to fish a plain bait, too. Some days, the fish give naked bait the nod. The point is not to be shy about experimenting to find a bite.

CHUMMING

You must chum to catch flounder. But chumming comes in many forms. At its most basic, and easiest, is to deploy a chum pot filled with clam or mussels over the side of the boat. Frozen mussel and clam chum is readily available at your tackle store. Be advised to pay attention to current and water temperature when buying chum before you leave the dock. In warmer water and/or in faster currents, you will go through chum more quickly. There's no formula for this, although I find a quart log of chum, solidly frozen and transported to the grounds on ice, lasts two hours max. So, for example, carry more chum during the full moon, when currents are faster, or later in the season when water temperatures are warmer. Keep it iced for best result. Doing so also allows you to re-freeze chum with good success. Chum that has completely defrosted and then refrozen will get freezer burn and not be as effective when you try to re-use it.

Another way to chum, and one in which you can be sure of providing the freshest scent in the water, is by cracking whole skimmer clams over the side. Skimmer, also called surf clams, can be purchased from some tackle shops. I prefer to find a commercial clam distributor and buy them by the bag. I shuck some for bait and use the bulk for chum. You'll need a billy club—a sawed off ball bat works well—and good hand eye coordination to chum with whole skimmer.

Assuming you're right-handed pick up your billy with your right hand and a clam with your left. Place the clam against the billy club, and bring both clam and club up over your shoulder. Now, in one motion, come down with both hands, releasing the clam and batting it hard enough to crack it. It will sink to the bottom and stay pretty close to your boat. The party boat mates are the absolute pros at this, and if you fish with these guys, you'll notice that they often throw two or even three clams up in the air and simply bat at them as they drop. This works too, but tends to spatter shell bits and clam juice all over the boat. I'm not a fastidious fisherman, but why add to the day end clean-up. Pick your poison. You can apply the same cracking technique to mussels. I do it a bit differently. Rather than bat at the mussels, I place a handful in a bucket and crush them with my billy club. Then I pour the mess overboard. Works pretty good.

Other methods of chumming also require props. They are proven fish attractors and the reason that fishing for flounder is often called flounder pounding. Get yourself a couple of old sash weights. Tough to get nowadays, since everyone's got thermopane windows, I fiercely guard the ones I still have. Check garage sales or ask a contractor whose renovating an old house to set some aside for you. If you can't find sashweights, small, eight pound mushroom anchors, rubber coated, are available at marine supply houses. An onion sack half-filled with rocks will also work as a pounder. In any case, tie a stout clothesline to your pounder and drop them over the side, lifting and dropping them into the muck. As you do so, you'll be stirring up puffs of sand, silt, and mud, and releasing small invertebrates, crustaceans, and fish eggs into the current to draw Mr. Blackback towards your baited hooks. In addition to creating a visual ruckus, and releasing scent and food, you are sending out vibrations. Flounder are very curious, and though they don't move too far to get food unless they absolutely have too, the pounding gets their attention. So before I move the boat to make another drop 20 yards away, I always pound furiously for a few minutes to see what develops. I do the same thing when I first get to a spot. During the normal course of fishing, though, a couple of lift and drops every few minutes is all that's required.

You can also stir'em up. Get yourself a stick, oar or push pole and stir the muck and sand. This is effective, though its harder work than pounding. In shallow water, a variation on stirring involves using your boat to stir things up. When I first arrive at a three or four foot deep fishing hole, I sometimes drive the boat around in a fairly high-rpm circle. Not enough to get the prop in the mud mind you, but enough so that the prop's wash kicks up the bottom and, hopefully, jump-starts the bite. In deeper water, drop your anchor 'til it just kisses the bottom, and drag it around in reverse for a bit to get the same effect. A final twist on stirring involves finding a clam digger. A bayman raking leaves a trail of sand and food down-current of his position. More than one of my clamming buddies has told me how they have caught flounder in the rake or in tongs. Set up down-current of such a gentleman—don't crowd him, he's working, your playing—or wait until he leaves and then jump in his grave.

In any case be aware of the current when chumming. Dump or bat your bivalves off the bow if you're in water deeper than 15 feet so that the current takes the chum closer to your hook baits. Deploy the chum pot from amidships. Stir from forward of the hook baits. In any chumming scenario, it's good to have the fish follow up the chum line and come across your baits just as though it was so much more of the chum itself. And just what bait should you use in your quest for as bucket load of tasty flatties?

BAIT

It's been discussed that clams, worms, mussels, grass shrimp and other crustaceans, copepods, and cephalopods, in both the mature and immature phases, are all food for flounder. All are worthy flounder baits, but there's some reality to consider: I wouldn't have a clue as to how to get my hands on some mummichog eggs or a batch of larval squid. Therefore, the range of baits you can tempt flounder with is limited to a degree, though still broad enough that some choices are in order.

First off, always have at least two kinds of bait. Just as we fish with a variety of terminal rigging until we determine what the fish want on a given day or tide, I'll also setup different rods with different bait. In fact, I start out with one bait on one hook of the tandem rig, and a different bait on the other. A second rod gets a different combination. You get the picture.

Clam is probably the most popular flounder bait and it works well.

I like fresh skimmer clam when I can get it but have put together respectable catches with frozen, pre-schucked bait as well. Cut clams into one inch strips in such a way that a part of the clam's gooey "belly" (intestine) is part of the bait. Flounder relish clam belly. Don't go with the "glob for a slob" theory. Flounder have small mouths, so keep the bait small. Wind the

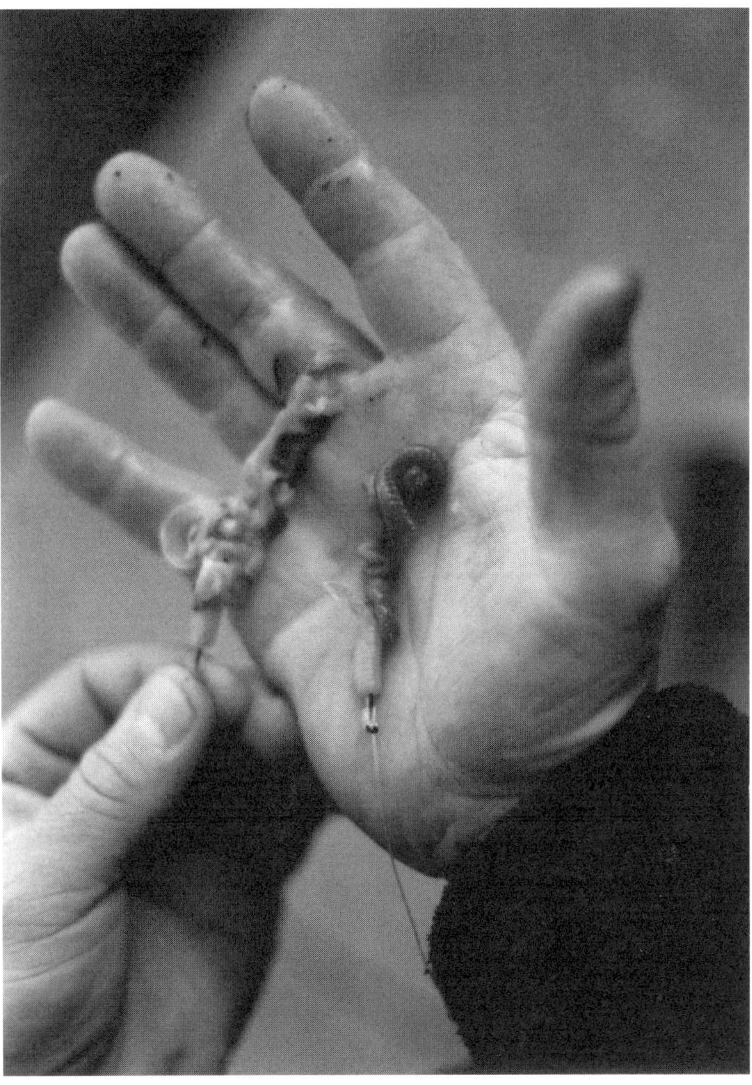

Winter flounder baits include worms and claim bits.
(Credit: NOAA)

tougher foot up the hook shank and arrange the belly around the hook point, leaving the point slightly exposed. This takes a little finesse, especially with cold, wet fingers, but is well worth the effort for a superior catch. You can fish clams au-natural, or you can doctor them a bit. I like a little of both. After all, variety is the spice of life.

One way of gussying up your clams is to dye them. Shuck fresh skimmer before your trip and soak them in a solution of kosher salt, water and food dye. Yellow and red are the colors that work best, just as they do for hook adornments and sinkers. Clams so dyed and salted can be kept in zipper bags or plastic containers for about a week in the refrigerator and still remain a viable bait. You can also freeze fresh dyed clams for later use, but don't defrost clams, dye them and refreeze them. I don't know about you, but my time on the water, even as a professional boating and outdoor writer who gets to do it for a living, never seems long enough. I don't want to take a chance on having a lackluster trip all because of a questionable bait that may have lost some of its scent and flavor due to freezer burn. In a pinch, fresh, or freshly defrosted clams can be dyed on the spot. Just pour some baywater and salt and the dye into a baggie or container and stir. Change your baits frequently to keep a fresh presentation.

Seaworms are always a good bet. Traditionally, there's been a worm dichotomy here on Long Island, in that bloodworms are deemed "better" on the South Shore and sandworms "superior" on the North Shore. I put no faith in this credo and simply prefer to use sandworms if I have a choice. The reason for this is hardly scientific, I just like the way sandworms look on the hook. I have confidence in them, and believe me, in any kind of fishing, confidence plays a huge role. Without enthusiasm, you won't work as hard, pay as close attention to details, or stay as focused. Happy hands do the best work.

To hook a seaworm for flounder bait, cut off the head with its nasty pinchers and discard. Then cut the worm into sections that are about one and a half inches long. Thread it up the hook, leaving about a quarter inch dangling to trail in the current. This may resemble a worm poking up from the bottom or a clam's siphon protruding to suck water. Or it may look like nothing, except something curiously good to eat, but that's what works. Change the baits every 15 minutes so that they're fresh.

Mussels make an excellent bait for flounder. The blue mussels which you can buy in a seafood market work OK, but my choice is bank mussels.

(Credit: NOAA)

These are the ribbed mollusk found clinging amongst the reed roots along the bank of your local salt meadow. You gotta get these yourself, although some bait shops procure them from time to time. Don waders or boots, grab a handheld garden fork, a bucket, and go a-harvesting. Whichever species you use, baiting with mussels requires patience. The meat is very soft-bodied, much gooshier than that of a clam, making them hard to secure to your hook. But with effort and a sigh you'll get it done. Take the meat out and begin threading it on the hook, wrapping it over and piercing it with the hook point. You may have to do half a dozen or more wraps and piercings before the bait will endure the short trip to the bottom without getting washed off your hook. But the patience will pay, as fresh bank mussel is a flounder delicacy if ever there was one. Like clams, mussels can also be dyed to add variety to your spread of baits.

FISHING

Flounder may be small fish, but the net preparation and effort expended in catching them can be large. So your boat is anchored. The chum's flowing. You're stirring the bottom. Your variety of baits is overboard. What now? Between cracking clams, moving the boat until you find fish, and changing baits, you try a number of techniques to see what the fish want. Start off with a dead-sticked rod for a perfectly still bait. "Rodney the Rodholder" is sometimes the best angler aboard. Next fish one or two rods in hand per angler. Work these baits differently. Try short, slow, lifts with pauses in between, This works best when the fish are sluggish, as in colder water, or for other reasons. The only "strike" you'll feel is the extra weight of the flounder on one of your lifts. Snap your wrist to set the hook and reel 'em up. Other times flounder like a bait that's jigged. Rapidly bounce your sinker, using six or eight short lifts followed by a short pause. On days when this appeals to them, the tale will be obvious, provided you haven't over-gunned them with bluefish tackle. You'll feel a definite twitch and surge. Again, a slight twitch of the wrist precedes swinging him over the rail and into the pail. These are the techniques you'll use whether fishing in the Amityville Cut, Centre Island, or Montauk Harbor. Find the habitats described earlier in your chosen area and have at it. As Ted Shuttleworth, a professional captain and one of the best fisherman around is fond of saying, "Fish have tails, they go where they want to." The point is, concerted effort close to home often pays off in a bigger catch than following the reports to the reputed nirvana of the week. (Published reports are a week old by the time you read them.) Unless you have some real solid info about a hot bite somewhere, direct info developed from a network of anglers and tackle shops and captains that you've cultivated over the years, remember that flounder inhabit all the waters of Long Island. For a shot at generally bigger fish, and bigger species, such as yellowtail flounder, there are some specialized techniques and areas however.

Bigger flounder, those over three-pounds and approaching six-pounds, can be caught in limited numbers in deeper, more open waters surrounding Long Island. My biggest was a just shy of five-pound yellowtail taken from Gardiners Bay. That fish was caught on a half a sandworm from a drifting boat. The technique for deep water flounder drifting is to use a stiff rod and a big sinker. For instance that behemoth I caught ate a bait submerged by an eight-ounce lead. As the boat drifts along the big weight hops and skips kicking up puffs of sand, attracting the attention of these big flatties. Instead of a tandem hook, I prefer a single number six sproat on a two foot stiff leader 30-pound test attached to the main line via a dropper loop. The sinker is deployed by an overhand loop about a foot below the dropper for the leader. The take is more like a fluke, aggressive generally and often requiring a bit of dropback to allow the fish to get to the hook. Once you catch one, short drift the area. That is, go back just upwind or upcurrent of the strike location and try again. If you keep scoring, you might try dropping the hook and putting a chumpot over. If you're in open water.

You see you can also catch these big flounder around the myriad nearshore wrecks and reefs around Long Island. Wrecks and reefs present their own set of challenges. If you drift them, you need to drift around the very perimeter. Big flounder don't live in the wreck like blackfish, they hunt next to the structure. If you get too close with drifting hooks your just gonna snag it and hang up. Skill in the use of GPS and depthsounder and your knowledge of how your boat responds to wind and current is paramount when drifting around such structure. But it can pay off. The artificial reefs offshore of the South Shore inlets, the rockpiles of Long Island Sound, particularly on the Connecticut side near the Norwalk Islands, and a number of wrecks like the *Gates City* near Moriches or the *Capital City* near Rye, have all produced outsized flounder for me over the years. Anchoring and chumming for flounder near wrecks, reefs and rocks was never productive for me. The chum brings on the bergalls like the plague, making it tough to present a bait to a flounder. Off course, you'll also draw some seabass and the odd blackfish off the wreck this way, but there are more directed methods for catching those species.

Targeting the biggest flounder isn't for everybody. Most of us, most of the time, will be happy catching our average fish in the shallower nearshore waters, because we'll be catching more of them. These fish offer protected water fun, an angling challenge, and tasty fillets for fishers of every age and economic strata. Who could ask for more?

Flounder Crib Sheet

Winter Flounder, a.k.a., flounder, flattie, blackback

Season: Available February –June and September-November

Location: Shallow harbors bays; bigger fish near deepwater structure

Baits: Clams, worms, mussels. Chum with clams or mussels.

Tackle: Light

High Hook Tip: Dig your own bank mussels for bait.

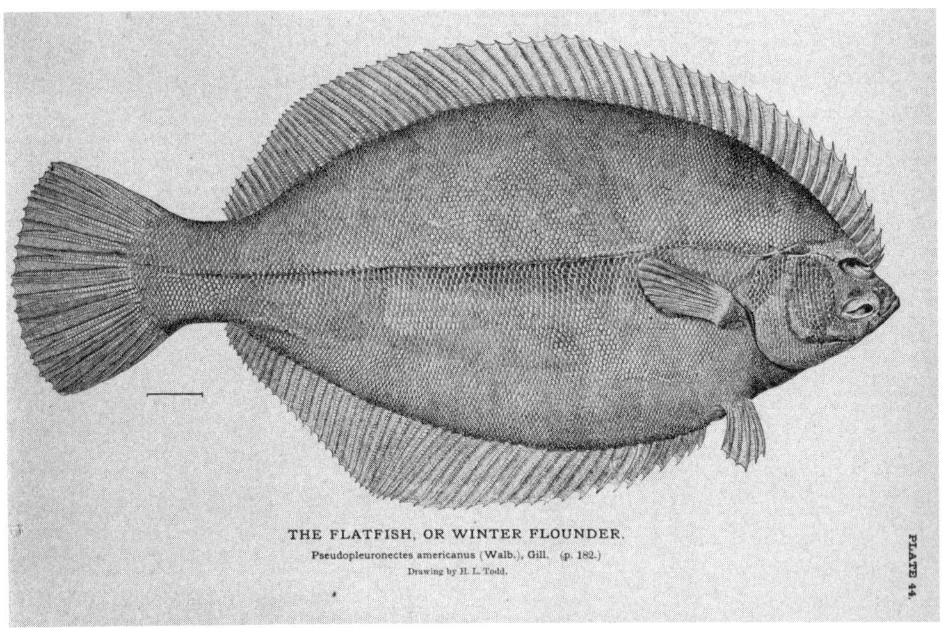

(Credit: NOAA)

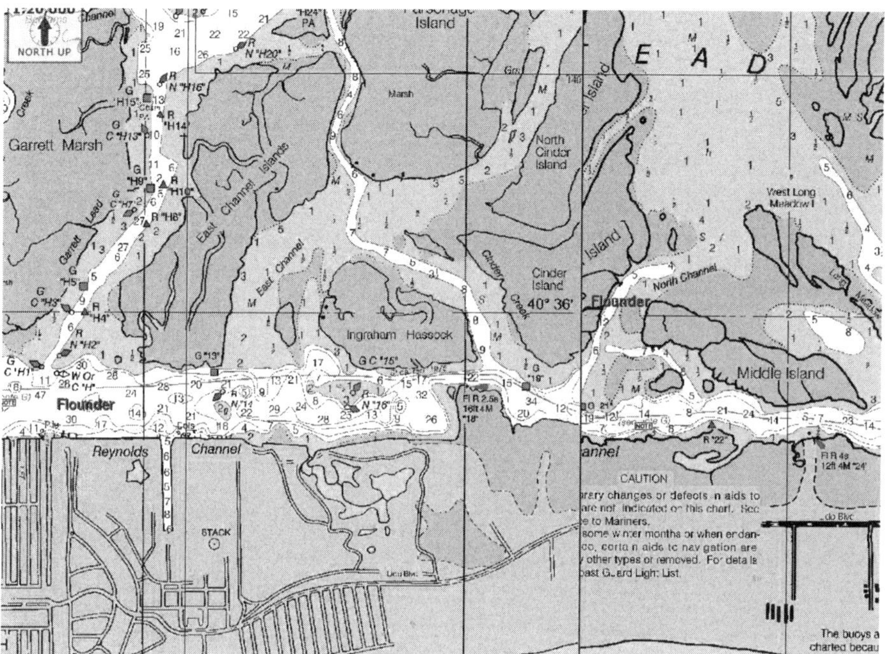

Mixed composition bottom, drop-offs, and edges that create current back-eddies are flounder hotspots. (Credit: Maptech)

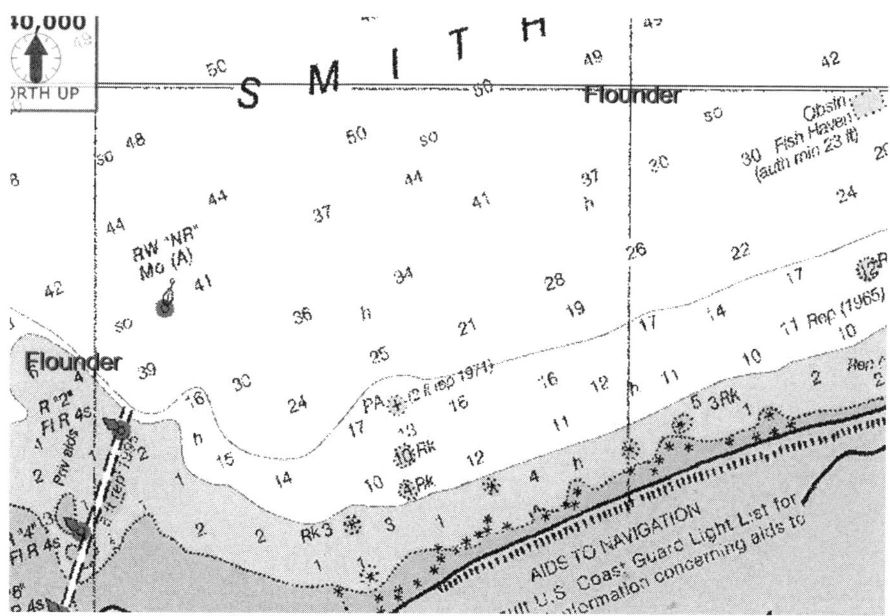

Work the flats outside the river at high water, and follow the fish deeper as tide falls in early season. Fish the deep soft spot later in the season. Note the SO symbol, indicating soft bottom.

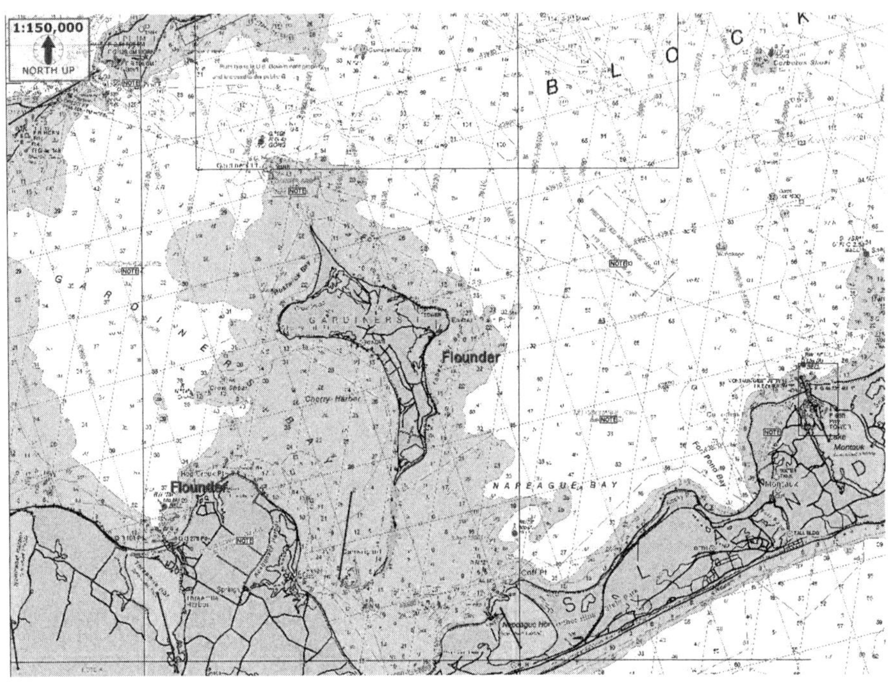

Try drifting Tobaccolot Bay with a big sinker for big flounder. Anchor at the Bell Buoy on falling water. (Credit : Maptech)

CHAPTER 2

Fluke

(Paralichthus dentatus)

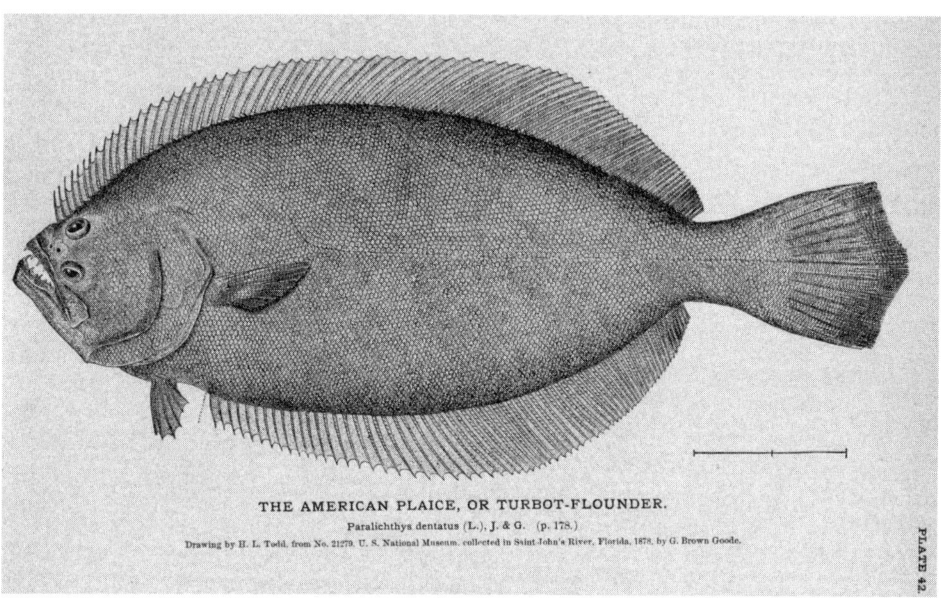

I love fluking. I mean, I've caught marlin in the Mona Passage, sailfish in three different oceans, and tuna the size of a Volkswagen beetle. I've caught Mako shark and swordfish that threatened the safety of the boat and crew, and I've won or placed in tournaments from Miami, Florida to Portland, Maine. And as cool as all that is, I love fishing for fluke.

Perhaps it's the time of year they show up in Long Island waters. The reports start trickling in during late April, as the sun begins riding a high arc. By May's end, the bite is on, winter's gone, and though the mornings are brisk, I'm in shirtsleeves by noon. The breeze carries the commingled scent of salt and blooming privet. Summer's here, without the humidity. And just a short boat ride away, some very game, very tasty flatfish are begging me to take my shot. Yeah, I love fluking.

TAXONOMY AND BIOLOGY

Fluke are flatfish that lie and swim right side down as adults. Like winter flounder, they start life as conically shaped juveniles, but slowly the eyes migrate to one side, called the eye side, which becomes pigmented. The "blind" side remains white, although occasionally you'll see a fluke with coloration on both sides, though this occurs more rarely than in winter flounder. Fluke are further differentiated by a row of large, sharp canine teeth. They use these to good advantage in capturing their prey. Fluke, also known as summer flounder, can burrow themselves into the sand in the blink

Can you see him? Fluke. (Credit: NOAA)

of an eye, a feat I've seen many times while stalking the flats. However, they tend not to do this as much as winter flounder. That's because the fluke, of all flatfishes, has the most amazing ability to camouflage itself both for its own protection, and to aid it in ambushing prey. The fluke's chameleon act is in two parts. Its skin can change color not just from nearly black to light brown, but through a range of tints and colors including red, blue, and yellow. Yellow especially, my research for this book has shown, and which also cleared up a childhood angling mystery. The family runabout for a short time was a 17-foot yellow outboard. While fluking in this boat, we boated a few, plopped them on deck and watched amazed as they turned nearly the same shade of mustard as the fiberglass deck. You can dazzle your friends, in fact, by carrying a colored bucket with you on a fluke fishing trip. Simply place a live fluke in a colored bucket with some water and wait. In short order, the fish's skin color will approximate that of the bucket.

There's another camouflage aspect to the fluke. Unlike a leopard, a fluke can change his spots. The skin varies to match the general appearance of the bottom, looking very speckled over shell or gravel, or nearly even over clean sand. Fishing's about more than catching and this kind of natural wonder is something I always try to appreciate, and share with my crew, while on the hunt.

Most of the fluke you'll catch will be less than three pounds. The IGFA World Record is a 22.6-pound fish caught at Montauk in 1997. I've caught plenty of fish between those extremes, up to 10 pounds anyway, and am confident that even the most ardent fluke addict would agree with me in calling five pounders, "nice fish, " and anything over eight pounds a doormat. Seeking these bigger fish in the deeper waters of the Sound and Ocean is your best bet. In fact, biologists tell us that the vast majority of fish over five pounds live in water deeper than 250'. (I've never took a break from tuna fishing to go fluking, but maybe I oughta!) In general, smaller fish will inhabit the shallower waters of harbors and bays. That said, my dad once boated an 11 pounder so far up a tidal creek his boat drifted into the sedge while battling the monster and I've spent some sorry tides in 60' of water throwing shorts back one after the other. But most of the time, the big fish/deep water paradigm holds true.

One reason for that may be the fluke's extreme sensitivity to dissolved oxygen levels in the water. The harbors and bays are warmer and experience less tidal flushing than open Sound and Ocean waters, and both of these facts results in diminished amounts of dissolved oxygen. Bigger fish need more oxygen, just as any larger organism does, and so the ratio of oxygen level to fish size may be more correct than comparing water depth. In any case, if you're fishing brown, turgid water with lots of dead weed floating in it—all signs of low oxygen content—chances are good your chances for fluke are low. Move to cooler, clearer, water.

Fluke can tolerate a wide range of temperatures, from just above freezing up to about 85 degrees. For our purposes, that means they can be caught when they are here. Fluke move inshore in April and back to the oceanic depths in October. The peak fishing usually occurs between late June and August. There are often brief runs of good-size fish in early May, usually coincident with the appearance of squid. Another good but short spurt of fish occurs in October, particularly along the open beaches of the South Shore, as the fish gather prior to migrating back to the edge of the continental shelf.

What does a fluke eat? Bony fishes make up the bulk of a fluke's diet,

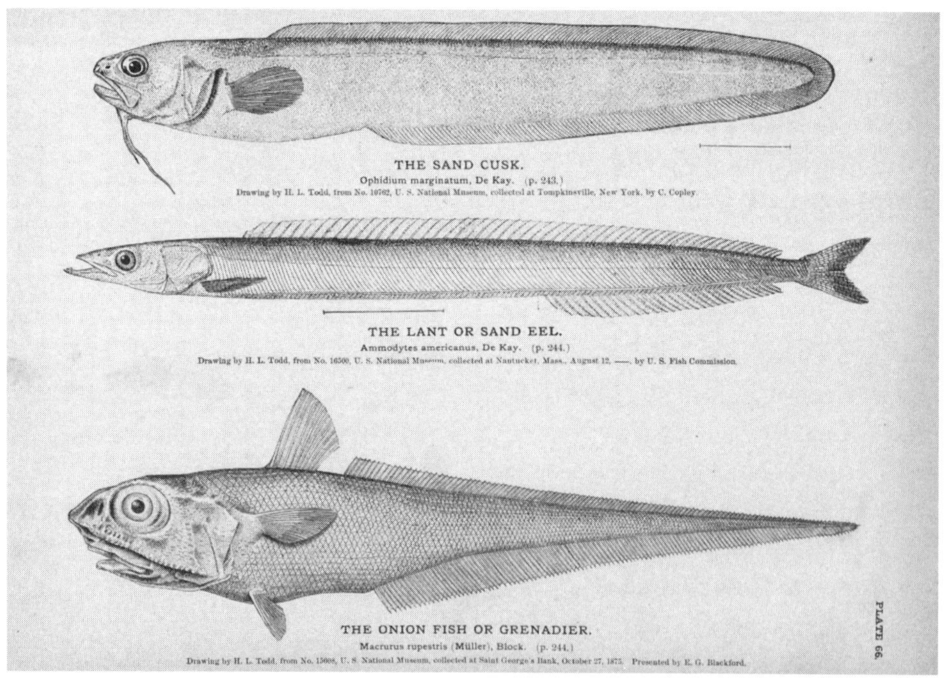

Sand eels are a major component of a fluke's diet. (Credit: NOAA)

and by a long shot according to the scientists. Sand eels top the list, though we'd be splitting hairs. In addition, fluke actively feed on spearing, killifish, snapper bluefish and grass shrimp (when they're feeding on shrimp, as evidenced by a stomach evaluation at the filet table or fresh-caught fluke spitting-up shrimp all over the boat, the meat has a bitter aftertaste). Squid is a very important food for fluke, as it is for most local species. Crabs, too, play their role, especially the calico crab, though crustaceans, they say, become a less important dietary component for fluke once the fish exceed 20" in length.

Where does a fluke live? Well we've already stated that they winter at the edge of the continental shelf and migrate inshore, sometimes even going up fresh and brackish rivers and creeks. That leaves a lot of real estate to cover. But we can narrow that down. For one thing, apply what we learned about dissolved oxygen counts and eliminate those areas from contention. Then look for moving water.

While fluke are speedy swimmers, sometimes chasing schools of bait to the surface, and even leaping out of the water, they are predominantly an ambush predator. They will use the current to bring the food to them rather than chasing it down and expending more energy in pursuit of prey than eating that prey can provide. So work the tidal rips, work the edges of wrecks and reefs, work the gullies, depressions, and bars. Here Mr. Fluke will be waiting for the dinner bell. Fluke adapt well to thick cover, thriving in eel grass and around pilings, jetties and wrecks. They can live in mud or in sand. The world of the fluke is wide and we can narrow the habitat we'll hunt for them in by looking at current and oxygen content. There is another discriminator, sort of by default, that will help you select prime fluking grounds. I'm talking about the most popular and productive—though not the only—fishing method: bait fishing from a drifting boat. When drifting, snags are more of a problem than they are than when fishing from a dead boat. Therefore, you'll seek out open bottom, either sand, sand/mud, gravel, cobbles or any combination, over which a strong current flows, the water is clean, and where the topography is such that bait gathers. If there's a wreck, rocks, mussel bed, grass bed or channel, or a hard edge nearby that you can skirt while drifting, you're looking good. Of course fluke "structure" isn't always so tangible. In 40' of water, a slight change in the bottom contour can be enough to set up a feeding opportunity for fluke. These areas can be found by looking for disturbed water, or rips on the surface. Rips can be as obvious as a wall of standing three-foot waves, as is sometimes the case in The Race, or as subtle as a barely perceptible seam in the surface, denoting disturbed water flow. These types of rips are common along the near-shore ocean waters outside our south shore inlets as well as in the deeper sections of the open Sound. Sometimes they're a result of subtly changing bottom contour and at other times, they denote an eddy outside the flow of the main current. These seam rips are often hard to see unless it's slick-calm. But once you find them, mark the spot. You can be assured that the rip, and the bottom contour causing it, is still there, even if you can't see it because of sea conditions. Just make sure the current's flowing.

Moving current brings up a point central to the theme of this book: as important as where to fish, is why you should fish a certain spot at a certain time. In fact, I believe that "why-to" is more important than "where-to." For instance, many hot spots can produce lukewarm action unless you happen to be there during the right stage of the current. To successfully fish for fluke, or any species, an understanding of current, and its potential effect on the bite, is imperative. This starts with distinguishing between tide and current. They are not the same thing.

Tide is the vertical rise and fall of water as it sloshes from one side of the Atlantic Basin to the other. Tidal Current is the horizontal motion of water induced by the tide being higher at one location and lower at another: Every schoolboy knows that water flows downhill. It's more complicated than that—tides rise and fall in waves and topography affects the strength and timing of current. This book isn't a treatise in oceanography, so we won't get in over our heads. What I will do is give you the pared-down, as-I-see-it explanation to illustrate how knowledge of tide and current can help you catch more fish. Any further study is up to you.

The first concept is that current strength and duration follows the tide at any given spot. It's behind it. For instance, at high tide, the current continues to flow in even after the tide has risen to its maximum height. When the current stops flowing—which can be anywhere from five minutes to over an hour later, depending on the location—a condition known as slack water occurs. Therefore, during a trip, don't ignore a potentially productive fluking spot based upon the time of high tide (or low tide); plan your itinerary around the time of slack water. Even if the difference between high, or low, slack and high, or low tide, is but five minutes, the spot may be worth a shot so long as the water's moving. As Bob Bossung, one of the

Bob Bossung with a nice keeper.

best fisherman I know, likes to say: "A lot can happen in five minutes." Bob is the king of calling for, "one more drift," long after most of us with even a reasonable degree of sanity are ready to rack the rods and head for the dock. He's a consistent high-liner as a result.

Secondly, learn how to follow moving water around the body of water you are fishing. As the current slows and stops at one place, it's just picking up steam at another location up-or down-tide. Therefore, the most successful fluke fisherman compare their inventory of spots against the times of moving water at those spots. When the current begins to slack at one spot, you move to another spot where you can fish the same stage of current that you were just catching on. I'm not suggesting leaving a good bite to find a better one. Rather, I'm saying that when the bite goes cold at one spot, you can move to the same set of conditions at another spot and hopefully resume catching. It's called pattern fishing. Being where the combination of

Here's Blane Bossung with a nice fluke.
Note net, and rigged backup rods, at the ready.

structure, water conditions, current, and bait, all of which play into a fluke's desire to work as little as possible in capturing prey, will catch you more and bigger fish than picking a spot based solely upon the fact that it's a "spot." Lets gear-up.

TACKLE AND RIGGING

My favorite fluke outfit is a 6'6" medium-weight graphite rod with cork grips. I mount a Penn International 965 loaded with 15-pound monofilament line to this conventional rod. If you like, spool-up with a superbraid for extra sensitivity and the ability to use lighter sinkers. The rod is light enough that I don't get tired holding it for a tide. The cork grips are more comfortable, because unlike EVA foam, I don't tend to squeeze them unconsciously. I like the Penn 965 because it can be fished in freespool, thumb on the line, to feed a fluke a "drop back" during the pickup, but can be engaged instantly by turning the reel handle. This is quicker and more natural than having to reach over and throw a lever to put the reel in gear. And when drifting fluke, you should be fishing in freespool because you'll catch more fish with the dropback followed by an instantaneous hookset than you will with the reel locked up. It's that very reason that I don't like spinning tackle for fluke fishing, or at least not for drifting baits. All of this will be covered in greater detail subsequently.

If the moon's full, the water is rough, or any other event is occurring that makes holding bottom with more than five-ounces of lead a problem, I'll switch up to one of my medium-heavy sticks, with a tip stiff enough to hold a big sinker without losing its touch. I'll mount the same reel to this, though spooled with 20-pound line. I always have at least two rods for each angler aboard, ones that will suit the anticipated conditions. I also never fish heavier than I have to. By the same token, I don't like going overly light, even when the situation allows for it. Many believe that ultralight tackle is the most sporting. But in my experience, fish may fight longer on noodle rods and wispy lines, but they fight harder on heavier tackle. Let the fish show all he's got, especially the bigger ones. Use appropriate, rather than light, tackle.

Terminal tackle for fluke is simple. The basic " fluke rig" is a three-way swivel with a sinker snap, a pre-tied leader with, say, a 3/0 wide gap hook snelled to its end, plus the sinker. Tie your line into one eye of the swivel, using a Palomar knot or Improved Clinch Knot. Pass the leader loop through the other eye, then pass the hook through the leader eye and pull tight, catspawing the leader to the swivel. Now snap on enough weight to hold bottom from a drifting boat in the depth and conditions you've chosen to fish. This rig has accounted for a lot of fish and it's low maintenance, meaning tangles are minimal. There is a rig I prefer, however.

Instead of a sinker snap, tie a Surgeon's Loop in the end of your line. (A Surgeon's Loop is like simply a double overhand knot. Loop the line through twice before pulling tight.) You'll attach sinkers by passing this loop through the sinker's eye and then dropping the sinker through the loop: a cat's paw. Next, tie a dropper loop about a foot above the surgeon's loop. To this loop, I attach, with the ubiquitous loop-to-loop catspaw, a 24" leader of stiff, 30-pound mono to which I have snelled a 5/0 sproat or wide-gap

Even with a basic rig, using a bucktail instead of a sinker for weight can up your score.

"kahle" hook. I prefer "stick" leader to leader material sold in coils because it's stiffer, and will stand out from the main line better. I'll usually dress the hook with a bit of bucktail, or most often, a B2-B4 (two-to-four inch long) squid skirt in either green or blue. If you like spinners or flashers, feel free to use them, with the caveat that they can attract grass and weed as well as fluke. If you think fluke will eat bait draped in seaweed, think again.

This rig boasts several advantages. For one thing, your bait drifts along above the bottom, rather than dredging through it like it often does when sinker and hook are connected at the same height, as of course they are when using the three-way swivel rig. This attracts more fluke, as the bait can be seen from further away and looks more like escaping prey, triggering the fluke's predatory instincts. It also minimizes the occurrence of crabs grabbing your bait, a common nuisance fluking with the three-way swivel rig, and it doesn't catch as much weed as the three-way, because there is no hardware. As for the squid skirts, these can be changed without having to cut-off and re-tie. Simply bite off the top of the squid skirt's mantle and slide it over the hook point and up the hook shank. I fish at least two rods while fluking, and use a different color skirt on each one, going as far as to bedeck every rig of every angler aboard with different colors. If a pattern develops, that is, if one color is catching better than the others, than it is a simple matter to convert all your rigs to that color. It's not as easy with other teasers. Finally, if you're afraid that fluke won't rise to a hook placed a foot above the sinker, allow me to relate some experience that might allay your reluctance. When seabass or weakfish are around, I tie yet another dropper loop above the first one, approximately three feet above the sinker, and attach a second hook and leader at that point in hopes of some mixed-bag action. (This, by the way, is the classic "Hi-Lo" rig used for a variety of species). Make sure the distance between dropper loops exceeds the length of both hook leaders or they will tangle. A company called Aqua-Clear markets some neat pre-tied Hi-Low rigs that are very effective and tangle free. In either case, I've often caught fluke on the high hook. Sometimes it outfishes the lower one. Enough said.

BAIT

Ham n' Eggs is the colloquial term for a pennant-shaped squid strip and a whole small fish, usually spearing or sand eel, placed together on the hook to catch fluke. This is the most popular, but hardly the only, bait that will put fish in the cooler. Cut the squid into strips, insert the hook point through one end so that it can stream out in the current, then hook the spearing through the eyes so it too can stream out. Drop it to the bottom. Simple enough. But like anything else related to fishing, attention to the finer points allows 10-percent of the fishermen to catch 90-percent of the fish. So it is here.

First, let's discuss preparing the squid for use as strip baits. Lay the squid on the cutting board and stretch him out. Cut off the head leaving the tentacles intact and put it aside, it's a good bait in its own right. Next, make a cut down the center of the squid's mantle, from the tip to where the head was attached. Only cut through one side of this "tube." With the long cut through one side of the mantle done, put down the knife and open the mantle like a book so it lays out flat on the board. Pull out the cartilage—this is the long plastic-looking thing within the mantle. At this point, there should be a flat, triangular sheet of meat on your cutting board. Also at this point, many anglers make what I believe to be a mistake. They flip the sheet of squid over and scrape the pinkish skin off so that they have a sheet of squid meat that is white on both sides. I advise against this, and prefer to fish the strips with skin on. The reason? Fish, all fish, are light on the bottom and dark on the top. So when I place my squid strip on the hook, I do so with the skin side up. This makes the strip more closely resemble whatever prey fish a squid strip looks like to a fluke.

Cut the squid, skin on, into pennant-shaped strips at least four inches long, with six or seven inches being preferred. Of course this depends on the size of the squid you have procured. If your bait shop is selling prepackaged "fluke bait," the squid may be small. Ask if he has the larger trolling squids used by offshore fisherman. Two or three of these is equal to a half-dozen or more smaller squids and you'll be able to cut longer strips. Don't go nuts though. While big baits do attract big fluke, you don't want the three-pounders struggling to get to the hook. As a rule, don't let your strip bait exceed the length of the accompanying spearing or sand eel by more than 25-percent. Make nice, neat cuts to produce nice, proportioned pennants. Ideally they should look like half-width pie slices that have been stretched in length. Ragged edges or a taper at both ends doesn't fish as well, because it doesn't drape and flutter as nicely, makes it tougher to place on the hook, and may spin. To hook the squid strip, or any drifted strip bait, really, insert the hook dead center through the wide end of the pennant. If you're careless, or hasty, and poke through to the side of center, your bait will fold over and may spin, causing grief and attracting less attention from Mr. Paralychthus Dentatus.

Cut only enough squid for the time being, leaving the rest on ice. Squid quickly cooks when left to itself on a warm day, becoming slimy and discolored. Present it to the fluke in the same condition you'd want to put it in your frying pan, sans breading, for a calamari dinner and you'll be fine. Also, while squid from the supermarket works, better bait shops sell local squid, which I have found to produce best. So much do I believe in this, that I try to stock up on local squid myself, by catching them in spring, when they are available from lighted docks at night. A word to the wise.

The fish portion of your ham and eggs offering is most likely to be either spearing or sand eel. Despite the scientific data stating that sand eels, a.k.a, sand lance, are the biggest component of a mature fluke's diet, I've had much better success with spearing over the years. Sand eels are a more durable bait, able to withstand more crab harassment than spearing, and they don't get mushy and useless as fast as spearing. Of course that's not going to be a problem for you, because you're going to keep your spearing on ice, right? Sure you are. Do so and you'll ensure a supply of good bait. Just don't bother re-freezing any leftover. It will quickly turn to mush during your next outing. Sand eel or spearing, each is placed on the hook the same way: insert the hook point through the both eyes of the fish and lay it flat against the squid strip. Place it through the gills or belly and your bait will not only spin, making a poor presentation, but will easily tear off before the fluke gets the hook in its mouth. You can seine your own spearing easily enough, though I haven't seen the difference between fresh and frozen spearing. Besides, better tackle shops offer local spearing for a few cents more than imported ones so it's hardly worth the effort, though seining trip to a local bay beach makes a wholesome family outing.

The squid and spearing combo is my most-fished bait for fluking, particularly when fishing in the ocean or the open sound. However, as soon as I catch a fluke or a sea robin my ham and eggs combo is likely to change. The first keeper fluke boated gets a strip cut out of his belly. Fluke belly is a wonderful bait and very durable. Same goes for a strip cut from a sea robin filet. Fluke seem to relish both and either one will stand up much better than squid. I've used the same sea robin strip to catch many fluke before it was too ragged and meatless to be worth a darn. To give your sea robin strip the proper enticing flutter, make sure to filet your sea robin filet. That is, use a razor sharp knife to pare some of the meat off the filet, leaving no more than one-eighth inch thickness of meat attached to the skin. Other fish worthy of use for strip baits include bluefish, mackerel and bunker. Bunker strips are particularly effective around the rocky points of the North Shore Harbors, areas such as Matinecock Point. This is particularly so if bluefish are, or have been, blitzing the bunker. Ever the opportunists, fluke will stay under the fray, getting a free meal out the choppers frenzy.

Another dead bait worth mentioning is smelt, which can be purchased in the frozen fish section of the supermarket. Some seven inches long, smelt are a big bait. While I have used them, I haven't done so enough to give you the finer points. But friend and sharpie Wayne Haskell, of East Moriches, swears by'em. And Wayne has caught some fluke.

A slow lift is often the best way to hook fluke, as Charlie Falvey proves.

As well as a strip and fish combo works for fluke, some days you just can't beat live bait. The ubiquitous killifish, a.k.a, killie or mummichog, is the most popular live bait for fluke, probably owing to the fact that they are widely sold and easily procured with the aid of an inexpensive trap. Hook them through the lips on either of the above mentioned rigs and let them do their thing. They are very effective when used in combination with a squid strip as well. Use a narrow strip, that's no longer than the killie in question. As always, I recommend starting out using a variety of baits until you figure out what's working best at the given time, tide, and location you are fishing. Things change tide to tide, time to time, and place to place, and Hi-liners never get stuck in a rut. Live killies, though they work great, have never been a big-fish bait. For doormats, I prefer a larger live bait.

It's interesting to wonder at the interconnectedness of nature when you consider that a mature bluefish eats fluke with relish while a big fluke will chase down and devour a snapper blue like nobody's business. And that's exactly what they'll do. I procure my snappers at the dock before I leave the slip, using a either a spinning rod or a cane pole and bait. If I use lures to catch the baby blues, I make sure it's a single hook jig. Removing treble hooks tends to tear up your baits. You'll need a good livewell to keep a bunch of snappers alive, a bucket of water won't do for more than a half-hour. Once you've got a bunch, head for the fluke grounds. Hook the snapper either through its eyes or through its nostrils. I like the nostrils, as they seem to last long on the hook and there's less chance of killing them by piercing the brain. Do not hook them through the lips, as it will impede the water flow to the gills and they'll likely drown. Instead of the high-low or three-way rigs mentioned, I prefer a different terminal setup for baiting fluke with live snapper. Tie a bead chain drail of enough weight to hold bottom to your fishing line using a Palomar knot. This is one case where I prefer not use the Improved Clinch knot because the twists you have to make in tying that knot are a pain in the butt to accomplish when trying to tie to a ball bearing swivel, which is what a bead chain essentially is. You make a twist, the swivel turns and undoes your twist. The Palomar is quicker and less frustrating. To the other end of the drail connect a 36" leader of 30 pound test line to which is snelled a 5/0 salmon (siwash) hook. The salmon hook is like a live bait hook, but with a bit longer shank. Fluke have teeth, and big fluke have bigger teeth, big enough to cut through mono leader. You can use a trace of wire to the same purpose, but I don't. It makes for another connection in your line and is more visible to the fluke. Besides, if you're paying attention to your bait's behavior, you should be able to setup on your doormat before he completely swallows the bait whole, exposing your leader to those nasty dentures.

BUCKTAILS AND OTHER LURES

Bait is great, but fluke voraciously eat lures. I've caught them while diamond-jigging bluefish in 100-feet of water, while throwing swimming plugs intended for stripers in the shallows of a salt marsh, and while salty-dogging weakfish in the swift currents of a narrows. It's a fun way to catch them and the best lures for targeting fluke specifically are bucktails.

By bucktails, I mean leadhead jigs, be they dressed with actual bucktail, nylon, marabou or feathers and the derivative leadheads dressed with the large array of plastic bait tails and imitation fish now available. This is shallow-water fluking best practiced in the shallows of Long Island's bays and harbors. I've caught them inside Oyster Bay this way, more often in Shinnecock Bay and the near-shore flats near Wooley Pond in Peconic Bay.

Use jigs between one-half and one ounce. I've had the best success with white and green, though yellow has its moments, particularly when peanut bunker or young-of-the-year weakfish are on the menu. As for plastics, both the shad bodied and slimmer profiled types work. Experiment and observe. If you see spearing while drifting an area, a Slugg-O or Fin-S fish is probably on order. However, if bay anchovies or snappers are spotted, the shad body might be better. Experimentation and observation are keys to becoming a better fisherman.

Your jig selected, tie it to the end of a 36" 20 pound leader. You can use a loop knot for this, such as the uniknot loop or perfection loop, on the basis that the loop allows the jig a more lively action than a tight knot. Some advocate this strongly. I use an Improved Clinch, on the basis that the working jig will be pulling the loop tight anyway. Take your pick.

For added appeal, tie on a teaser by making a dropper loop halfway up your leader, cutting the loop close to the knot to make a short trace on

Here's Blane again. He was smaller then but the fish was bigger!

which you'll tie the teaser. I like to use a saltwater fly, like a Deceiver in green and white. Teasers look like a baitfish being chased by the bucktail, and thus spark a competitive, predatory response from Mr. Fluke. You can tip the hooks with a small, slim strip of squid or fluke belly or with the tail section of a spearing or sand eel for added effectiveness.

Connect this leader system to your main line using a barrel swivel and a pair of Improved Clinch knots. If the swivel is a ball-bearing model—it needn't be since buckies don't spin and impart line twist, so save your money—you might find the Palomar Knot easier to tie. If bluefish are present, you might consider tying the leader to the main line with an Albright Knot. More than one bay blue has seen the swivel as a morsel and cut me off while bucktailing. I fish this terminal rig from a seven foot spinning rod loaded with 12 pound line. This is shallow water fluking, where most of the fish will be less than three pounds. That's the rigging and setup. The how-to of bucktailing fluke is detailed later in this chapter.

FISHING

Let's start with that live snapper swimming at the end of your drail-weighted leader over, say, the cobbled bottom in front of Gurney's Inn at Montauk, along the myriad jetty fronts at Long Beach, or just outside the beach at Bayville. The weight touches down and you develop a feel for it caroming off of rocks and scraping over shells. You also feel the staccato pulse of the hooked snapper, his every tail swipe transmitted through the leader, damped somewhat by the sinker, and finally thrumming its way up your taut line and into the subtle flex of the rod tip and varying pressure on the foregrip. Pay attention. This is your bait, swimming merrily along. When the rhythm alters, something's going on. If you stop feeling this, the bait either got off or died. What you are hoping for is the change that gets my heart pumping and my pulse racing. That change is your bait suddenly, and frantically, pulling like a fish twice his weight. You are witness to a death dance, as ultimately a snapper bluefish, hamstrung by a weighted drail, has little chance outrunning a highly developed predator like a fluke. It's up to you now, so don't blow it. Let the fluke catch your bait. Wait for a solid whack, then wait some more. You'll feel a few sharp tugs in succession after the fluke grabs the bait and moves it deep into its maw. Strike, you angler! Cross his eyes! Lift the rod over your head while reeling in any slack. Big fluke will try to bury themselves into the bottom once they know they're in trouble. They are difficult to extricate if they do. If it happens, keep the pressure on. Carefully. You are fishing from a drifting boat. An eight pound fluke firmly embedded in sand can exert more pressure than eight pounds as the boat moves away and he stays put. It's now when you question everything. Did I tie my knots right? Was that leader new or was it used last trip? Did I nick the line on the trim tab, boating the last fish? All of your skill and experience comes into play at a time like this, as you gauge the strain on the line against the reel's brake setting and the additional, oh-so-gingerly-applied extra pressure of your thumb. Ha-ha, you've got him now. The pressure eases momentarily and you're right on top of him, reeling in the slack. He dives for the bottom in a rod bending surge. Denied! You pump, reel, pump, reel. I see color! Get the net! Thump, thump, thump on the deck. Well done.

It's not always like that, but doormat fluke do generate angler adrenaline. When fishing with smaller live baits such as killifish, the drill is similar, but for the strike which, because of their smaller size, means it's time to set the hook. Remember, a fluke's mouth is tough, relative to the fine-wired hooks necessary for proper bait presentation. Don't be afraid to set the hook, reel in some slack and set it again. You don't have to rear back like a Saturday morning TV fishing host, but a firm jerk or three ensures that point and barb get sent home.

Fishing with dead baits is a different ball game. For example, once you're squid and spearing combo hits the sandy ocean floor in front of "The Castle," east of Shinnecock Inlet, or off Prybill Beach in Glen Cove, you'll be attentive to a different message telegraphing up your line, through your rod, and into your hands. What you'll feel, or should feel, is a steady, constant pressure as the sinker is dragged across the bottom with the bait trailing just above and a couple feet behind. A revolving spool reel is recommended because you'll, once again, fish with the reel in free spool and your thumb acting as the brake. That's because a fluke, like most fish with teeth, will usually attack its prey from behind. (Fish without teeth, like striped bass, usually attack head-first. That way when they swallow their prey, the baitfish's gills don't get caught in their gullet.) I've seen fluke attack my bait many times when fishing for them in clear, shallow water locations, like the flats near the Moriches Coast Guard. Here's what happens.

As the bait drifts by, the fluke pounces on it from behind, his teeth clamping down and his body arching and thrashing in a flash. He's crippling the prey like a cheetah taking down a gazelle. This is often felt as a tap-tap-tap, causing your rod tip to jump in a series of rapid-fire raps. The fluke still has to chew his way up to your hook. Remember you're fishing from a drifting boat. The "crippled" bait is still moving away from the fluke.

Firmly clamped on, he chews his way up towards the hook in the attempt to swallow his meal. Your job is to help him eat it. Allow line to free-spool out from under your thumb. This dropback makes it easier for the fluke to swallow the bait and get to the hook. If you set up on him without a dropback, you'll more than likely reel-up a half-eaten bait, the fluke will go back to his haunt, and that's that. You coulda been somebody.

Instead, freespool the line back and wait. How long? Well sometimes the fluke will make that easy for you, revealing the fact that he's swallowed your bait by a sudden hard tug. At other times, you need to use your instinct and powers of visualization and after doing so, clamp your thumb back down and lift the rod smoothly and s-l-o-w-l-y. If the fluke is on, you'll feel a hard tug, or just the fish's weight, at which point you should engage the reel, reel out any slack, and set the hook. If you don't feel the weight or the tug while lifting, immediately drop the rod tip and resume dropping back. I've had fluke "play" with my bait countless times, grabbing it and letting it go, before I finally made my lift when he had eaten the hook. Though I've lifted and dropped-back on the same fish as many as seven times, most times you get two shots at the same fish. After that, its time to reel up and check your bait. If it's chewed, change it. If its still there, change it. Might as well put on some fresh, you've reeled it up. Maximizing your chances by paying attention to details is what separates the sharpies from everyone else.

Now, fishing bucktails and jigs for fluke requires yet another technique. The jig and teaser, as described above, is dropped to the bottom and jigged in short rapid hops, no more than a foot off the bottom. Actually, the shorter you can make the hops and still keep the jig working, the better. This is where a stiff, fast-action graphite rod really shines. If you spooled up with 20 pound braid instead of 12 pound mono, your ability to work the jig properly will be enhanced. You gotta have the right tools for the job.

If you're used to drifting and dreaming with strip baits for fluke, you are going to be surprised by how hard fluke strike a jigged bucktail. The take comes on the upsweep, (unlike stripers, which eat buckies on the drop more often than not) and with a jolt. Raise the rod and start reeling. More often than not the fish sets the hook on the take. As a bonus, you'll gut or gill hook very few fish when jigging bucktails for fluke. The shorts you catch can be released without harm and you won't waste any time unhooking boated fish.

DRIFTING

Since most of your fluke fishing occurs while on the drift, boat handling is as important to bait presentation as your terminal rigging or your dropback and lift technique.

Fluke lie in lanes along the bottom, often holding over a very small area. Once you catch, you don't want to keep on drifting, hoping for another bite. You'll be more effective if, after boating a fish, you drift for another 100' or so, then pick up, run back up to where you started, and make the same drift again. Back in the day, we'd drop a marker buoy when we caught a fish. This not only marked the spot where they were holding, but gave us a target to drift towards. Wind and current shift, so starting your drift at point A the first time doesn't mean you'll hit point B on subsequent drifts. Having a mark to aim for lets you fire up the motor for moment and correct the course of your drift with a burst of power. Nowadays, I use the GPS chartplotter to mark where I'm catching, using the instant waypoint (save present position) function. It lets me see the exact line of all my drifts and doesn't alert other boats to where the fish are holding like a marker buoy does. Of course, repetitively dipping the net in the water tips off the more observant fellow anglers. A word to the wise.

GET THE NET

No matter which method you use to catch fluke, your score will be upped by focusing on structure and current and by using their nature as voracious predators against them. When your catch is hooked, beat, and at the surface; when you see that beautiful, big brown fish, have a net ready. Fluke have an uncanny ability for shaking the hook if you try to lift them aboard.

When your doormat is at the boat, keep his head in the water, lead him head-first into the net. I've seen lots of things on the water over the years, but a fluke that can swim backwards isn't one of them.

Fluke Crib Sheet

Fluke, a.k.a, Doormat, Summer Flounder

Season: April-October

Location: Bays, Harbors. Bigger fish in open sound and near-shore ocean, particularly near structure.

Baits: " Ham 'n Eggs" combo of squid and either spearing or sand eel; smelt from fish market; live killies; live snappers; bucktails or plastic tails.

Tackle: Medium

High Hook Tip: Strips of false albacore belly are killer baits.

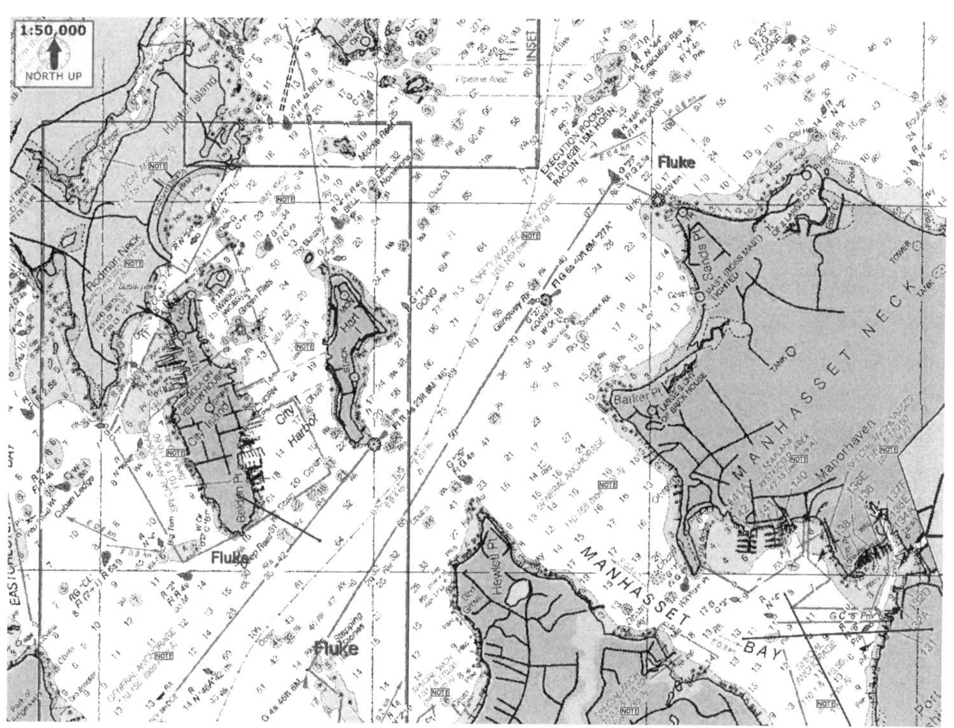

The Western Sound's numerous points and islands hold fluke.

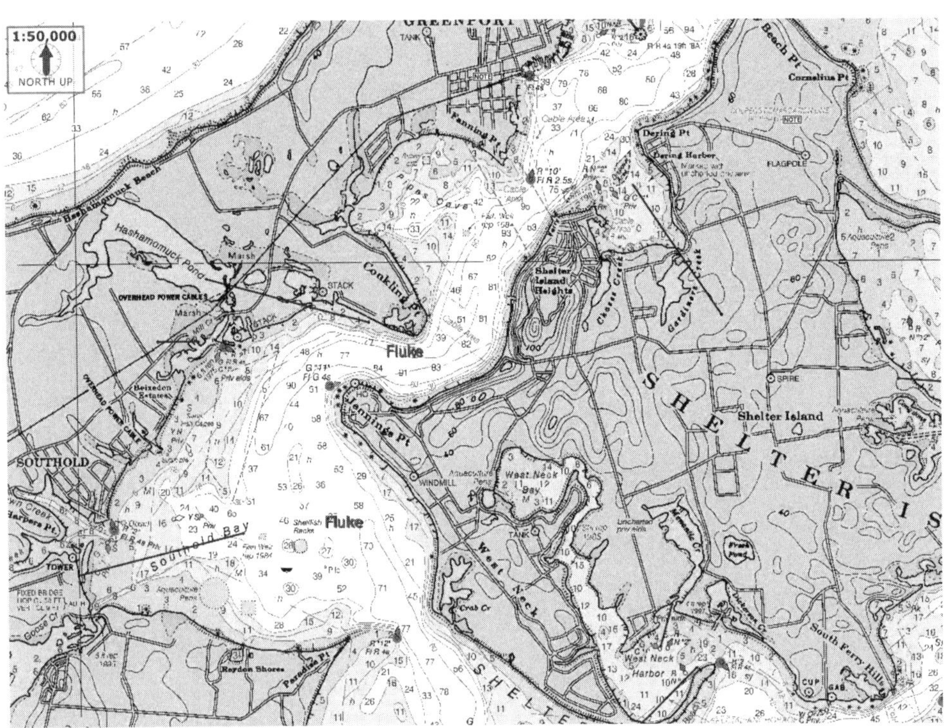

The Super Bowl of Fluke occurs at Shelter Island in May, when doormats gorge on post-spawn squid. This is a short-lived run, so gear-up!

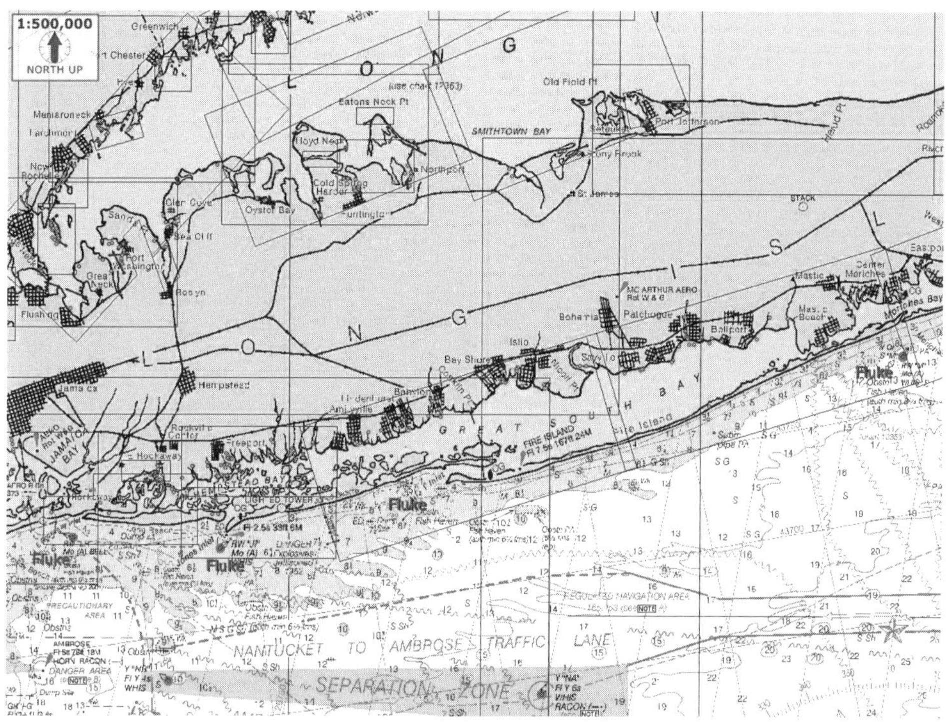

On the South Shore you'll score more and bigger fluke by fishing outside in 40' to 60' than you will in the bay.

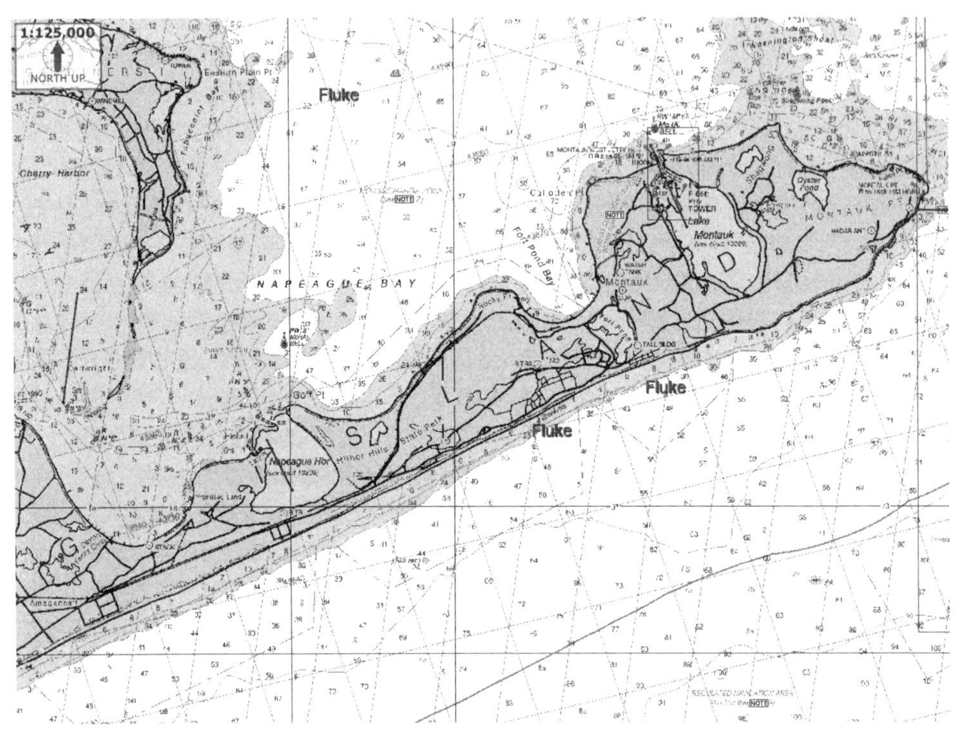

Gurney's (the Breakers) and Trailer Park are doormat city.
Fish Gardiners if there's a heave on the Ocean.

CHAPTER 3

Bluefish

(Pomatomus Saltatrix)

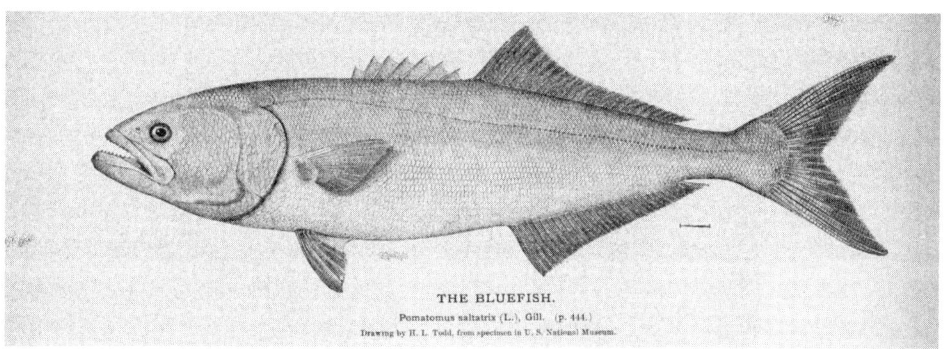

THE BLUEFISH.
Pomatomus saltatrix (L.), Gill. (p. 444.)
Drawing by H. L. Todd, from specimen in U. S. National Museum.

"The blues are running! The blues are running! Dad, can we go on the *Capt Al*? Pleeeeeez?! How about the Hempstead Harbor pier? Magnolia Pier? Manorhaven Park? Captree? Shinnecock Canal? We'll go early, you can tie our rods off at the end of the pier—that's the good spot—and I'll take a spinning rod and snag some bunker from the cove near the old barge plus we'll bring the diamond jigs and cast for them and if the live bunkers don't work we'll use chunks under bobbers. Can we? Will you? Will we? Pleeeze?"

As a kid nothing got my blood running more than bluefishing. And why not? They were, and are, the hardest fighting fish in our inshore waters. They often school in large numbers, so you can really blitz them and catch fish after fish, enjoying arm-wearying, drag-searing run after arm-wearying, drag-searing run. Blues invade our harbors and bays and they run thick, marauding the deep waters of the Sound and Ocean. There's an element of danger, as a bite from a big blue can net you some stitches (been there, got the scar). They can be caught from boat or shore, by a variety of methods and with minimal investment in tackle, making them an everyman's quarry. I even like to eat 'em, provided they're fresh and under five pounds. Yes, the bluefish just may be the perfect gamefish.

TAXONOMY AND BIOLOGY

Numerous in every ocean excepting the Polar seas, bluefish are a globally pursued sport fish. On the East Coast of the US, they are caught from Maine to Florida, though at the extremes of that range, big fish are rare. Lucky for us, the largest biomass of the biggest bluefish spend the warmer months between Cape Cod and southern New Jersey. That makes Long Island, "Bluefish Central."

Brian Falvey (L) and Charles Falvey (R) with a "cocktail" bluefish popped-up on light tackle.

Bluefish are stout and long-bodied, about one-fourth as deep as they are long. More sea-green than blue, this top color fades to a silvery white, flat, belly with a blunt edge. The bluefish's mouth shows rows of conical teeth. Its lower jaw is under-slung and its tail is broad and deeply forked. All of this translates into the hammer-striking, rod-bending excitement for which bluefish are beloved.

The All-Tackle World Record bluefish weighed 31 pounds, 12 ounces and was caught off Cape Hatteras, NC. The New York State record was caught in the Atlantic Ocean in 1998 and weighed 25 pounds even. You can expect to catch blues ranging from 14 or 15 pounders down to young-of-the-year snappers measured in inches, rather than by weight. The size of the fish you catch depends largely on the school you happen to be fishing at any given time.

Bluefish are oceanic, warm water fish preferring a minimum water temperature of 55 degrees and are rarely present when water temps dip below 50 degrees. On the hot side, biologists say 86 degrees is the warmest water they can tolerate. While some of our backwater harbors and creeks may get that warm in some years, it's not likely for most of us to fish for bluefish in such tepid water. Besides, bluefish need lots of oxygen, so still, hot waters like that, which can not hold lots of oxygen, are a poor place to seek bluefish.

Bluefish can swim at speeds up to nine miles per hour. Compare that to striped bass, whose maximum swimming speed is just over four miles per hour. That's one reason to like bluefish as a gamefish. Another is that bluefish possess the rare ability to force water through their gills by swimming with their mouths open. This ram ventilation allows them to maintain speed and power for longer intervals than other fish, most of which need to gulp water to extract oxygen. This explains why a bluefish fights so hard. The hook in his mouth, holding it open, doesn't hurt his ability to get oxygen like it does other fish. In fact, it's the opposite. Under stress, such as being hooked, a bluefish normally opens his mouth and swims fast. The striped bass is the only other local sport fish with this ability.

Bluefish are primarily sight feeders, though they react well to smell. Field studies have shown that an attacking bluefish accelerates towards its prey, extends its lower jaw and than turns 90 to180 degrees. This hard turn helps explain the jarring strike we anglers normally experience when a blue bites. It also explains the mysterious bite-offs where we never felt a thing:

The fish made his 180-degree turn toward you, putting slack in the line. So keep on your toes, despite the fact that blues often hook themselves.

In the winter, the blues move south and offshore, wintering off the Carolinas and Florida in two distinct groups. As our waters warm, both stocks head north, with the first fish starting to show in Long Island waters in late April. Generally these are larger fish, two foot or more in length and weighing an average of eight pounds. These first-of-the-year blues are very skinny—"all head," I like to say—hence the nickname "racers." Following these fish in May, is a huge influx of "cocktail blues," sometimes called "tailors." (In Australia, where bluefish fever runs as hot as it does on Long Island, bluefish of all sizes are called "Taylor.") By June, fish of all size classes, including "choppers" or "alligators," which may exceed 15 pounds in weight are present, though the very biggest fish won't be common until October and November, after they've fattened up at the expense of our local baitfish population. They are here for the spawning run, which occurs offshore, in the deep waters of the Atlantic. And following the migration and exertions of the spawn, they are ready to eat. And eat. And eat some more. In fact, the bluefish is one of the few wild animals in the entire world that hunts for sport. Blues routinely eat until they are swollen, then regurgitate their food so they can continue the attack.

Bluefish fry find themselves drifting North in the Gulf Stream. Currents and winds carry them inshore where they feed primarily on tiny crustaceans until they are about five inches long. These young "snappers" then begin feeding on smaller fishes, living in the protected waters of bays, harbors and creeks until fall. (Interestingly, a study conducted in the Hudson River concluded that between 50 and 80 percent of juvenile striped bass mortality is a result of bluefish. In short, snappers get fat on baby bass.) At this point, some of these fish may be 10" long before they make the migration south. Interestingly, bluefish school in a size-specific way. That is, 10" fish tend to all school together, one pound fish tend to school all together, and 10 pound fish tend to school together. This is most likely a result of the fact that bluefish readily eat bluefish. By sticking to the same size class in schools, they can better protect themselves from their bigger siblings. Why should you care? When bluefishing, if you catch a five pounder, chances are that all the fish in that school will be the same size. If you want bigger fish, you need to find a different school.

As the fish mature, squid, fish and eels comprise the diet. Menhaden, known locally as bunker, are a primary food source, particularly in Long Island Sound. But you have to consider what's around. Bluefish eat squid, eels, and mackerel, particularly in spring, when those fish arrive in good numbers and particularly offshore where squid and mackerel spend most of their lives. Spearing too, are candy to blues, the biggest ones often spitting handfuls all over the deck upon capture. Its important to know because, while I've had porgies and seabass cut in half by bluefish as I was reeling them up; and while I've caught a number of fluke who had a crescent-shaped bite out of their tail area; and while my dad once rigged a Milky Way bar with a wire leader, cast it out and "popped" it like a plug and caught an 18 pounder; while the bluefish's habit of reckless abandon during eating is well-known; you still have to remember that we are fishing. The thing that better fisherman know, is that despite their rep as swimming meat grinders, "matching the hatch" will make your bite ratio rise. This becomes more critical when using artificials then when using bait, as we'll discuss later on.

Fisheries scientists tell us that the stock of bluefish today is about half of what it was in the early 1980's. Don't blame the commercial guys: 90 percent of bluefish landings are by recreational anglers. Release what you're not going to eat or use for shark bait.

That jives with my experience. Was a time where you just could not avoid the blues. (Something you might want to do when targeting other species, for instance.) Today, with perhaps the exception of the North Shore Harbors, there are days when it's hard to find them. Of course, the information in this chapter should keep the occurrence of that scenario to an absolute minimum.

So if bluefish are superfast swimmers, ranging from the open sea to the most protected harbor, where do you begin to look for them? "Look for the birds," is common advice. Sure, terns and gulls wheeling and diving is often sign of a bluefish blitz going on. But you can't always count on that. So, barring birds, think like a bluefish. What does he need? He needs to eat. So look for bait.

If you fish in the Sound, that means keeping track of the bunker schools. Often, the best bluefishing on the North Shore is deep in the harbors, amongst the sailboat moorings. On the South shore, the same applies. One of my most memorable fishing trips was a bluefish blitz that occurred at the head of Bergen Basin, within the confines of JFK airport.(This was before our current geopolitical situation and the security measures that go with it.) We were in a tin boat, a short cast from a wire-topped, chain-link fence, jets screaming overhead, and the blues had literally turned the narrow waterway—canal really—red in the process of decimating a bunker school. Don't overlook the backwaters.

You'll also find bluefish where current and structure combine to disorient and/ or congregate baitfish. This comes in handy when the sun is way high, as bluefish will often sulk in deeper water during the hottest times of day. On the North Shore any of the harbor points on moving water—I like Prospect Point—or the roiling, rolling waters of Plum Gut are good bets. On the South Shore, the Inlets, of course, are great, but don't neglect others. Any place water flows off a flat (Shinnecock's East Cut) is funneled (Reynolds Channel) or is accelerated by flowing between two opposing points of land (The Narrows, Bellport)is a good spot to look for blues. In deeper water, the high spots, like Cholera Bank are great spots for blues, as is The Triangle in Mid Sound.

Finally, look for slicks. Bluefish feed so rapaciously that they often leave a slick so thick you'd think someone dumped cooking oil overboard. The slick results from the oils released by the chopped-up baitfish. You can often smell these slicks, though the exact scent is beyond my powers of description. I will say that a slick doesn't smell like fish, so much as like fresh, sweet, fruit. Spend sometime chasing bluefish, and before long, you'll have no need to rely on weak simile from me. When your nostrils are filled with the pungent scent of predator eating prey, you'll know it.

TACKLE AND RIGGING

Bluefish tackle is as diverse as bluefish habitat. You can use a cane pole to catch snappers and you need a stout outfit to beat a 12 pound chopper. Some of you may balk, believing that 'sport' involves catching the biggest fish on the lightest tackle. I disagree. Large line capacity, a smooth drag, and a moving boat allows an angler to land big fish on wispy tackle. However, that fish may not survive a release, even if he swims away after you resuscitate him. And if you are gonna keep the fish for the table, so much lactic acid will have built up that the meat is basically spoiled. Besides, fish pull harder on heavier tackle. They may pull longer on the noodle rods, but they pull harder on stout stuff. You want a big bluefish to show you all he's made of? Fight him on 20 pound gear from shore or an anchored boat.

Vitriol expelled, I'll divide bluefish tackle into several categories. Since so many of us like to chase the birds, let's start off with gear for that. You'll want a medium–heavy spinning rod between six and seven feet long. To this you'll mount a medium weight reel loaded with 15 pound line. (Or equivalent diameter in a super braid.) Terminal tackle consists of a snap swivel on which you'll attach your lure, typically a diamond jig of between one and three ounces with a surge tube tail, or a popping plug. If you use the tube tailed jig, make sure your snap swivel is a good-quality ball-bearing model. If not, your line is going get very twisted, very quick. A large snap, no swivel, is fine for poppers. Use single hook lures—replace the tail hooks on poppers with single hooks one size larger than the treble you removed. That keeps the lure in balance Trying to remove a treble hook from the toothy maw of a live bluefish is tough—and dangerous. I do not use a wire leader on this setup. I find that blues chase the moving jig or plug, hitting it

Charlie Falvey boating a bluefish. Note the homemade lip gaff.

from behind. The lure itself provides the bite-off protection. Yes, occasionally another blue will bite you off as he tries to steal the "bait" from his brother's mouth. It's rare, and a cost of doing business. Besides, the wire detracts from the lure's action and can cause tangles during the cast. Pick your poison.

For bottom fishing with cut bait, chunking, or live bait fishing, I suggest conventional tackle. Revolving spool reels offer better line control than spinning reels. For instance, you can let a bait out a little deeper, or give a live bait a little more room to roam around, all while keeping a relatively taut line. Plus, you're likely to catch bigger fish while baitfishing than you will by chasing the birds. Conventional reels, with their stiff frames, heavy-duty gears and larger drag washers are the way to go. Spinners just don't have the beef to hold up to gorilla after gorilla like a conventional reel does.

What size tackle am I talking about? You could use a medium weight six foot rod and a levelwind reel loaded with 15 pound test if you're in open water where you don't have to pull a fish away from obstructions like jetties, bridges, other anchored boats; heavy weight isn't needed because the water is shallow or there is little current; and/or you know the fish aren't that big. At the other end of the spectrum is a heavy 30 to 50 pound class rod, six and a half to seven feet long, to which is mounted a 3/0 reel loaded with 40 pound test. This would be the gear for full moon tides, deep water, heavy weights and big fish. I usually bring the first setup whenever I go baiting blues, as a backup, and because if conditions warrant using it, it's a lot lighter to hold for a whole tide than the broom stick outfit I described.

But if I could only bring one rod on a bluefish expedition in which I expected to be baitfishing, I'd start with a seven foot medium-heavy graphite rod with lots of backbone, but with a soft enough tip for flipping out a chunk or lobbing a live bait. To this I'd mount a heavy-duty, medium weight conventional reel—I'm partial to models that allow going from freespool to in-gear by simply turning the handle. Load this reel with 20 pound test line.

Terminal rigging for bluefishing with bait also depends upon several factors. If you're fishing in the deep, fast waters above Hell's Gate, or in the rips at Montauk, or you are drift fishing rather than anchored, I'd suggest the classic Three-Way Rig. Tie a three-way swivel to your running line. To the next eye of the swivel, attach a two foot long 50 pound mono leader.

Using an Albright Knot, connect a six inch trace of wire leader to which is connected a 6/0 hook with a wide bend—a beak style is a good choice, as is an Octopus hook. You can use all wire for the leader, simply Haywire Twist piano wire to the three-way swivel, or snap on a store-bought cable leader, but the heavy mono-trace combo ups your chances of a stray bass also hitting the rig. Bass can be more line-shy than blues. To the third eye of the swivel connect an 18" section of 20 pound mono and tie a Surgeon's Loop in the end for a sinker connection. Using the catspaw, you can slip the loop through the eye of the sinker and change weights easily as conditions change. If you're fishing a wreck, rocky area or "sticky" bottom, tie an overhand knot in the sinker line just above the loop. Overhand knots allow mono to cut itself, so if you get hung-up, you may be able to break off the sinker, save the rest of the rig, and get back in the action more quickly. Of course, you should always have several back-up terminal rigs ready in any case. You don't want to be searching for swivels or frantically tying knots in the middle of a short-lived blitz, perhaps the only one for the day. The more time you've got an offering in the water, the more fish you will catch. It's not rocket science.

An alternative Three-Way rig, one I've come to favor, uses less hardware, i.e., less weed catchers and less "flash" to attract a bluefish that might bite you off instead of biting your hook. Clinch knot a barrel swivel to your running line. Tie a dropper loop about a foot long, in the middle of a four foot length of 60 pound fluorocarbon leader. ("Flouro" is less visible, mimicking the refractive index of water.) To the dropper attach your hook and wire trace, using an Albright or, using both strands of the dropper as one leg, tying a Palomar Knot to the wire trace's loop. At the terminal end of this leader, tie a surgeon's loop to attach your sinker.

A fishfinder rig lets you feel the pickup while the fish feels nothing. However, this is not a rig for "deadsticking." If you want to hit the bottom and put the rod in a holder—as you might when young people or novices are aboard—use the Three Way. If you want the best shot at fish, and are willing to actively fish, use the fishfinder. You can make a fishfinder most simply by sliding an egg sinker up your main line and tying a barrel swivel to the end of the line as a stop. I don't do this. Burrs from the molding process, inside the egg sinker, chafe the line. Instead, I prefer to buy the nylon fishfinders, (buy the black ones, not the white ones with the silver snaps, to prevent bite-offs) with a sinker snap attached. This is slid up the line, a barrel swivel is tied on as a stop and a foot-long trace of wire leader with a 6/0 Octopus style hook is attached to the barrel swivel's other ring.

Now, when the current slows, or you are fishing shallow water—say Reynolds Channel, Shinnecock's East Cut, Port Jefferson's Middle Grounds—you'll use a simpler rig. Tie a barrel swivel and leader as described above and skip any sinker attachment. In slow current, or shallow water, you'll simply drift the bait back with the chunks-perhaps adding a split shot or rubber-core sinker to fine tune the depth of the bait's drift.

For live bait fishing, you'll want to add another setup to your arsenal. You can buy live baits in many ports nowadays, but you can also catch your own if you're fishing where concentrations of bunker are reliably available. I'm speaking of course, about the North Shore Harbors, where bunker seem to be prevalent. A heavy duty spinning outfit, say an eight-

Large "racer" bluefish, all head and skinny, rampage the back bays in early spring. Heady Creek, Southampton.

footer with lots of backbone, is great for snagging bunker and fishing it live right there, where you snagged it. Mount a reel capable of holding 200 yards of 20 pound line. You need this beefiness because you're gonna chuck a 5/0 to 7/0 weighted treble hook out into the school of bunker, allow it to sink, and then rip it back with sweeping snaps of the rod in hopes of snagging a bunker. You can tie up a leader, using 60 pound mono, using dropper loops to attach an unweighted treble or two about a foot apart, above the weighted snag hook. This lets you snag more than one bait at a time, fishing one live immediately, and saving the others for fresh chunk bait.

Some guys will snag the bunker, and let it swim with the weighted treble: they just stop reeling once they feel the menhaden get impaled. I like to do this. The weight slows the snagged bait down, making him easy prey. All predators, bluefish included, are genetically programmed to attack the weak and wounded. That's nature's way of keeping the stocks healthy. We fisherman have to hone-in on the ways of the fish world if we want to be hi-liners. So this method often works. But not always.

One problem with fishing the snagged bunker right on the snag rig is that you have no choice in hook placement. You don't know if he's caught in the head, side, tail, whatever. The best place to hook a live bunker for bluefish is under the backbone, just aft of the dorsal fin. Bluefish generally attack from behind. Moreover, this aft hook placement lets the bait breath better and live longer. Therefore, real sharpies often have two rods. One's a snagger, as described above. The other is a similar outfit, though rigged with a single hook—treble or not—on a trace of wire leader. The bunker is snagged, boated or beached, and then transferred to the other rod. I like this method when boat fishing with a crew. Upon finding a school of bunker, one guy "makes bait" with the snag rig, filling the livewell, while the others immediately begin fishing. Once enough baits are caught, or after a fish is boated, the snagger fishes himself and one of the anglers keeps up the snagging. Organization and teamwork will really improve your catch, whether bleufishing, tuna fishing or flounder fishing.

Traditionally, when live baiting, I've fished a seven foot, soft-action, medium-heavy conventional rod with revolving spool reel capable of holding 200 yards of 20 pound monofilament. More recently, my good friend, Capt. Tim Hermus, of M & M Charters out of Westhampton, has turned me on to using spinning tackle. Hermus pulls more big fish—I'm talking bass here too—out of Moriches Inlet than anybody I know. The setup he uses is a stiff-backboned soft-tipped spinning rod to which is mounted a Penn 560 Slammer Liveliner. This setup's advantage over conventional tackle is that it doesn't require an "educated thumb" to prevent a backlash when a fish picks up your bait and runs. Instead, the line peels out smoothly and, since a spinner's spool doesn't revolve, backlashes are basically eliminated. The caveat mentioned above still applies: Hermus wears out several reels a season, as the gears and guts of most spinning reels just aren't as tough as those of quality conventional reels.

The terminal setup for live bait is basic, and the same whether using bunker, herring, eels, whatever. For shallow water and light current, simply tie a barrel swivel to the end of the running line and attach a foot-long trace of 100 pound piano wire leader and your hook. You can attach a rubber core sinker if you need a little weight. If currents are strong or you need to get your bait deep, skip the barrel swivel and tie a bead chain drail of enough weight to keep your bait down. Attach your leader and hook to the drail's other end. Use short-shank "live bait" hooks, in sizes ranging from 5/0 to 8/0, depending upon the size of your bait. For instance, I'll use smaller hooks, like 5/0 for eels, than I do for shad or big bunker where I might go as big as 8/0. But I never use a hook smaller than 5/0 as I feel it doesn't expose enough point and bend for a proper hookset. Use as big a hook as is reasonable and your hookup rate will soar.

If you have novices aboard, non-fisherman out "playing," or just want to load up on bluefish either for shark bait, dockside bragging rights, or for the "thrill" of reeling 'em up three or four at a time, add a wire-line outfit to your arsenal. Wire is deadly effective for putting meat in the box. Plus, there are times, such as midday, when the blues sulk and go deep, when wire becomes the most effective way to catch them. Particularly with an umbrella rig. This is charterboat-style fishing, where the captain and boat actually do the catching—the crew simply pumps and winds (and grunts and groans!) But lots of folks love it. So get yourself a couple of heavy-duty 30 to 50 pound class rods, Six-foot-six-inches in length, and make sure they have carbaloy or roller guides. I prefer carbaloy ring guides over rollers, because there is no maintenance involved. Rollers need periodic adjustment and constant lubrication. Wire will quickly groove and ruin any guides but the above two. Also, look for an underwrap (thread between the guide and rod blank) or ask your tackle dealer to show you what underwrap is. The pressure of wire can "punch" through today's tubular rods if no underwrap is present. My wire rods are custom Altenkirch sticks, solid glass, and have been in service for over 20 years. It pays, long term, to buy quality tackle. Mount a 4/0 trolling reel with at least a 3:1 retrieve ratio (you'll have lots of line out and a slow retrieve reel will make your time fishing drudgery. Don't be sold a slow retrieve "powerful" reel. Blues are tough, but they're not bigeye tuna). Load this up two-thirds full with 50 pound mono backing and connect 300' of 50 pound stainless-steel wire, using either an Albright knot or a barrel swivel. Mark the wire at 100' and then every 50'. You can use colored electrical tape, or tight wraps of telephone cable, as depth indicators. Or you can let the tackle shop do it. Wire isn't just about going deep, it's about precise depth. Your lure will be one foot deep for every 10' of wire let out (or 10' deep for every 100' out). The marks, therefore, let you posi-

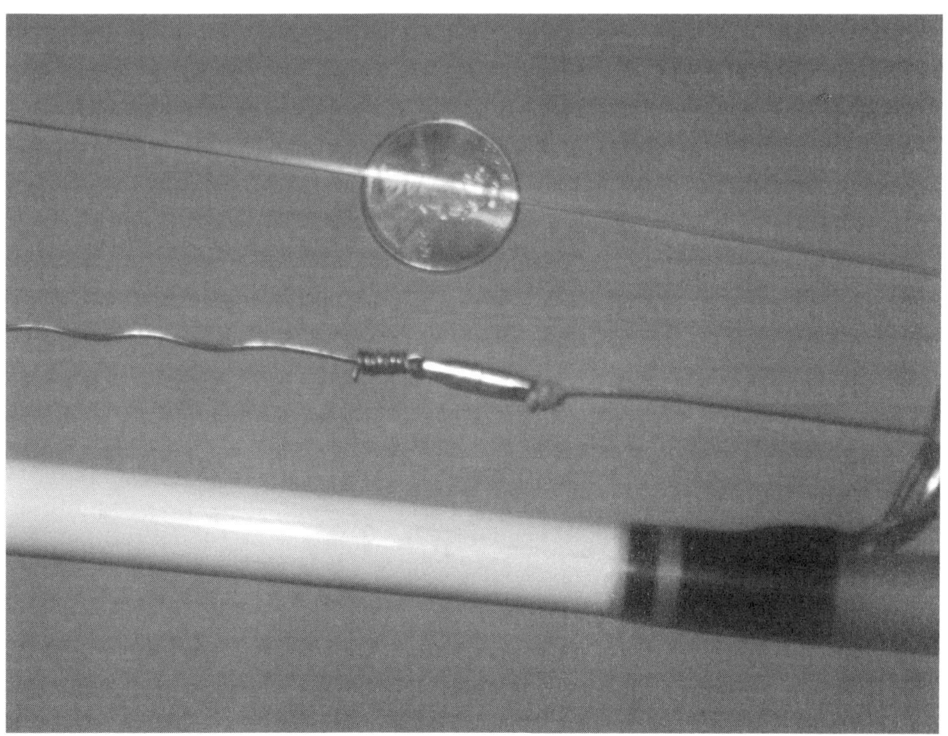

A wind-on swivel makes a smooth connection between wire line and leader.

tion the bait in the water column. As an aside, placing a drail between the lure and the leader will get you down another foot for every ounce of lead. That tip lets you get a little deeper while retaining a large spool diameter (less line out) and thus helps maintain a faster retrieve.

Haywire Twist a 50 pound ball-bearing barrel swivel to the terminal end of the wire. The Haywire Twist is an easy knot, once you know the trick. Make a loop in the end of the wire and twist the two "legs" of the loop across each other evenly, at a 45 degree angle, and twist both of them at the same time. Simply wrapping one leg of the loop around the other makes a sloppy connection, tough to go through the guides and makes a weaker connection as well.

I like the "wind-on" swivels in this application. Their lower profile eases them through the guides, lessening the chance of a backlash while letting out the line. You can also cut the rings off a ball bearing swivel and tie your line and leader to the holes in the remaining barrel to achieve the same streamlined effect. Then Clinch knot a 20' length of 60 pound fluorocarbon leader to the swivel's other ring. Finally, Palomar or Clinch knot a ball-bearing 150 pound snap swivel the end of the leader. Use the best components for your wire outfit's leader system. No cheap swivels or line and tie the knots with precision. You can use it several times over–and re-use the hardware all season—if you do.

FISHING

If you're chumming and chunking, steak your mackerel, bunker or herring by making three-quarter-inch wide vertical cuts. Then simply impale a bunker or mackerel chunk on the hook, with the hook bend passing under the backbone and the point coming out the other side, remaining exposed. With big chunks, like those from the shoulder of a large bunker, I'll cut the chunks in half. You want some hook bend and the point exposed. Now let the bait out into the current, keeping an eye on the depth and speed of the chum-chunk flow. In shallow water, slow current situations, you want your bait to drift back naturally with the chunk-chum. Throw a few chunks overboard and watch how they drift. Now let out your bait, pulling line off the spool to match the speed and rate of sink of the chum chunks. A split-shot can be used to fine-tune your bait's rate of sink.

In deeper water, or faster current where you are using the three-way or fish-finder rig, allow your bait to hit the bottom. Then let out line, thumbing the spool and lifting the rod tip, "walking" your bait back into the current. Again, check out how fast the chunk chum is sinking and at what angle. You are trying to get your bait back to the location where the chunks have hit the bottom, or nearly so. Be ever-vigilant for a pickup, though, as a strike can come at any time. When the bait reaches what you estimate to be the "spot," let it sit for a minute. If no strike, reel it back in and start over. Within the limits of your reel's line capacity, experiment with how far back to let the bait go before reeling up. Sometimes the fish will hang back, particularly when you first start chunking. As the slick develops, the fish will often swim up it and hit your hook baits closer. This is what you want and an indication that you are chumming rather than feeding. Be attentive and think about what's going on. Don't over-chum. It takes experience, but it's well worth developing the feel for how much chum it takes to attract the fish without feeding them so much that they hang back in the slick. Why should a bluefish swim further to get to your bait if he doesn't have to? Too much chum can be worse than no chum.

When the fish picks up the bait, let him run for a moment, dipping your rod tip. Now engage the reel and come up with the rod—hold on! That bluefish is gonna peel some line. Your rod tip will throb, flexing and relaxing, as the combined forces of drag slip, line stretch, and rod bend all take up the strain. Do not let up. Bluefish wear a big hole in their mouths where the hook is. Keep the rod tip up and the pressure on. Pump the fish back to the boat by reeling only on the down stroke. Pump up, reel down, pump up, reel down. Expect at least one other run, and when it comes, keep the tip up at 45 degrees or so and let him pull drag. Then resume pumping and reeling. Watch our for a last minute surge at the side of the boat.

You can gaff your bluefish, though I prefer to swing 'em aboard. Grasp the leader, rotate your wrist to take a wrap or two around your palm, and in a smooth motion that allows the line to stay taught, haul him aboard in a fluid arc. They chew up nets, so use one at your peril. Or bring more than one.

Here are another couple of tips for handling just-caught bluefish: if you grab them by the tail and lift so that the body bends at a right angle from the tail and hangs down, the blue will go into paralysis (until you let go). Another way is to grab them by the eyes like a bowling ball. In any event stay away from the teeth and ice down any fish meant for the table. Bluefish that's been "poached" on the deck of your boat or in a bucket isn't worth feeding to a cat. But ice 'em and bleed 'em and you might be pleasantly surprised.

There are those who disdain live-baiting for bluefish, figuring why bother, but I'm not one of them. Sure, there are times when I'd rather nail a bass or a tiderunner weakfish, but watching the drama of predator and prey play out at the end of my line is a pursuit that never disappoints, regardless of the quarry. Particularly when fishing calm, shallower water.

Your bunker or herring, impaled with a 7/0 short-shank O'Shaughnessy aft of it dorsal, is lobbed just up-current of a point, bar, or drop-off. Thumb on the spool, rod tip high, you zone in on your bait's every tail-beat as you let the current take it back to the edge. You've got his rhythm down, and you watch your line, attentive for a flattening angle, indicating your bait trying to surface in an attempt to escape an unseen predator. You're ears are in gear, listening for slurps, tail slaps. Your nose picks up the scent

Bunker were once touted as food. They make better bait.

of fish, mixed with the brine air. You wait. The bait swims faster. You give some line. Frantic now, the bunker is circling, pulling hard. Don't strike yet. Brake the spool with your thumb, dip the rod tip: the lamb to the slaughter. A pause, as your bait is struck—then the line begins to move again. Fast. Engage the reel, reel out any slack and come up….Fish On!

Yes, live-baiting bluefish is exciting. And you can be the director of this drama anywhere from Execution Rocks to Shagwong. Of course, you won't always hook fast on the first pickup. If you don't, let the bait be. Often the blue, or one of his brethren, will pick up a missed or maimed bait. Another reason for not head-hooking a bait when targeting bluefish is that they'll often ignore it if that's all that's left. With an aft hook position, your chances of having half a bait that's still appealing rise greatly.

Diamond-jigging is another tried and true technique for bluefish. Its particularly effective in deeper water like Cholera, The Eaton's Neck Triangle, or near-shore wrecks like the Panther, and especially when spearing are on the menu. A tube-tailed jig, heavy enough to hit bottom without getting blown away by the current, is knotted to the end of a 60 to 80 pound mono leader. Using heavy conventional tackle, and a reel with a minimum 4:1 retrieve ratio, you drop the jig to the bottom. Here's where you become a fisherman.

Some days, all you need to do is drop the jig, and when it hits bottom, immediately begin reeling as fast as you can. Wham! Fish on. This was called squidding when I was a kid, though the term has fallen from favor. But its not always that simple.

Sometimes the fish are holding at some point above the bottom, so you drop, jig and reel all the way back to the surface, counting the turns of the reel handle. After getting hit, you subsequently drop down to the bottom—your reference point—then reel back up the same number of turns to the depth where you got a strike. At this point, you can engage the reel and jig the lure at that depth. Alternatively, reel up a bit more, let the jig fall for a couple seconds, then reel up a few turns and repeat this yo-yo action in the strike zone. Your bottom machine may mark fish at one depth, but they may be striking at another. Trust the bite.

Other days they like you to jig the jig. That is, bounce the bottom, creating puffs of sand. This imitates the action of sand eels. A wonder of nature, sand eels rise like ghosts, out of apparently barren bottom, remain visible momentarily, and then vanish back into the sand as quickly as they appeared. You must do your best to imitate this action. Think like a sand eel. Make it happen. Believe.

Trolling wire line for bluefish is also deadly. You can use a variety of lures. Bucktails laced with porkrind, bunker spoons, large single tubes, you name it. Ideally you'd pick a lure that imitated what the blues are suspected of feeding upon: a large spoon for bunker, a bucktail dragged through the sand for sand eels, etc. Day-in, day-out, however, you can't go wrong with an umbrella rig. Invented in Montauk, right here on Long Island, umbrella's are deadly. Basically, the only time I won't stream one in my wake is if the water's real weedy. Despite their effectiveness, they are the great rakes of fishing tackle.

Umbrella rigs range from simple two-hook spreaders to six-armed rigs capable of deploying 12 tubes. I like the four-arm rigs that feature four hooks and four teasers. And I like to customize them. Teasers, the hookless tubes, are attached to the loops in the middle of each arm. On the corners, I use hooked tubes. But I don't simply connect the hooks to the snaps at the end of the arms. Instead, I tie short leaders, about 10" long, using 80 pound mono to each hooked tube. At the leader's other end I tie on a black barrel swivel. The teasers and these corner hooks all sport the same color tubes. I then tie a three foot leader to the ring on the weight molded to the frame. To the end of this, I tie a different color hooked tube. When going through the water, the hooks on the corners are further back then the teasers and the center hook is further back than the corner hooks. This makes the rig more closely resemble a school of baitfish. Also, I believe the off-color lure dropped back down the center looks like a straggler—a wounded, slower fish, one that a predator like a bluefish is likely to hone in on. I've also used a longer eight or 10" rigged tube in this drop back position, believing it resembles a predator chasing the "school." Here, I'm trying to incite the bluefish's competitive instinct to bite. In any case, the leaders give the hooked tubes better action. Don't just snap tubes on the frame. Use leaders.

I usually fish one red umbrella rig and one natural umbrella rig, again using an off-color hook dropped back. Its easy enough to change colors and I keep a supply of hooks and teasers aboard for this purpose. Green has also worked well, as has white. But red and natural are my go-to colors.

To put an umbrella rig in the water, set the boat on the intended course. Throttle up to about two knots. Grasp the rod in your right hand, thumb on the spool, clicker off. Hold the rig by the leader, close to the frame in your other hand. Shake-out any tangles or twists. When all is hanging clear place the rig in the water and simultaneously let out line under the control of your thumb—almost complete free spool is what you want. If you put the rig over with strain on the line—the reel in gear—it's going to trip over itself and tangle. Just remember: boat under way, place in water, thumbed free spool, and you'll be fine. Once the rig is submerged it will deploy smoothly the rest of the way

Now, before you let out line and start fishing, look at how the rig is swimming while it's there next to the boat. Are the teasers lazily rotating? Are the hooks swimming snakily? Adjust your boat speed until they are. Now you are ready to fish.

Allow the line to go back, figuring about 10' of depth for every 100' of wire you let out. I usually throttle the boat up a bit to get the lures out faster, than return to the "fishing speed" I observed next to the boat once the mark for the intended depth has passed through the tip top. Engage the reel, put the clicker on and start working the structure.

Wire line trolling involves intense visualization on the skipper's part. You have to "see" what the lure is doing 50' down and several hundred feet behind your boat. Eight little fish are wiggling their way through the murk, (usually) just above the shell-strewn bottom. You veer a little to make the lure pass as close as you dare to a boulder. As they approach the drop-off—the boat's already past it—they come into view of the bluefish, lying in wait, noses to the current. They see the lure from below, suddenly appearing over the ridge. No takers on the first pass? Try shifting into neutral for a moment as the lure passes the structure. The decrease in speed causes them to sink a bit. Shift back in gear in gear, they suddenly surge forward. This approximates how a school of baitfish swims, in fits and spurts, as anyone who has watched spearing in the shallows knows. You can also try stemming, if there's enough current. Troll the boat past the structure, say a reef or rockpile, till the lures are right on it. Now throttle down to a speed that keeps the boat motionless, its nose in the current, neither moving ahead nor falling back. The current will keep the tubes swimming, and you're leaving a tasty meal right in "the hot zone" for a prolonged period. Stemming is particularly effective after you've made a couple of successful passes and determined where the fish are hitting. By using it, noting your line depth, you can often repeatedly hook up and get right back on 'em like clockwork. I remember slaughtering bluefish using the stemming technique at the Smithtown Bay Reef one trip, and have done so at Jessup's Neck and the South Race in Peconic Bay with regularity. But the technique can be applied anywhere you have structure of reasonable profile and current.

A lot of new guys ask me how I turn the boat around so quickly with wire line and rarely seem to get the rigs fouled-up. Number one, I accelerate through the apex of the turn that keeps the lures riding a little higher. Second, I'll often take up—or have a crewmember take up—a dozen turns on the inboard lure. The inboard lure slows down and falls during a turn. So if I'm turning to starboard, the starboard lure comes up a bit—not too much—just enough to keep it from hitting the bottom. It's when one of them hits the bottom and stops that lines cross, lures tangle, and tempers flare.

Wire line tackle is expensive, rivaling that of offshore gear. It also requires practice both with boat handling, and line handling. For instance, when letting out wire, its better to thumb the side of the spool than to thumb the wire itself. Figure it out, though, and you'll be rewarded not just with lots of fish, but you'll catch fish when others can't seem to catch them.

Now, when the birds are wheeling on a feeding school of bluefish, nobody has a problem finding them. But even the best anglers can have trouble catching them, and the problem is invariably other anglers. In short, don't run full throttle into the school. A nice easy pace, get within casting range, and idle down. If you find yourself upwind of the school—too bad. Let the others fish and go around and come back without dispersing the school. Courtesy allows everyone to get in on the action.

When I see birds diving, and fish busting, my heart races, despite having seen it hundreds of times. But I take a minute to watch for a pattern. Very often the fish will run the bait to Point A then to Point B then out to Point C in a repetitive pattern. If you can see this pattern you can get one step ahead and be waiting, motor shut down, rod in hand, ready to cast.

When that time comes, throw your lure. If it's a popper, the time to start reeling and popping is the instant the lure hits the water. This means turning the handle and flipping the bail a split second before the lure splashes. Sometimes a straight, water-pushing, high-speed retrieve works best. Other times you reel and pop, reel and pop. Sometimes, as exciting as top-water bleufishing can be, they won't take a popper as readily as a jig worked through the depths.

At those times, switch to a Hopkins or Diamond Jig with a tube tail. For these, I like white tubes first, contrary to my color preference for umbrella rig tubes, with natural coming in second. These observations are based on nearly 30 years of logbooks that I have kept. I know what works–and what has worked for a long time—for me. Take it as you will.

I like to let the jig settle to bottom depth, before engaging the reel and beginning my retrieve. The most productive has always been a fast, rhythmic, jig and reel. If I feel a touch and don't hook up mid-retrieve I will pause for second, allowing the jig to sink for a minute. This I believe imitates a fish that has just been wounded. Often, I get a strike the next moment as I again begin reeling.

Birds working, a crisp, October sunrise, and acres of busting bluefish comprise imagery, and incentive, to keep me fishing 'til I can no longer hold a rod.

Bluefish Crib Sheet

Bluefish, a.k.a, chopper, tailor, racer, snapper.

Season: April-November

Location: Deep ocean to backwater harbors; near wrecks, dropoffs, areas of high current and concentrations of larger bait, i.e, bunker, herring.

Baits: Live bunker, herring, shad, mackerel; chunks of bunker, herring, mackerel, etc. Actively takes a variety of lures.

Tackle: Medium to Heavy (mature) Ultralight and cane poles (snappers).

High Hook Tip: When chunking, impale several bunker hearts (Brownish-maroon globule in bunker guts) just below point of hook. It makes them crazy.

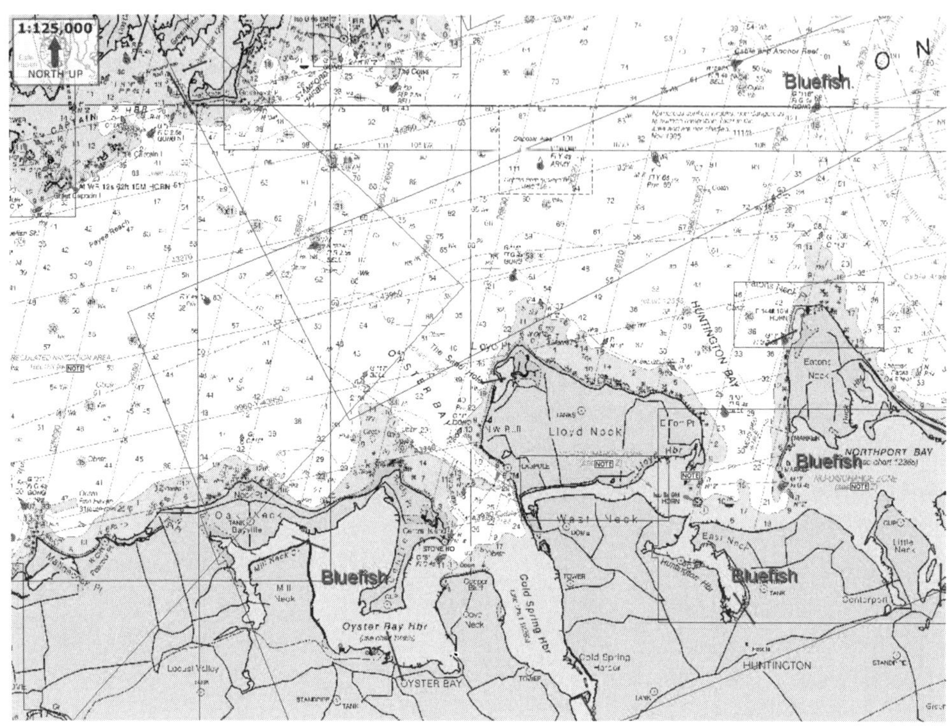

In mid-Sound, Buoy 11B is a great spot. Big blues also roam deep into the inner harbors, amongst the mooring buoys.

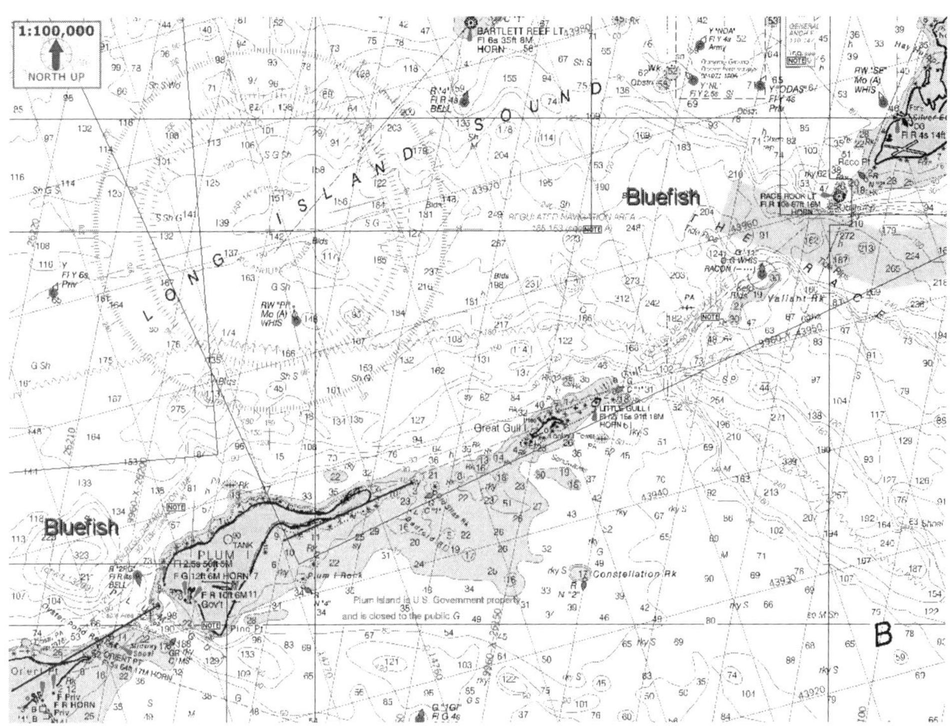

Plum Gut (lower left) and The Race (upper right) offer world-class bluefish action.

CHAPTER 4
Striped Bass
(Morone saxatillis)

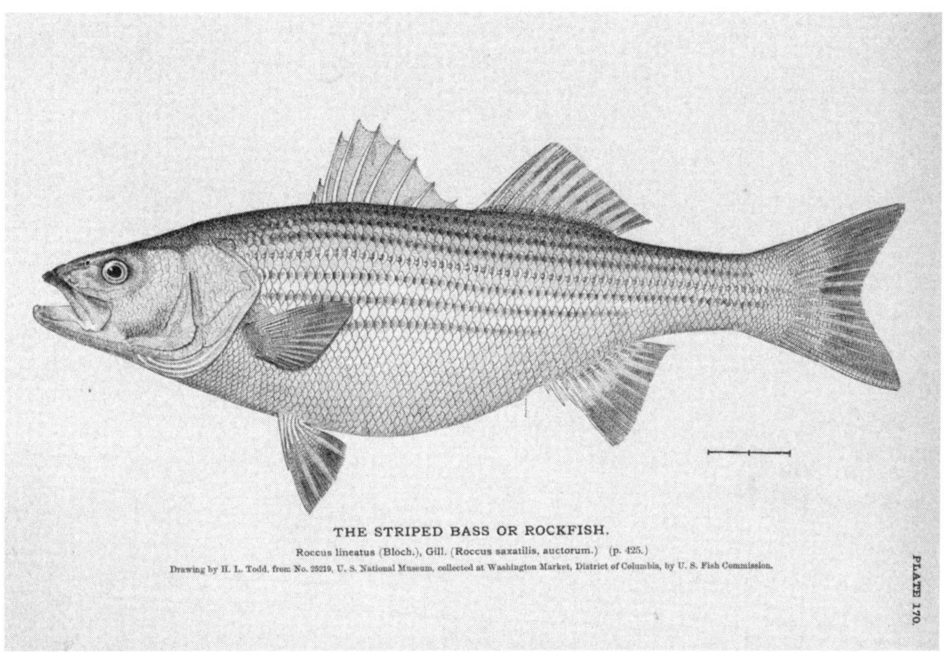

Credit: NOAA.

Few fish have attained the status the striped bass enjoys. That's primarily because no fish that can be caught close to shore offers so much: stripers fight well, grow to large size, are pretty to look at, and taste darn good. Secondly, there's a whole generation of anglers, those who fished in the early 1970's and before, myself included, who watched the stripers go from abundant and common —my grandfather complained when he caught a double header of bass on a spreader rig while we were flounder fishing off Bar Beach—to nearly zip. By the time the Bicentennial rolled around, only sharpies were catching fish with regularity. By 1984, Congress had enacted the Striped Bass Act, strict limits were imposed, and most anglers were fishing for other species. This dearth of fish transmuted the striped bass into its mythical status. It's human nature to want what's hard to get.

While this was going on, a small group I like to think of as The Faithful continued the quest, egged on rather than deterred, by a diminutive population of fish. Red-eyed and salt-smeared from too many night tides, those who caught stripers in those days of no-kill, catch-and-release-only bass fishing were revered by anglers. Remember, it wasn't like today, where most anyone clam chumming can drill a keeper with some effort. Bass were fewer and farther between—at least for the bulk of us. (Hard numbers: there were an estimated 1.8 metric tons of recreationally caught bass in 1986, half a ton commercial. In 2005 those numbers had increased to 12 metric tons and three metric tons respectively.)

I'm not one of The Faithful. I went fluking and weakfishing and blackfishing and spent a lot of time chasing tuna, sharks and other pelagics during this period. But I count several members of The Faithful as dear friends. The Faithful taught me a lot, setting me on a road I have traveled for over 25 years now, a highlight of which was the capture of a 54 pound bass in 1998. (Still my only bass over 50 pounds.) But every tide is an adventure, because if The Faithful taught me anything, it's to approach striper fishing as hunting rather than as a conglomeration of techniques, fancy knots and rigging methods. Think like a bass and you'll catch a bass, Martin Landy used to tell me. It's the theme of this book—think like a fish to catch that fish—and is what I hope to share most with you in this chapter. The Faithful gave me the ball and I ran with it. Now I'm handing-off to you. What was freely given is given freely.

TAXONOMY AND BIOLOGY

Striped bass are bulky fish, three times as long as they are deep. Characterized by seven (and sometimes eight) dark lateral stripes, they have a lateral line, which they use to sense vibrations in the water. The lateral line is usually covered by the third stripe down from the dorsal fins. The bass's most typical coloration is a dark greenish back fading to a white, fat belly. That said, you'll often catch fish that are more silvery overall as well as those that are a light tan under the stripes. The latter are sometimes colloquially referred to as "sand bass."

Striped bass have a large mouth, with an under-slung jaw and three rows of small teeth ringing the jaws. As anyone who has reached deep into a striper's maw to unhook a swallowed bait knows, they also possess two rows of teeth on their tongues. These tongue teeth do a number on your forearm when unhooking a gut-hooked striper, the scabby abrasions that result resembling skateboarder's "road rash."

The striper's distinct looks make it easy to distinguish from other species. However, young fish, under a foot long, often co-mmingle with white perch in tidal creeks. It can be very hard to tell the difference. But look close: there is a space between the two dorsal fins of a striper and no space between the two top fins of a white perch.

Stripers are beautifully evolved for their environment.

Striped bass grow to over 100 pounds and more than five feet long. The largest documented catch was a pair of 125 pound fish caught at Edenton, North Carolina in 1891. The current IGFA All-Tackle World Record Fish is a 78.8 pound fish caught at Atlantic City, New Jersey in 1982. The New York State rccord is a 76 pound fish caught off Orient Point in 1981. My good friend, Bill Bennet, a retired baymen, remembers haul-seining

This "50" ate a trolled tube the author tipped with an eel filet.

stripers off East End beaches, some of which exceeded 60 pounds in weight. The big fish DO live here. Dozens of fish over 50 pounds are reported each year and sharpies, who have made a study of the bass's habits, regularly catch 30-plus pound fish.

The average size, according to biologists, is between three and 35 pounds. I'd narrow that down a bit and say that the bulk of fish caught recreationally on Long Island weigh about nine pounds, measuring some 30" long. That's an observation, based on the preponderance of schoolie fish caught. A female that length might weigh in at 12 pounds or so, the "girls" being fatter. (Almost all stripers over 30 pounds are female.) Furthermore, most fish over 20 pounds live in open waters of the Sound and Ocean, whereas fish under 20 pounds predominate in the bays and harbors. So where you fish—and how you fish—often dictates the average size you can expect, facts to be covered in depth later in this chapter. Still, big fish are caught "inside," meaning you can bang a slob at any time, so keep the faith.

The striped bass spends its entire life within sight of land. Sure, they'll sometimes pass through "offshore" waters, taking the shortcut between Sandy Hook and Montauk, for instance, rather than follow the beach, during migration. But for the most part, they are a fish of the coast.

Bass spawn in brackish and freshwaters. Though the bulk of the stock comes from the Hudson River and Chesapeake Bay, they spawn in smaller tidal creeks and streams, even some right here on Long Island. Mother Nature doesn't place all of her eggs in one basket. Spawning begins in April in the Chesapeake Bay and mid-May to June in the Hudson River. Interestingly, tagging studies have shown that most of the bass in Long Island Sound are Hudson River fish and most of the bass found along the South Shore's Atlantic Coast are Chesapeake fish. At Gardiners Bay, and on east into New England, both stocks co-mingle.

A female bass, surrounded by smaller males, broadcasts her eggs. The males broadcast sperm. Within 48 hours, a three millimeter long larvae hatches. After a week, the yolk sac is absorbed and they are swimming and feeding. At 80 days the signature stripes form. At one year, they weigh about a pound and measure a foot long. At three years they are mature, weighing about five pounds and measuring 20" in length.

While it's known that stripers spawn in freshwater, and that young fish spend most of their first year in or near the brackish nurseries they were hatched in, pinning down overall migration patterns is tough. There are fish that leave the Chesapeake and Hudson and head north and east along the coast, returning to their natal waters each fall. Some fish do not return, however, choosing instead to over-winter in local coves and creeks, lying in a torpid state in the mud. (I know several people who, while gigging for eels through winter ice, have speared 25 pound bass.) Still others head offshore, again taking to the bottom in a semi dormant state. What is certain is that prior to laying-up for the winter and also after the exertions of the spring spawn, the bass will be most concentrated and feeding most actively. That's probably why June and October are nominally the best months to fish for stripers, with the nod going to October. It's all about the fall.

Taking a look at water temperature tolerances, scientists tell us that striped bass can live in waters as cold as 33 degrees and as warm as 95 degrees. Research also shows that adult bass are most active when water temps are between 44 and 69 degrees. My personal logs show that until the

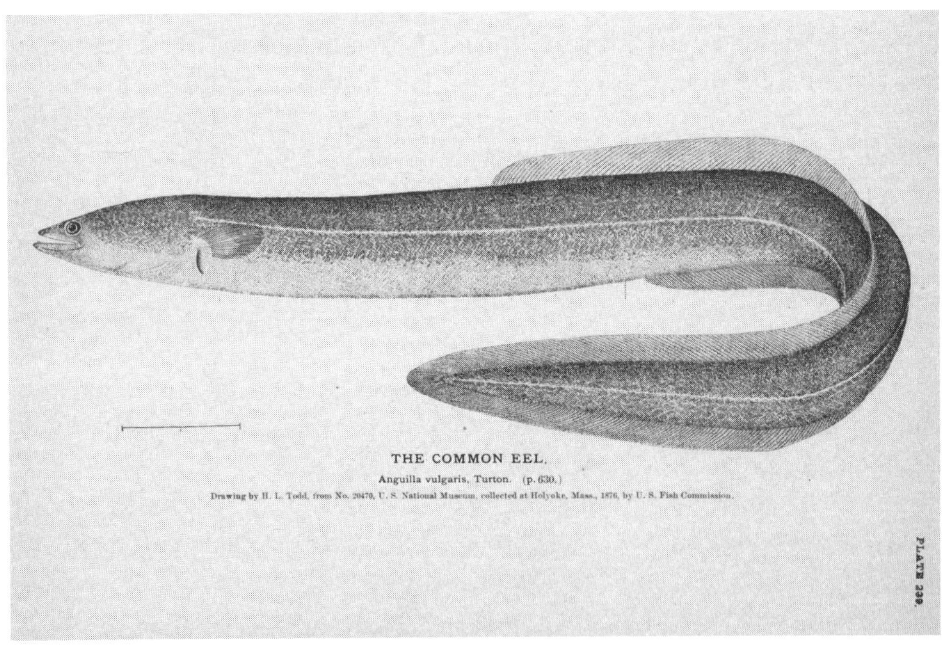

Stripers are opportunistic; eels are a favorite meal.
(Credit: NOAA)

water temps hit 50 degrees in the spring, the fish are unwilling to strike a lure, even if they are present, though they will sometimes slurp a dead bait or a worm. I've found temps in the low 60's to be ideal for actively feeding bass, regardless of the method with which you choose to pursue them.

In the fall, my observation has been that once the water temp dips below 48 degrees you still may catch fish, but most will be small "rats" under 24" in length. An abundance of small fish caught on rod and reel heralds the end of the fall run.

Striped bass are opportunistic feeders and the list of prey species is extensive. The most important food fishes are the clupeids (herrings and bunkers) and spearing. But that's just because these are the most abundant in our waters most of the time. Stripers eagerly devour eels, crab, squid, lobster, seaworms, mollusks, blackfish, porgy, bluefish, flounder, fluke, bergalls, eels and the list goes on. I know of some live bait bass specialists who regularly fish the groins and bulkheads for whatever small "trash fish" they can get, only to head for the rip or inlet and live line them for big cow bass. Here's a tip: Cut open the belly of any fish you catch and kill to find out what the bass have been eating. It may expand your horizons as to striper bait selection. At the least it may help you with lure selection.

Striped bass habitat is as diverse as their diet. They can be found along the quiet sedge islands of Jamaica Bay and they thrive in the fast, deep, currents and rocky terrain of Plum Gut. The quiet water fish will generally invade the flats, mussel, and grass beds during flood tide, dropping back to the deeper channels during the ebb. I caught my share of 20 pounders in this type of environment, and nothing's finer. But more and bigger fish, will be found in the rough stuff. Rocky points and reefs, cobble or mussel strewn bottoms, fast currents, breaking surf, these are the areas nature has blessed the striper to thrive in. Tough scales and bony head provide armor against shell and rock. Large fins and a broom tail allow it to swim with control in waters where smaller, less-well endowed creatures are tossed about like Dorothy going to Oz. With gaping mouth and flaring gills, it can suck up a fleeing or disoriented baitfish from the maelstrom. They call them rockfish down Maryland way, and with good reason. Look for your cow in the rough stuff: rough bottom, rough water, or both.

Taken a step further, you should look for bass when the current and or wave action is having the most effect. For instance, once a tide is nearly fully flooded, the current is slowing, the water depth has now increased, and so less turbulence is created as it flows past a point or over a bar. I've found

This guy thinks like a fish. Capt Scott Horowitz show’s off a slob.

mid-tide coming and two-hours into the ebb to be prime time, in general. Of course this kind of thing is very location-specific. I mention it to get you thinking like a bass. She needs water rushing over structure to bring the bait to her. She also needs to be able to set up where she can burn very little energy, rushing into the fray to grab a fish, then darting back to a position of relative calm—the gully behind a bar, the lee-current side of the boulder, etc.—where she can use that big tail to lazily stay on station. Just because they can swim in the swift currents and white water doesn't mean they want to. Like any other predator, a striped bass cannot expend more energy catching its prey than the energy supplied by that prey once it's eaten. Fish don't practice deficit spending. Think like a bass and you'll catch more bass.

It's also important to note that striped bass are a schooling fish, and will often school with fish of different sizes. Sometimes, when catching a bunch of rats, it's wise to fish a little deeper, or on what you perceive as the school's perimeter, in an attempt to catch a bigger fish. The little guys are more aggressive, bunching tighter and competing more fiercely. The slobs will often hang back or down, defending a preferred position and waiting for a meal to come to them. Of course, other times, it's just a school of rats, hence the colloquialism, "schoolie bass." The bigger bass travel in smaller schools, and even as solitary individuals. Supporting this, I've pulled many a cow out of a spot, sometimes two, then proceeded to beat the water to a froth trying to catch another without success. Many pieces can often only support a couple or three big fish—unless it's the fall and you stumble upon a migrating school. Fall is different.

TACKLE AND RIGGING

If you stood in the middle of a tackle shop, extended your arm, finger pointed, and spun in a circle, you'd be indicating the type of tackle that can be used to catch striped bass. They are caught on everything from wispy ultra-light gear to trolling tackle that could best a Mako shark if in the right hands. The tackle choices I am going to describe are the ones I use for spinning, wire line trolling, and fishing with live and dead bait. Feel free to use them as suggestions, a springboard if you will, to enhance the method of capture that suits you best.

The best way to catch a big bass is with live bait. You can buy live bunker and eels in many ports. If you want to catch your own bunker, and you don't want to learn to throw a cast net, you can snag them. A heavy duty spinning outfit, say an eight-footer with lots of backbone, is great for snagging bunker and fishing it live right on the spot. Mount a reel capable of holding 200 yards of 20 pound line. You need this beefiness because you're gonna throw a big weighted treble hook out into the school of bunker, allow it to sink, and then rip it back with sweeping snaps of the rod in hopes of snagging a bunker. You can make a leader, using 60 pound mono, with dropper loops to attach an un-weighted treble or two about a foot apart, above the weighted snag hook. This lets you snag more than one bait at a time, fishing one live immediately, and save the others for fresh chunk bait.

Some guys will snag the bunker, and let it swim with the weighted treble: they just stop reeling once they feel the menhaden get impaled. I do this sometimes. The weight slows the snagged bait down making him easy prey. All predators, striped bass included, are genetically programmed to attack the weak and wounded. That's nature's way of keeping the stocks healthy. So this method often works. But not always.

One problem with fishing the snagged bunker right on the snag rig is that you have no choice in hook placement. You don't know if he's caught in the head, side, or tail. The best place to hook a live bunker for striped bass is through the nostrils, making sure the hook bend goes under the hard bony section. Bass, lacking big, cutting teeth, swallow baits head first. They often grab a fish by the side and swim away with it a bit, before turning it headfirst to swallow. That ensures that the bait's flared gills don't get lodged on the way down the gullet.

To ensure better hook placement, real sharpies often have two rods. One's a snagger, as described above. The other is a similar outfit, though rigged with a single hook—treble or not—on a trace of 60 pound fluorocarbon leader. The bunker is snagged, boated or beached, and then transferred to the other rod. I like this method when boat fishing with a crew. Upon finding a school of bunker, one guy "makes bait" with the snag rig, filling the livewell, while the others immediately begin fishing. Once enough baits are caught, or after a fish is boated, the snagger fishes himself and one of the anglers keeps up the snagging. Organization and teamwork will really improve your catch.

Ideally, I prefer conventional tackle for live-lining stripers, using a reel capable of holding 250 yards of 30 pound mono mounted on a six and a half foot long rod. Conventional reels allow you to fish in free spool, your thumb on the line, so the bass can run with a bait without tension before you set the hook.

Spinning reels with the "bait runner" feature work really well for live-lining stripers. I was introduced to this setup by my friend Capt. Tim Hermus, M & M Charters, Westhampton, New York. With these reels, you fish the bait with the bail flipped over. When a bass picks up, he can take line, yet there's no need to thumb the spool like with a conventional reel and no fear of a backlash. When its time to set the hook, you throw a lever and the reel becomes engaged. It makes fishing bait a lot easier, though you might find that the reel's gears don't hold up over time like the beefier ones in conventional reels do. Hermus goes through several a year, though he fishes every day and it's a business expense for him. Take your pick.

Terminal rigging for live bait depends upon what you are fishing with and where. I prefer a short-shank, live bait hook in sizes 5/0 to 8/0, the smaller hooks for smaller baits like eels, snappers, and small herring. The larger hooks are for bunker, shad or that keeper-size flounder. (Hook flounder through the "shoulder" just aft of the gill plate.) Basically, I want a hook with a big enough bend to go through the bait and leave some of the bend, as well as the point and barb, exposed. Keep a variety of sizes on hand to handle different baits.

I'll clinch knot this hook to a 36" leader of 40 pound mono—or 60 pound fluorocarbon. Flouro is not as abrasion-resistant as mono, so I usually up the strength, particularly if I'm fishing the off the boulder-studded shore of, say, Wading River, around bridge pilings like at Goose Creek, or any other rough spot. The leader gets attached to the main line in one of several ways depending upon the conditions in which I'm fishing.

If I'm in a shallow water or low current situation, I'll tie a barrel swivel to the end of my main line and connect the leader there, using no weight, or perhaps a small pinch-on sinker if deemed necessary. For fishing the swift waters like the South Shore Inlets, I'll tie a bead-chain drail of sufficient weight to hit bottom to the main line and connect the leader to that with a perfection loop. For deep water, like Plum Gut, the Montauk Rips, Hell's Gate, the Triangle in mid-Sound, I'll use a three-way rig. That is, tie a three-way swivel to my main line. Tie the leader to one the remaining swivel eyes. To the third swivel eye tie a section of mono line. Then tie a large Surgeon's Loop in the end of this trace so you can catspaw the necessary bank sinker to its end. This sinker line is best if it's lighter than your running line since if you get snagged, you can often break it off leaving the sinker on the bottom, and retrieve your bait, hook and swivel, and get back in the action with the least time spent re-rigging. Tying an overhand knot in the center of this "sinker leader" is another way to help you break free of snags. Mono cuts itself when tied in an overhand knot.

I personally do not like a fish finder rig for live bait fishing. I do use them for chunk fishing, when the water is deep, or if I am fishing a "dead stick" (rod in the rod holder: Let 'ol " Rodney" catch 'im, as me and the boys like to say), as when the bite is slow and I want to fish a second rod to up my chances. With live bait, the fish finder has no advantage to my way of thinking, in that a bass expects there to be resistance when she grabs a live bunker and starts swimming away with it. But with chunks or bellies, that same fish expects to simply flare her gills, suck in the morsel, and keep swimming pretty as a picture. Think like a bass, catch more bass.

So, when chunking or clam bellying, use the same conventional gear described above—you can drop down to 15 pound baitcasting gear if conditions and weight requirements warrant— then slip a black fishfinder with sinker snap onto your main line. Then tie on a black, 80-pound barrel swivel to connect your leader. Some guys slip a bead on the line to prevent the fishfinder from abrading the knot at the swivel. I do not. Instead, I check my terminal rigging every time I reel up and re-tie at the first sign of abrasion or fraying. Pretty much every time I've failed to re-tie when I noticed something wrong, I've hooked up—then lost a fish.

If the water is real quiet, or shallow, say under 15' deep, you can tie the leader directly to a barrel swivel at the end of the main line as described above, perhaps using a split shot or rubber-core sinker if needed to tweak the sink rate. The point is to get your bait drifting back and sinking down in the current at the same rate as your chum, which we'll explore in greater detail later in this chapter.

Wire line trolling gear is responsible for lots of logged kills in my records. Whether dragging spoons or jigging bucktails, the stuff is deadly. But you can't just use any rod and reel to fish wire. Wire will quickly groove all but carboloy or roller guides. I prefer the carboloy ring guides as they require less maintenance than the rollers. Pick your poison. Rods for wire line use should also have an underwrap beneath the guides. This keeps the guides from pushing through many of today's tubular rod blanks under the heavy, no-stretch pressure wire can exert. In fact my wire sticks are seven-foot solid glass blanks for that very reason. Built by Altenkirch, they sport cork grips and carboloy ring guides—with an underwrap. These blanks are rated to 80 pounds but with a slow action, bending in an almost even arc from foregrip to tip when dragging a lure. This action is particularly suited to trolling big plugs and bunker spoons, as it lets you see how the lure is working. As long as that rod is throbbing along, your lure is swimming. Stiff, fast action give less indication of being "weeded-up." Nor do they impart the correct action to the lure.

Carried to an extreme, some sharpies have special bunker spoon rods. These measure 10' long and have a parabolic action. In the shop, tip pressed against the ceiling, they will bend in a perfect arc. But when a big bunker spoon is being pulled behind the boat, these rods do something very unique. The don't just throb like my shorter sticks, instead the tip and middle of the rod pulse like the phased waves you'd see displayed on an oscilloscope. The tip-top dips, the middle humps, the base dips. It's as though a ripple is passing through the blank. This rippling pulse imparts an action to the lures that drives bass nuts. You won't find bunker spoon rods on the racks–you'll have to find someone to build them for you.

What reel to use for wire? Get a Penn 4/0 Special Senator. The red one, not the black one. You want the high-speed retrieve ratio, as many times you'll be fishing some 300' from the boat. Without it, making lure changes or clearing weeds is just a chore. Have the reel about two-thirds loaded with 50 pound mono backing and topped-off with 300' of stainless-steel wire. I like the stainless, it's cheap and lasts a long time. Other guys prefer monel or lead core, which are easier to handle, but more expensive.

In any case, find a good tackle shop to load your wire if you are unsure of how to do it. In short, you'll need to tie an Albright knot, or haywire twist a ball bearing barrel swivel, to connect the wire line to the backing. The swivel must be small enough to pass through the tip-top so choose it wisely. I like the newer "wind-on" swivels for this purpose, or you can cut off the rings from a 100 pound barrel swivel and tie the mono and twist the wire into the remaining holes in the barrel. That's what we did before the wind-on swivels came about. Goes through the guides like a snake.

Next, you'll need to mark the wire at 50' intervals so you can tell how much is let out while fishing. Multicolored telephone wires can be barrel-wrapped around your wire line for markers, or strips of colored tape can be used. The wires last longer, but are harder to do. (Lead-core line often comes pre-marked.) Next, haywire another ball-bearing swivel to the end of the wire line. Now clinch knot a 20' long section of 60 pound mono or fluorocarbon leader to the barrel swivel. Tie a 100 pound ball-bearing snap swivel to the end of the leader. You want such a long leader so that you can have a few turns of mono on the reel spool when boating a big bass. If you fish from a large boat, with higher freeboard, use a 30' leader. The mono's stretch provides a measure of cushion that the wire doesn't at this critical time. Plus, you don't want to be grabbing wire line when it's under tension unless you are wearing gloves. The long leader makes leading a fish to net or gaff easier on the hands. You are ready to fish.

A word on the amount of wire to use. I suggested 300' because that works for me fishing mostly out of my home port of Shinnecock. Wire gets your lure down 10' for every 100 feet you let out. So 300' lets me fish 30' down. But, you also will sink a foot for every ounce of weight you add between leader and lure. So by adding a 10 ounce drail, I can fish 40' deep with only 300' of wire. (Tip: Sometimes I use more weight and less wire to get down where tight turns are necessary). The point is, if you're trying to kiss the bottom in 60' of water, by all means use 600' of wire. At the other end of the spectrum is my good friend Bobby Bossung. A dedicated member of The Faithful, Bossung has a pair of wire outfits, besides his Bunker Spoon rods, that are specially rigged for night fishing in 12' of water or less. The reels are loaded with 100' of wire. The advantage is, at night, when its hard to see or feel the depth marks going between your fingers and out the guides, all Bossung has to do is listen for the barrel swivel go click-click-click-click-click through the guides. Then he knows his 100' is out and his lure is riding just above the bottom. My point is, consider where you are going to fish trolled lures and adjust the outfit accordingly.

Casting for stripers is the ultimate inshore sport in my book. Swimming plugs, popping plugs, bucktails, and leadheadded jigs with rubber bodies of all types fall into this category for me. This is spin fishing. Even if you're as good as Roland Martin with a baitcaster, I recommend a spinning outfit as the way to go for this fishing. You'll be hunting fish, following the tide from spot to spot, casting out to knock on the door and see if anyone's home. Often, you only get one shot at a fish, casting at the swirl she left as she gobbled a fish carried by the tide or throwing in the direction of a tail slap that you heard, but didn't see, halfway through your last retrieve. A spinner lets you shoot rapid fire, like a pump shotgun, time after time, and take advantage of those opportunities better than a baitcaster. It also gives you a faster retrieve ratio, which is helpful in keeping your popper moving while reeling out the slack between "pops" (twitches of the rod's tip during retrieve).

For quiet water situations, where long casts aren't required, say working the myriad sedge islands along the State Boat Channel with a popper, or drifting and casting a lead head plastic tail to be bottom bounced along the perimeter of Garvies Point, a seven foot medium heavy rod with a fast action will do fine. Mount a 12 pound class spinner and load it with 12 pound mono or the equivalent diameter spectra. For mono, I usually tie the lure direct, without a leader, using either a perfection loop or a large snap (not snap swivel) to ensure the lure's action is not impeded. With the spectra, you'll want to use a double Uniknot to connect a section of 20 pound fluorocarbon leader and then tie on a snap.

That setup works well—even on surprisingly big fish—as long as the boat is not anchored and the water around is clear of snags, like rocks, bridge abutments, whatever. If the water's clear of obstructions and I can let the fish run, and I have fresh line and good knots, I can whup a 20 pounder on this rig, though it's really intended as a schoolie setup.

For tougher spots, and when I need plenty of backbone to resist the powerful run of what I expect to be bigger fish; for hauling a three-ounce pencil popper; for sending a popper way out onto a flat from a boat anchored at the edge of the shallows; for drifting and casting bucktails in 40' or more feet of water in the Ocean or Sound; I want a different rod, my favorite rod, the one I use most and have caught the most (though not my biggest) bass on: my eight foot, fast action graphite rod. To this is mounted a quality spinning reel capable of holding 200 yards of 15 pound mono. And that's what I fill it with: 15 pound test. A quality reel, a smooth, properly set drag, and you can beat any striper that swims with this rig. Of course, when I fish boulder-strewn bottom rather than sandy South Shore terrain, I opt for my nine-footer, loaded with 17 pound line. It makes it easier to "persuade" a cow that just gobbled my $16 Gibbs plug that it's not in her best interest to head back behind the rock where she was stationed. (Though if you can move the boat, you've got a shot at these fish, even with lighter gear.)

Finally, let's talk about rigging for that North Shore of Long Island specialty, practiced for decades, especially by anglers plying the western reaches of the Sound: worm trolling. How long have people been worm trolling? Dating back to the 1800's, rich men living along the Gold Coast hired dorymen to row them along the beaches in front of their palatial mansions during the wee hours of a summer's night.

Unlike wire line trolling, worm trolling is shallow water fishing. Get yourself a pair of medium weight baitcasting outfits loaded with 15 pound line. Tie on a size 2/0 baitholder hook directly. The idea is, in the dark of

FIG. 1.—The strike.

Trolling for stripers dates back to the 1800's.
Anyone recognize the yacht club burgee?

night, to place a trolled sandworm, or bunch of sandworms, as close to the stones as possible—hopefully right past the hungry maw of a waiting cow. I'm not saying you have to use an aluminum boat for the job, but most worm-trolling sharpies do. Threading your way through submerged boulder fields at night, even the most experienced wormer may bump a stone now and again.

FISHING

Live-baiting for stripers is the best way to consistently score with big fish. And the best big bass bait on Long Island is the menhaden, a.k.a, bunker. While you can snag your own as mentioned above, uninjured fish make better baits, if for no other reason than that bunker are tough to keep alive in a livewell. Bleeders not only die quickly, they can cause the other baits in your well to die as well. So learn to throw a cast net, hook up with a baymen working a pound net, or, source a baitshop or marina selling live, net-caught bunker. To keep a dozen baits healthy for a tide, figure two gallons of rapidly changed water per bait. That means a 50 gallon well, minimum, and a high-flow pump. What "high-flow" means depends on the size of your boat. That is, the amount of head, or height, the pump has to lift the water to the livewell will affect the actual performance of the pump. At a minimum, I'd call for a 800-GPH pump to feed a 50 gallon well located two feet above the intake.

Hook your bunker in the snout, between the eyes and nostrils, running the bend of the hook under the hard bony plate. Slip it over the side, let the sinker find bottom, then leave the reel in free spool and thumb the line. You can put the clicker on to prevent a backlash if you like. Tune in to your bait. Feel his every tail pulse through the line and rod. Note the pattern or direction he swims in. You want to be able to visualize him swimming merrily along. Feel the thumb pressure required to keep him from pulling line. Do so and you'll better know the difference when he changes the pace when being stalked by a bass. Of course, I could simply tell you that the bunker will start to swim erratically and faster when a striper zeroes-in on him, but that's not the whole story. When he's being chased, a one pound bunker can bend the rod and pull some line. Also, small bass, sometimes no bigger than the bait you are fishing, will harass your bunker. You need to distinguish between these actions and the action of a decent-sized bass picking up the bait and moving off with it. Strike when the bait is running hard, but not caught, and you may miss a fish or pull the hook out of your bait and lose it.

When the striper does grab your bait, she'll move off in a surging, usually short, run. Drop the rod tip, point it in the direction the bass is moving, and let her take all the line she wants . You just bowed to the cow. This is often followed by a pause, with maybe some movement thrown in, as the bass positions the bait to be swallowed head first. Wait. The fish will run again, faster and more steadily. Keeping the rod down and pointed at the fish, engage the reel, wait for the line to come tight, reel out any remaining slack….NOW! Bring the rod up with brisk jab rather than a heave-ho. Reel down, remove any slack and short jab a few times to really set that hook. Let her pull drag when she wants, just keep the rod tip up. Pump-up and reel down whenever she takes a break.

With a big bass, or any large gamefish, your rod tip will tell you how to beat the fish. The fish will run, pulling out line against drag. Eventually the line will stop going out, but the fish will still be fighting and pulling, in equilibrium with the pressure of rod and drag. At this point watch that tip! As soon as you see the bend in that tip unbend a bit—you have to watch because you can't always feel it—that's the fish resting. Get on her now! Pump and reel, pump and reel.

If you miss, and we all miss at times, immediately put the reel back in free spool and re-fish the bait. Since you were paying attention to how your bait feels at the end of the line, you should be able determine if your bait is healthy, injured, or gone. If it's still there, chances are good the bass that first attacked it will come back for it. If you don't get a hit and your bait feels kaput, reel up and change him out, taking a quick glance at your leader while doing so. Stripers gill plates are very sharp, and your line and leader can get nicked by a fish that hit but was missed.

Where to fish that bunker? If you fish him right where schools of bunker are evident, the weight he's dragging around will make him swim clumsily, quickly distinguishing him from the other bunker in the school as easy prey. If you take him to another spot or piece of structure where there are bass, but no bunker evident, the lack of a school for your bait to blend in with also makes him stand out. The only time I've known bass to pass-up a bunker is during a cinder worm hatch. You're hard pressed to catch a linesider when the water's filled with these little curly worms. (Although fly fishing buddies of mine do well fishing Worm Blob, Bucktail Worm, and Windram Worm patterns.) Otherwise, if you've got live bunkies and bass are present, don't worry about matching the hatch.

As good a bait as bunker are, eels are probably the most popular live bait used for stripers on Long Island (Fresh clams are live, but they fish like dead bait). They are more widely available, being sold in most tackle shops, and they are much easier to keep alive than bunker: eels kept cool and damp will live for days. You don't need water, and in fact, placing a dozen store-bought eels in a bucket of water is the best way to drown them that I know of. Instead, for a tide's fishing, simply place them in the bottom of a bucket or cooler. If its real hot out, add some ice first, and suspend the eels above

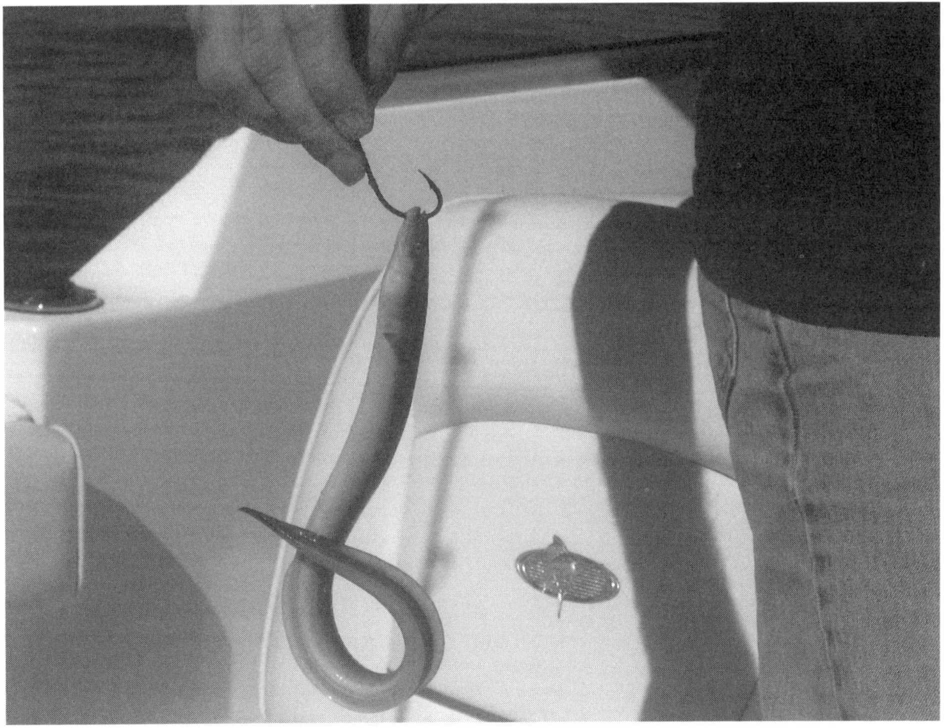

Eels are great nighttime bait in summer—but work in daylight during the fall run.

it –the meltwater will drown them—on a tray, or even a folded towel. This will keep them cool.

To place the eel on the hook, insert the point through the lower jaw and out the upper jaw. They stay very feisty this way, and it's a secure hooking method, resistant to the inevitable bumps from fish that hit, but miss a few times, before finally gobbling the bait. You don't want you're eel to get knocked off the hook during a preliminary skirmish.

Eels can be quite active and hard to grasp. There are several methods used to counter the squirming. Some anglers keep a box of sand at hand, and dip a wet hand in it before attempting to grab the eel. Others chill their baits in a cold cooler before use to slow them down. Others will toss the eel to the deck to stun it—I've done this—in order to make the eel easier to place on the hook. Most times though, I use a soft terry-cloth rag. Placing it in my hand like a grip, I reach into my bucket, and grasp the eel right behind the head—it takes a few tries—with a firm squeeze. Once I have the eel like this, I have enough leverage to control him and place the hook. Once the hook has penetrated, I don't let go. Instead, I let the grasping hand, still clothed in the rag, slide down the eel to near its tail. I keep the eel stretched-out, between hook and this hand, and in a smooth motion swing the line and terminal gear overboard, releasing the eel at the last moment. Let them hang idly from the hook, and you'll have problems.

TIP: Between drifts, or any time you have reeled a hooked eel back up, DO NOT allow it to dangle in the air. That is, after placing the rod in a rod holder, after initially hooking the eel, or whatever, make sure the eel is lying in deck, in the bottom of a bucket, or is otherwise supported. If you let them wave like flags flying from your rods they will knot themselves into a ball that would defy Houdini.

Fishing eels is more subtle than fishing bunker. If you are fishing light-tackle in a harbor, you'll likely be able to feel the eel pulling a bit. And, in that situation, when a bass starts chasing him, you'll have some notice. In that case, allow the fish to run with the bait, and set the hook when your instinct tells you it has been swallowed. This may be indicated by a pause after a short run, but, unlike a big bunker, a bass can easily inhale an eel.

In deeper water, with heavier tackle and weights, you may have no indication of the take until the bass has gobbled your eel and begun to swim away. Point the rod at the water, wait a beat, then cross her eyes! Let your gut guide you. Trust your instincts while fishing and over time they will become sharper.

Other live baits ranging from flounder to bergalls can be fished in similar fashion to those described above for the more popular bunker and eels. Keep the general principals in mind, hooking the bait near the head, though for flounder I like to hook them through the shoulder just aft of the eyes being careful not to hit the backbone. Larger flounder or porgies will be harder to swallow and thus you'll have to allow the fish to run a little longer before setting the hook. Smaller snappers or bergalls may be instantly inhaled. Pay attention to your bait's action at all times and you'll learn the difference between an active bait and one that's being chased, one that's been swallowed and one that's been eaten by a bass that got away without feeling the sting of steel from your hook. Develop those instincts!

Dead bait fishing can be a deadly striper tactic. The dead bait method that's arguably the most widely practiced for stripers is clam-chumming. I say dead bait, because live clams don't wriggle or require an elaborate live well. But fresh skimmer clams, which are very much alive, make better hook baits than frozen clams any day of the week. There are numerous wholesale fish markets on the Island where you can purchase fresh skimmer, or surf clam. And you can also gather your own if time and motivation are available. If not, frozen clam will suffice. Live or frozen, be sure to include some of the succulent "belly" along with some of the tough leathery "foot" on each hook bait.

Chumming can be done with frozen clam, purchased as logs that fit standard chumpots. Simply load a log, drop the pot and your slick is started. There's another twist to this method, taught to me by my father, and the one many sharpies still employ. Step one is to have your belly chum defrosted. Step two is to reach in, grab a handful and drop them over the side. Step three is to watch and wait as that handful of chum sinks out of sight in the current behind your anchored boat. Step four is re-apply another handful of chum only after the previous handful has disappeared.

The madness behind this method has two advantages. It helps prevent you from over-chumming, in which case you'd be feeding the fish, instead of just attracting them. Over-chumming is worse than no chumming. But, primarily, dolloping out clam bellies a handful at a time helps you present your hook baits better. By watching the rate and angle of descent of the handfuls of chum, you can deploy your hook baits to match that angle and rate. Free-spool back the baits by pulling line directly off the spool, adjusting till they match the sink rate, angle and speed of the chum. You can use your thumb, or the clicker to prevent a backlash. To further fine tune the bait presentation, add or remove weight using rubber-core sinkers placed a foot above the bait on your leader. Once you've got the hook baits and chum flowing out in sync the drill is to keep pulling line and feeding the bait out until it starts to bounce and tumble along the bottom aft of the boat. At this point reel back in, replace the bait if it's washed-out or "crabbed," and start over. The idea is to make your hook bait appear as much as possible as one of those free-floating globs that the bass are lazily scoffing up.

Of course energy, desire and the right crew are paramount to "handing-out" your chum. Lacking these, you can send a frozen log in a chumpot to the bottom, impale a glob of clam on your hook, and send it out until it hits bottom. Leave the reel in free-spool, your thumb holding the line. Time for a sandwich? Put the rod in a holder, still in free-spool, and use the reel clicker to hold the bait. Still fishing works, but the active method of chumming has been more successful for me over the years. Besides, dead-sticking while clam chumming results in many gut-hooked fish, most of which are throwback size. Attending your tackle with vigor and focus is not only more productive, it's better for the fish.

Bunker-chunking is an age old technique, practiced, perfected, and more commonly used at Montauk and in Long Island Sound, whereas clam-chumming is more prevalent in the South Shore Bays. I've chunked for bass with success around the Island. The technique is similar to what I described above for handing-out clam chum. Prepare by cutting up a flat of bunkies into bite size morsels. Toss these in a bucket, and after anchoring up-current of bass-holding structure, start handing them out, waiting for each handful to disappear before throwing over some more. (You can wait, depending upon current velocity and depth, as much as a minute, between handfuls. Experiment. Just remember you are chumming, not feeding.)

Steak your bunker or herring into hook baits by making three-quarter inch wide vertical cuts. Then simply impale a bunker or mackerel chunk on the hook, the hook bend passing under the backbone, and the point coming out the other side, remaining exposed. With big chunks, like those from the shoulder of a large bunker, I'll cut the chunks in half. You want some hook bend and point exposed. Now let the bait out into the current, keeping an eye on the depth and speed of the chum-chunk flow. In shallow water, slow current situations, you want your bait to drift back naturally with the chunk-chum. Throw a few chunks overboard and watch how they drift. Now let out your bait, pulling line off the spool to match the speed and rate of sink of the chum chunks. As with clam-chumming, split shot or rubber-core sinkers can be used to fine tune your baits rate of sink.

In deeper water, or faster current, where you are using the three-way or fish-finder rig, allow your bait to hit the bottom. Then let out line, thumbing the spool and lifting the rod tip, "walking" your bait back into the current. Again, check out how fast the chunk chum is sinking and at what angle. You are trying to get your bait back to the location where the chunks have hit the bottom, or nearly so. Stay on your toes: a strike can come at any time. When the bait reaches your estimate of the "spot," let it sit for a minute. If you don't get a strike, reel in and start over. Within the limits of your reel's line capacity, experiment with how far back to let the bait go before reeling up. Sometimes the bass will hang back, particularly when you first start chunking. As the slick develops, the fish will often swim up it and hit your hook baits closer. This is what you want and lets you know that you are chumming rather than feeding. Be attentive and think about what's going on. Don't over-chum. It takes experience, but its well worth developing the feel for how much chum it takes to attract the fish without feeding them so much that they hang back in the slick. Why should a striper swim further to get to your bait if he doesn't have to? Too much chum is worse than no chum.

When the fish picks up the bait, give way, letting her run for a moment, dipping your rod tip. Now engage the reel, reel in any slack and come up with the rod tip in a smooth, firm motion. Hello! Your striper is gonna pull and run. Your rod tip will throb, flexing and relaxing, as the combined forces of drag slip, line stretch, and rod bend all take up the strain. Do not let up. Your every movement should be smooth as a squid. Keep the rod tip up and the pressure on. Pump the fish back to the boat by reeling only on the down stroke. Pump-up, reel down, pump up, reel down. Expect at least one other run, two or three for a big fish, and when it comes, keep the tip up at 45 degrees or so and let her pull drag. Then resume pumping and reeling. Many big bass are lost during a last minute surge, when she sees the boat. At this time, you don't have stretch in the system like you did when the fish was out and away, pulling drag. Be ready and, again, smooth is the word. Have a big net on hand for landing striped bass. I like a 30" rectangular hoop with a 48" long net. Always net 'em head first, leading the fish in with rod or leader. You can lip a big bass, if the need arises, say the net is lost or too small for a whopper you didn't expect to catch. With the fish relatively calm at boatside, head in to the current, grab the leader for additional control. Now, reach down and have your other hand poised—thumb ready to insert into the bass's mouth. Usually there is a little "sparring" as the fish's mouth open and closes and you try to insert your thumb. Smooth—don't excite the fish. When you see your chance, insert your thumb and hook it down on the lower jaw inside the bass's mouth. The other four fingers are on the outside of the lower jaw, in a fist against which your thumb pressure has pinned the lower jaw. In a smooth motion, lift her up, over and in. It requires some strength to one-hand lip-land a big bass. But some of you might be surprised to learn that with the lower jaw pinned open as described, the fish will hang limp from your hand.

At this point I usually reach in with my other hand and remove the hook. If that can't be done easily while holding the fish, I'll lay her on the deck to do so. DO NOT drop the fish from the hanging off your thumb position. You're gonna hurt a fish meant for release, bruise the meat of a fish meat for the table, and if the hook is still in her, there's a good chance of it snagging your hand as the fish drops away. It hurts, trust me.

LURES

My absolute favorite way to catch striped bass is with spinning tackle and artificial lures. You won't catch as many fish as the chummers and chunkers. And you won't catch as many big fish as those swimming live baits. But the fish you do catch will be more memorable.

You can obviously throw poppers at a school of fish busting the surface—I would, and do when the opportunity presents. However, when I talk about fishing with poppers, I'm talking about cruising a stretch of water like a lion stalking the plains. You are seeking opportunity. Look for rips, riffles, current splits, water spilling around a point, any situation that appears as if it would give the bass an advantage over its prey.

Finding such spots requires time and effort exhausted in reading the water. Most of these spots will only be bass-worthy under certain conditions of wind and tide. Your job is fish, fish, and fish some more, until you build an inventory of such spots. Write them down and when it time to fish, check the wind and tide. You'll be able to head right for 'em, at least in your local waters. When fishing new ground, apply the same principle of reading the water to the new area.

Bobby Bossung and Rocky weigh-in with plug-caught bass.

A key to this water reading thing is looking for wind against tide scenarios. Bass hang on the down-current side of structure from Manhattan to Montauk. Throw in a wind opposing the current and usually the water will be rougher, the rip will "stand up," giving the bass even more of an advantage over prey. Stripers will seek these spots and move to them as conditions change. You need to do the same thing. This is where thinking like a fish really does pay off in catching more fish. It's a mindset, a way of making yourself integral to the life and death drama that's been occurring beneath the surface of our waters since the glaciers receded. To successfully plug for stripers you need to consider yourself the apex predator of the food chain, thinking: Where will dinner come from today?

Poppers make for the most excitement. I like a variety of these surface lures, ranging from the tried and true Creek Chub Striper Strike (the silver, nicknamed "chrome death" is deadly, especially once some of the chrome has chipped off, revealing the tan base color). to newer lures such as the Smack-It! Floating types—Troublemakers, Smack-It's—are easier to work than sinking varieties like the Creek Chub, although the latter can be cast effectively, even into a breeze of wind.

I keep my color selection simple: dark and light. I see no reason to have every color of the rainbow available. In my tackle locker you'll find black, blue with white belly, yellow, and the classic red-head pattern. The other colors all work, go buy 'em, but I do darn good with the above selection. As for size, I use a few smaller, three-quarter ounce lures on occasion. But mostly I'm heaving one and a half to two ounce lures with my eight foot, 15 pound class spinning outfit.

While wind against tide churns the water, making baitfish helpless and giving bass an advantage that they will usually seek out, wind against tide gives you an advantage, in addition to being a clue as to the presence of fish based on what type conditions they need to eat. When wind is against tide and a rip is clearly delineated, it narrows down your search for a suitable spot to probe considerably. The second advantage is that by setting the boat down-current and up-wind of the rip, your lure presents in the easiest and most natural fashion. It's easier, because the cast is downwind. It's more natural because baitfish generally swim with the current. So by casting down-wind and up-current, your lure can be cast farther and when retrieved, is moving in the direction a bass expects her dinner to be moving.

Okay. So we have structure. We have wind against tide. Another fine point for throwing a popper for bass is: quiet water, quiet lure; rough water; noisy lure. For example. You approach a seething rip, one that's standing a good foot above the surrounding water. Moreover, it's what I call a stepped rip. The main standing wave is humping and breaking in place, spitting out whirlpools down-current and bulging with whitewater up-current. Another line or two of non-breaking riffles run in parallel. The wind is honking, Spume's flying. In such conditions retrieve your popper aggressively, coming back with the rod tip hard, and fast enough so that the lure's broad, cupped, face shoots a jet of water at each pop. You should be at the bleeding edge of ripping the lure from the water's surface and having it missile back towards your face (Watch it... it has happened!) You need to get the lure noticed in these conditions. Besides, any bait getting washed through such a maelstrom is likely to be tumbled, so you are matching the hatch.

On the other hand, your rip may consist of a simple seam in the water. It belies the presence of a very minor bottom change. It has just a yard-wide slick behind it, revealing some piled-up water, but there's no spume. It's quiet. In these conditions, the retrieve to use is a slow and gentle. Crank just fast enough and twitch the rod just hard-enough so that the lure gurgles along back towards you. As the lure approached the rip itself, slow even more, to just a tad faster than whatever current maybe running and give a few twitches. With practice, you'll find that you can make the lure hang on the rip line for a two pops instead of just the one you'd get with a steady retrieve.

Of course these are guidelines. You need to vary your retrieve between these extremes to find out what the fish like at the moment. But making lure action match water action is the best starting point.

The strike when popping a rip—or point, or boulder, or any place structure is causing water to change speed and direction, can vary in type but is always exciting. Here's the drill. You throw past the structure and begin your retrieve the instant the lure hits the water. As you're popping it back towards you, you notice a wave behind the lure. It's a bass, pushing water and chasing down your lure. Keep popping, keep retrieving. The wave disappears and suddenly the water explodes next to your lure. Missed! Keep popping keep retrieving. The worst thing you can do is stop reeling because you thought the fish ate your lure. The action of working the lure will hook the fish. Pop...reel...pop...reel...BAWHOOSH! Another explosion and this time a broom-size tail sticks out of the water and comes down with a slap. You kept reeling, so you came tight. That bass that just stood on its head is now pulling. Set the hook again. With the slack reeled-out, firm pressure and a lifted rod is all that's necessary. Keep the rod tip up, allowing her to run. Pump and reel to regain line when she rests. After three or four runs, the second one usually the longest, she'll start to wither. But watch out for that last run under the boat, being prepared to stick the rod tip underwater if necessary to avoid getting chafed-off.

Swimming plugs are another effective tool for hunting bass with spinning tackle. Whereas poppers are a daytime lure, swimmers shine at night. Swimmers come in a huge variety. There are hinged, so-called "broken back" lures and rigid lures. I prefer the rigid ones. Lengths range from three inches to over a foot long. Mostly, I stick to five and seven inch models. Like poppers, I keep a limited number of colors available but have a variety of "dark and light." I fish dark on dark nights, either due to clouds or the lack of a moon. I recommend fishing lighter colors on bright nights. Dark means black, brown, and blue, perhaps with some white or silver belly. Light means yellow and white, and again I prefer a light-bellied lure.

You can fish the same rips, edges, points and drop-offs gleaned from your inventory of popper spots. In fact, the gleam of the moon, or ambient light from shore or your boats navigation lights, often make the froth and seam of a rip quite visible at night. Unlike poppers, swimmers work best when worked across the current, not directly down current. This affects where you decide to anchor or set up for a drift. Get up-current of the structure a bit, (or at least even with it relevant to the current) so that the boat is about 30 degrees "ahead" of the target area. So positioned, you can cast so that during the retrieve the lure is vectoring: working across the current toward you while being swept down-current and across the edge (bar, hump, hole, etc.). Ideally, the lure is heading back to the boat at a 45 degree angle to the current just as it crosses the edge. Allowing the lure to get straight down-current and reeling it back across the edge against the current isn't that productive. Adjust the cast for wind and current speed, and you'll get it. TIP: Steve "Rocky" Rapoon, one of the best bass fisherman I know—hey, "Rock's Rip" in Shinnecock is named for him—taught me this one. As soon as a swimming lure hits the water, take four or five really fast cranks to get it down to depth and working in the strike zone sooner.

Rocks tip works. Since you're retrieving across the current, and a swimming lure doesn't begin to dive until water pressure against its lip builds up, you can miss a lot of opportunities by lazily tossing it out and then being slow to flip the bail and start the retrieve. We are talking the difference of two seconds here, but in a three knot current your lure moves six feet per second. That's 12' of un-fished territory over a "spot" that might only be 40' wide. Smart anglers maximize the lure's soak time at the proper depth.

After getting the lure down to depth with a few fast cranks, the best retrieve speed for swimmers is slow as you can go and still keep it working. You can feel when a swimmer is working right as it makes the rod tip pulse in short, staccato bursts. These indicate the lure's seductive wiggling action, as it shakes it moneymaker over the structure where it will hopefully be devoured by a hungry cow.

Anglers fishing swimming plugs are rewarded with a jolting strike. You're out there casting, retrieving as slow as you can go, the rod tip's pulses indicating the lure is working properly. It's all quite serene. Then the reel handle stops cold in your hand and the rod is nearly wrenched from your grasp. Unlike a popper, in which there is slack in the line during much of the retrieve, a swimming plug working across the current allows no slack. The line is always tight, so that when the strike comes, you feel all the power the fish possesses.

At this point, the fish is probably down-current of you and thus has great advantage. Even when resting, she'll "pull" drag because of the current. The first run will be long, longer than you may expect. In fact you may have to move the boat and drift down with the fish if she's more than 20 pounds. Smart anglers are prepared with a float that they can tie to the anchor rode and so dump it overboard. That done, they follow and fight the fish, then come back for the ground tackle after thumping a slob into the fishbox. Nice.

Jigs are another fun and effective way to catch stripers with casting tackle. Be they bucktails, diamond jigs, or plastic bait tails rigged on lead heads, jigs are ready striper lures. Unlike swimmers and poppers, jigs are great for probing deep water. (They also work good in the shallows.) Whereas the plugs are good for surfacing fish, or unseen fish holding in less than 15' of water in our back bays and harbors, jigs can be presented effectively in deep water. They are the preferred artificial at The Triangle, Plum Gut and in the South Shore Inlets for this reason.

Diamond jigs, and their cousins the Crippled Herrings, Hopkins, etc, are favored by some North Shore sharpies for taking fish off structure in the deep mid-Sound waters. But they work Island-wide. These are daytime lures best fished close to the bottom while drifting or anchored over bass-holding structure. There are two ways that I fish them.

The method called "squidding" is my favorite. A reference from the turn of the last century when anglers used hand lines and lures called "block tin squids" –molded tin jigs—squidding is simple, but has a few nuances. At its most basic, squidding means dropping the jig to the bottom, engaging the reel, then reeling up. In my mind I like to visualize the jig spurting out of the sand as replicating the action of a sandeel. As such, I only work the bottom portion of the water column. That is, after the jig hits, I immediately reel up say 10' then re-drop the jig and start over, repeatedly. Retrieve slowly. Most hits come just as you begin reeling up or during the drop. TIP: Count the turns of the reel handle. That way, after you catch a fish, you have an idea where the next one will strike.

Nuances include being attentive to when the jig hits the bottom. The instant it does, engage the reel and begin the retrieve. You don't want a "dead" lure sitting on the bottom, lest you let the fish know it's just a hunk of metal and not a tasty sand eel. Secondly, be poised to engage the reel and set the hook during the drop. I freespool the jig to the bottom with the rod tip pointed down. My thumb is feathering the line coming off the spool heavier than, for instance, I do when dropping a bait rig to the bottom. The idea is to slow the drop just enough to keep the line taut but still let the jig flutter. My other hand is ready to engage the reel. Doing so allows me to react to the subtle, sometimes barely perceptible bump, as a hitting bass interrupts the descent of the jig. Fish that hit in the drop are hard to hook so be ready.

The second way I like to work a diamond jig is to jig it. Call it eponymous fishing. Again, drop down to the bottom and immediately engage the reel. Now work the rod tip in sweeping lifts, allowing the jig to flutter on the descent. Don't just flail away though. Again, many times the fish will hit on the drop. Dip the rod tip fast enough to produce flutter, but not so fast as to create a loop of slack in the line. Be ready for that pickup on the drop!

Bucktails, and their plastic-tailed, lead-headed cousins, work great day or night. Bucktails should be dressed with a strip of pork rind. The plastic tails need no added adornment. I prefer red rind above all, but keep green and yellow aboard in order to mix things up. For instance, if I know, from talking to other anglers, or from my own observations, that the bass are eating baby weakfish, I might give yellow a shot. TIP: Always place pork rind on the hook with the white side down and the colored side up. That better imitates a real fish, which are light bellied and darker on the back.

Matching the hatch aside, I've found that buckies and plastic tails are most effective when the smallest size that lets you hit bottom are used. I rarely use a jig more than three ounces in weight and most times use a two ounce size, even dropping down to ounce-and-half when current and depth permit. The smaller the jig, the livelier the action. So be prepared to swap lures as conditions change so you are always using the minimum weight that allows you to hold bottom. "Find the bounce!" as friend and striper sharpie, Frank Lenihan likes to say.

Both leadheads and bucktails can be fished vertically, like diamond jigs, but they are more effective when worked horizontally back to the boat over structure. Cast up-current, or at an angle to the current. (Casting down-current means your retrieve will be against the current, an unnatural presentation.) Let the lure find the bottom. You may be waiting for 10 seconds or more before flipping the bail or engaging the reel. Once you think bottom is found, reel in the slack and with gentle, subtle, slow, lifts of the rod tip, begin working the lure back to the boat. The rhythm is going to vary depending upon conditions, but something like a one-foot lift of the rod followed by three or four slow turns of the reel handle is a good jumping-off point. You want that lure puffing the bottom, rising gently and then flutter-tumbling back down to puff sand again. Once again, many strikes come on the drop, or in the minute pause between drop and the next lift. Keep slack out of the line as much as possible: you are retrieving slowly, but you must also retrieve steadily. It's a practiced art to go slow and still keep the lure working. It requires concentration. Be attentive, keep at it, and you'll get the feel. Especially once you catch your first slob on a spin-cast buckie. The surging runs and powerful shakes starkly contrast with such subtle lure presentation. Variety is the spice of life. And success breeds success.

TROLLING

It's tough to beat wire line trolling for bass. You can use a variety of lures. Bucktails laced with porkrind, bunker spoons, large single tubes, you name it. Ideally you'd pick a lure that imitated what the fish are suspected of feeding upon: big spoons or plugs for bunker, a bucktail dragged through the sand for sandeels, an umbrella rig to replicate spearing. During the day, the go-to lure is the umbrella rig. Invented in Montauk, right here on Long Island, umbrella's are deadly. Basically, the only time I won't stream one in my wake during the day is if the water's real weedy. Despite their effectiveness, they are the great rakes of fishing tackle.

Umbrella rigs range from simple two-hook spreaders to six-armed rigs capable of deploying 12 tubes. I like the four-arm rigs that feature four hooks and four teasers. And I customize them. Teasers, the hookless tubes, are attached to the loops in the middle of each arm. On the corners, I use hooked tubes. But I don't simply connect the hooks to the snaps at the end of the arms. Instead, I tie short leaders, about 10" long, using 80 pound mono to each hooked tube. At the leader's other end I tie on a black barrel swivel. The teasers and these corner hooks all sport the same color tubes. I then tie a three foot leader to the ring on the weight molded to the frame. To the end of this, I tie different color hooked tube. When going through the water, the hooks on the corners are further back then the teasers and the center hook is further back than the corner hooks. This makes the rig more closely resemble a school of baitfish. Also, I believe the off color lure dropped back down the center looks like a straggler: a wounded fish, one that a bass, being a fine predator, is likely to target. I've also used a longer eight or 10" rigged tube in the drop back position. I believe it resembles a predator pursuing the "school." This incites the striper's competitive instinct to bite. In any case, the leaders give the hooked tubes better action. Don't just snap tubes on the frame. Use leaders.

I usually fish one red umbrella rig and one natural umbrella rig, each with an off-color hook dropped back. It's easy enough to change colors and I keep a supply of leadered hooks and teasers aboard for this purpose. Green has also worked well, as has white. But red and natural are my go-to colors, just as they are for bluefish.

To put an umbrella rig in the water, set the boat on a course headed to drag your baits over structure. Throttle-up to about two knots. Grasp the rod in your right hand, thumb on the spool, clicker off. Hold the rig by the leader, close to the frame in your other hand. Shake out any tangles or twists. When all are hanging clear, place the rig in the water and simultaneously let out line under the control of your thumb—almost complete free spool is what you want. If you put the rig over with strain on the line—the reel in gear—it's going to trip over itself and tangle. Just remember: boat under way, place in water, thumbed free spool, and you'll be fine. Once the rig is submerged it will deploy smoothly the rest of the way

TIP: Before you let out line and start fishing, look at how the rig is swimming while its there next to the boat. Are the teasers lazily rotating? Are the hooks swimming snakily? Adjust your boat speed until they are. Now you are ready to fish.

Allow the line to go back, figuring about 10' of depth for every hundred feet of wire you let out. I usually throttle the boat up a bit to get the lures out faster, than return to the "fishing speed" I observed next to the boat once the mark for the intended depth has passed through the tip top. Engage the reel, put the clicker on and start working the structure.

Wire line trolling involves intense visualization on the skipper's part. You have to "see" what the lure is doing 50' down and several hundred feet behind your boat. Eight little fish are wiggling their way through the murk, (usually) just above the shell-strewn bottom. You veer a little to make the lure pass as close as you dare to a boulder. As they approach the drop-off—the boat already past it—they come into view of a cow bass, lying in wait, head to the current. She sees the lure from below, suddenly appearing over the ridge. No takers on the first pass? Try shifting into neutral for a moment as the lure passes the structure. The decrease in speed causes them to sink a bit. Shift back in gear in gear, they suddenly surge forward. This approximates how a school of baitfish swims, in fits and spurts, as anyone who has watched spearing in the shallows knows.

You can also try stemming, if there's enough current. Troll the boat past the structure, say a reef or rockpile, till the lures are right on it. Now throttle down to the point at which the boat is motionless, bow into the current, neither moving ahead nor falling back. The current will keep the tubes swimming, and you're dangling a tasty meal right in "the hot zone" for a prolonged period. Stemming is particularly effective after you've made a couple of successful passes and determined where the fish are hitting. By using it, noting your line depth, you can often repeatedly hook up and get right back on 'em like clockwork. I often crushed the bass using the stemming technique at the Ponquogue, the Throgs Neck Bridge, and the bars outside the South Shore Inlets. But the technique can be applied anywhere you have structure of reasonable profile and current.

A lot of new guys ask me how I turn the boat around so quickly with wire line and rarely seem to get the rigs fouled-up. Number one, I accelerate through the apex of the turn; that keeps the lures riding a little higher. Second, I'll often take up—or have a crewmember take up—a dozen turns on the inboard lure. The inboard lure slows down and falls during a turn. So if I'm turning to starboard, the starboard lure comes up a bit—not too much—just enough to keep it from hitting the bottom. When one of them hits bottom and stops, lines cross, lures tangle, and tempers flare.
While umbrella rigs are a daytime lure, you can jig bucktails on wire line day or night. Jig? With wire? Yep, as long as your fishing relatively snag-free water. Here's the drill.

Snap a bucktail to the snap at the end of your leader. Set your boat's speed and course as previously described. Dress the buckie with a strip of pork rind. Drop the lure back until it is bouncing the bottom. Engage the reel and begin jigging the rod, allowing the lure to kick up puffs of sand as it leaves the bottom. The explosion of sand, the flutter of the pork rind, and the pulse of the deer hair combine to drive bass nuts. This action from a trolling boat creates a loop of slack in the line with each jig. The moving boat quickly removes this slack, but unless you're careful the loop will often wrap your rod tip. To avoid this, and to prevent you from getting exhausted from jigging—it's hard work—you want to hold the rod differently from any other kind of fishing. Instead of holding the rod upright, hold it upside down, the butt in one hand and the fore grip in the lower hand. Like a broom. Now you can "sweep" the tip to impart action to the jig and clean-up on the fish. It's much less strenuous and you won't wrap the tip with the inevitable slack loop.

Jigging bucktails works day or night. Fishing big lures, such as Stan Gibbs lures, Danny Plugs and even Big Rapalas is a better way to fish after dark. As with bucktails and umbrella rigs, the main idea with trolling plugs on wire is to present your lures at a specific depth over specific bass-holding structure. With any of these techniques, you might catch by simply trolling around the Sound or Ocean mindlessly—there are worse ways to spend time on the water. But you'll be fulfilling your role as Apex Predator better if you target specific spots for specific reasons. Successful fishermen make themselves a part of the eat-or-be-eaten process, not third parties hoping for the best. So have a plan before you drag these plugs around.

Ironically, I have found that trolling big plugs are more effective at dead slow speeds into the current. I know I have harped on fishing lures with the current throughout this book, but these big plugs have a more tantalizing action when worked into the current. The rod tips tell the story. When the lures are working right, the tip throbs seductively. To get this action trolling with the current requires you to go too fast for bass's liking. The current, pushing at the lure's tail in the same way it pushes your boat's stern when going slowly and with the current—it doesn't want to remain straight. And of course you can't "steer" your plugs like you can your boat. Therefore, head over structure and into the current when trolling the big wood after dark. Watch the rod tips and adjust the boat speed until that seductive wiggle is apparent. And after you have scored, missed a fish, or marked some fish on the bottom machine, try stemming. TIP: These big diving plugs need to be "tuned." If you're not getting the right action out of them, put the lures overboard next to the boat where you can see them. If it's not wiggling enough, the eye may be bent. Bend the eye a mite—just a mite, until it's parallel to an imaginary center line of the plug.

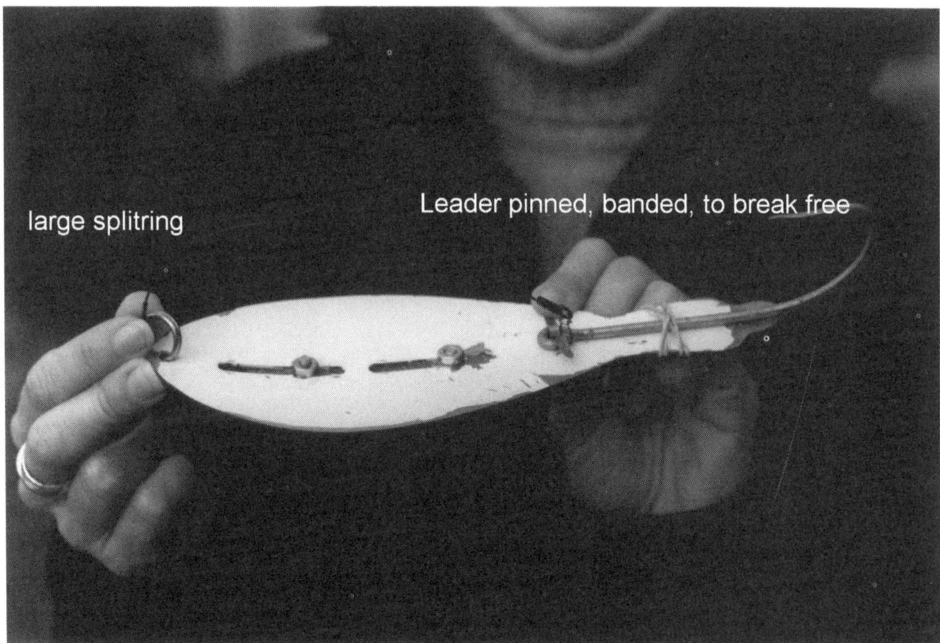

Bunker spoon: Rigged with a break-away hook, a big bass can't get leverage to throw the hook.

As always, my color selection is simple: dark for dark nights and light for bright nights. Blue, black, white and yellow are all you need. I carry four of each though. Why? Because these big wooden plugs can get waterlogged after a while. When that happens, the action is hindered and it's time to switch lures. Therefore, I have enough on hand to keep "dry" lures fishing without running short on the shade that's working best that night.

Bunker spooning with wire line is a specialty technique, one perfected and practiced most by those working the western South Shore. Many a cow has come on a bunker spoon trolled at spots like the infamous Pink Hotel. But I've used the technique out east to great success and know of anglers Island-wide who swear by it.

As previously described, you're best served using a set of specially built bunker spoon rods. Only these will impart the best action to the lure. You also want to be advised that a bunker spoon doesn't just wobble and roll, but swings through a three or four foot arc back there at the end of 200' of wire. The implication is that a pair of lures can tangle even when you're trolling dead straight. The extra length of the bunker spoon rods helps prevent this. But real spoon sharpies use horizontal rod holders to increase the spread. You can buy right-angle rod holder adapters that fit your boat's regular rod holders. Or you can bolt-on a pair of surface mount holders at 90-degrees to the boat's centerline. Either way, a safety line is required to ensure the rod, deployed horizontally out over the depths, doesn't go splash.

Once set up with the right boat gear and rods, you need to pick a spoon to fish. Bunker spoons range from foot-long slabs of metal down to palm–sized lures. The big ones are my go-to lures and I use white or chrome exclusively. Also, I recommend always fishing the same size and shape together. Different lures work best at different boat speeds, as indicated by your observation of the lure next to the boat prior to dropping it back and by the action of the rod tip once the lure is deployed.

Bunker-spooning is another structure-specific technique. I've found the most success running the lures parallel to a bar or edge, or as close as I dare past a boulder, remembering that the spoons swing horizontally in an arc. The rods are fished in the holders, clicker on. At the strike, it's imperative that two things occur. One, the skipper gives the boat a little throttle to take out the slack. Yes, you are fishing from a moving boat, the drag of the lures keeping the line taut. But, like phone wires stretched between utility poles, there is a sag between rod tip and lure. Goosing the throttle takes this out allowing for a better hookset and gives the fish less chance to shake the hook.

Simultaneously, the angler is reeling in the slack, waiting to set the hook until the line is bow-string tight. Bunker spoons are deadly, but they have a flaw. Hook in mouth, the large surface of the spoon is usually lying alongside the bass's head after the hook-up. This gives the fish a tremendous amount of leverage with which to twist the hook out. Its imperative that the angler be attentive while pumping and reeling to maintain tension, using shorter, quicker pumps than might be typical. Also, the skipper needs to be watching the line, applying throttle where necessary to keep out the sag. The only time I take the boat out of gear while bunker spooning is when the fish is leadered and I'm needed to gaff or net it. An involved effort and team work makes for effective spooning and a memorable catch.

Wire line tackle is expensive. It can cost nearly as much as offshore gear. It also requires practice both with boat handling, and line handling, and as skipper, acting as team leader to make it all come together. Work at it and you'll end up being the hi-liner at your marina.

Striped Bass Crib Sheet

Striped Bass, a.k.a., bass, cow, linesider, striper.

Season: April- November, sometimes December

Location: Bays, Harbors, Inlets, Deep Sound and nearshore Ocean, especially around rocks, bars and rough water.

Baits: Live bunker, herring,porgies, bergalls, seaworms and clams. Whole squid, chunked fish, bunker heads. Any and all artificial lures.

Tackle: Medium casting and spinning to heavy conventional and wire line gear.

High Hook Tip: With a gloved hand, you can jig bucktails on wire without need of crew. Drive the boat looking where you are going, jig with the gloved hand, and be ready for a strike.

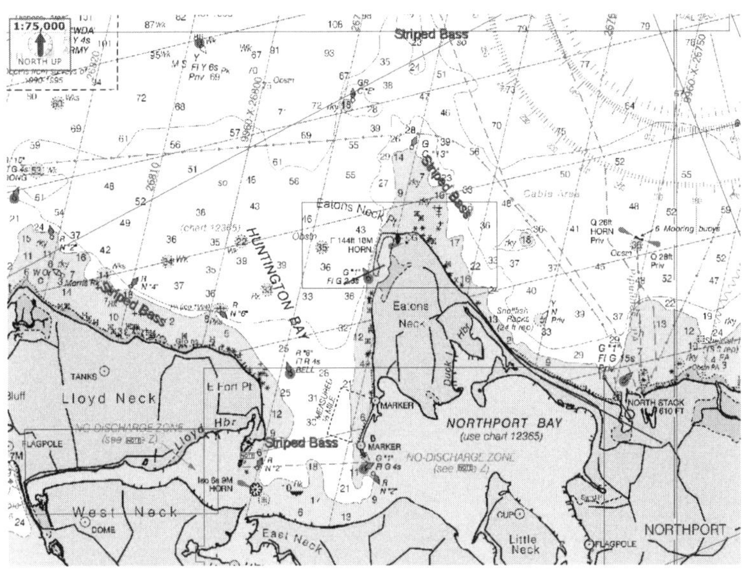

Boulders, points, and reefs, the North Shore is prime Striper country.

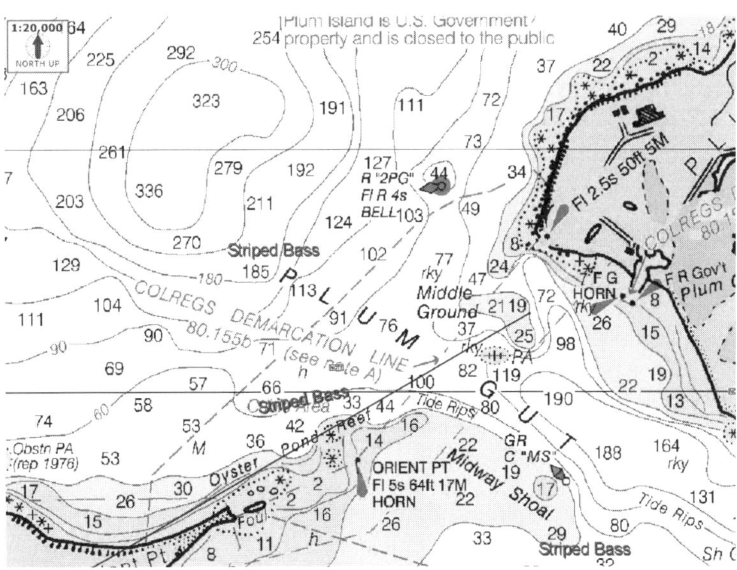

Jigging, baiting, trolling…Plum Gut is striper heaven

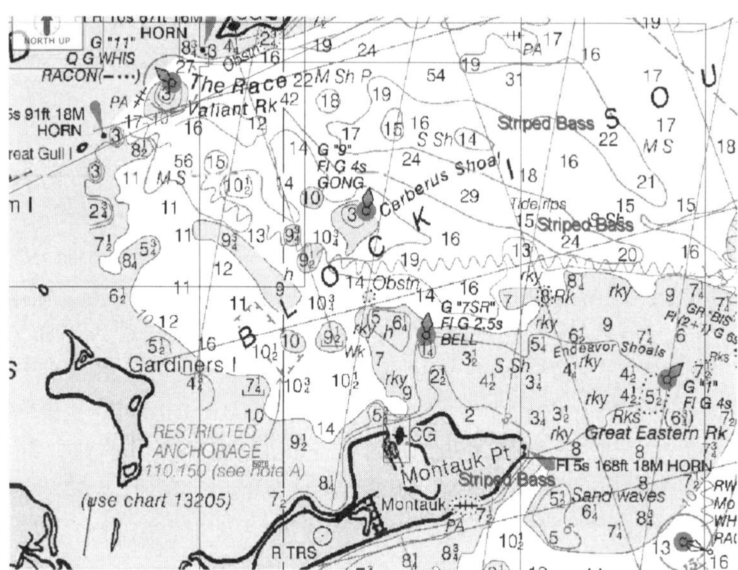

If Plum Gut is heaven, Montuak is Nirvana. Fish outgoing water and pick a spot!

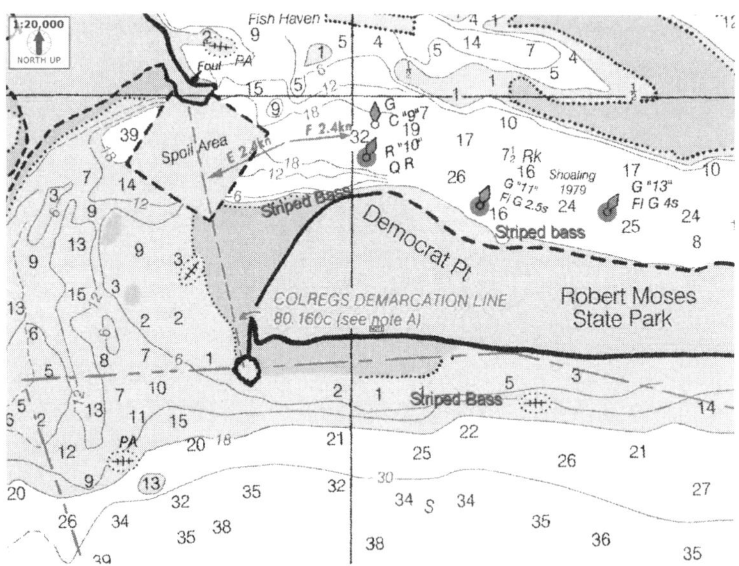

"Demo" at Fire Island Inlet offers great structure accessible by 4WD. The "Spoil Area" in the inlet is a deep hole.

We see early-season bass holding at a hole because we "peaked" the transducer in manual mode. In AUTO mode, the screen showed no fish.

CHAPTER 5
Weakfish
(Cynoscion regalis)

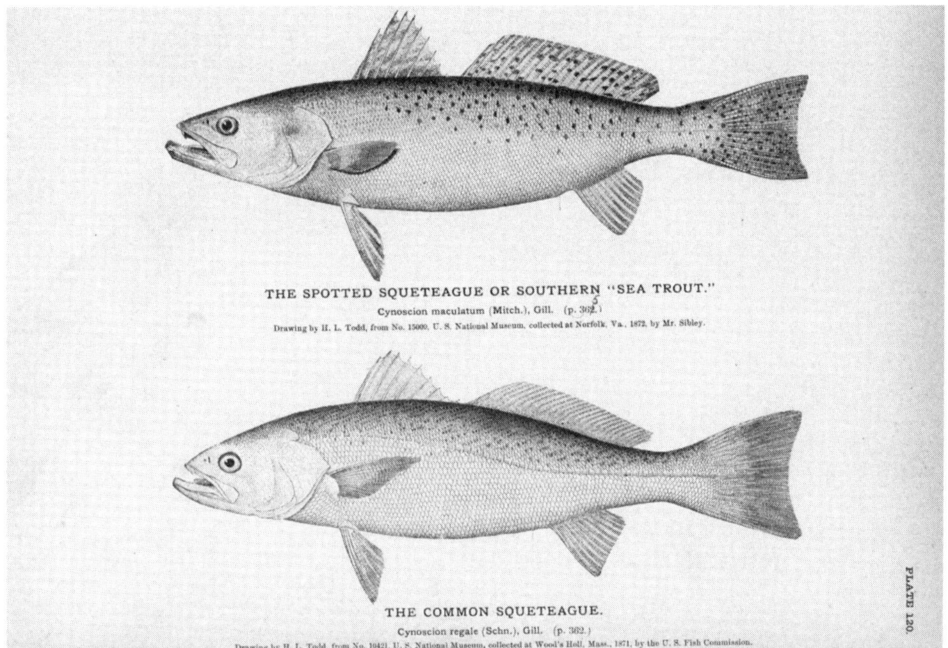

Fresh-caught, slick, and flopping on deck, the weakfish gleams with every color of the rainbow. It is the most beautiful of Long Island's game fish, rivaled only by the Mahi-mahi that lives far from shore. The weakfish's beauty conceals a beast: Tough, bull-dogging runs mark the way this fish fights. The name weakfish, derives from a fragile mouth structure, which, when horsed, or fought on too-heavy tackle, will rip out, leaving the angler with a fish story instead of fish box glory. It takes a light touch to consistently boat weakfish. Delicious flesh, strength and determination at the end of a line, light tackle as a requisite, and the wonder of nature's ability to awe us with beauty, make the weakfish a premier sporting fish.

TAXONOMY AND BIOLOGY

Weakfish are elongate fish, about four times as long as they are wide. Noticeable is a broad tail and a proportionally larger caudal peduncle—the fleshy stub that connects tail to body—than many other species. Likely, it is from here where their strength in battle flows.

The weakfish's snout is conical and its lower jaw is under-slung. Both upper and lower jaws are studded with a row of small, sharp, teeth. A pair of canine teeth, fangs really, protrude from the upper jaw.

Right along the spine, weakfish are usually dark green. Their fins are tipped with bright yellow—hence the nickname, "yellow fin." Along the sides, weakfish can range from brown and copper to blue and purple. This base color changes with habitat, ambient light conditions, and as I mentioned, there is a brief period following capture in which they seem to flash through all these colors before turning the dull silvery grey of death. Overlaying the base color are diagonal bands of dark, linked spots. Given the complexity of their coloration, it is unlikely to mistake weakfish for any other species.

Weakfish over 15 pounds are rare, according to biologists. However a 19.2 pound "tide runner" was caught in the Atlantic Ocean off Jones Beach in October, 1984. That fish is tied with another fish of identical weight, caught at Delaware Bay, for the All-Tackle World's Record. Most fish taken will be between one pound and six pounds, though plenty of double-digit fish hit the scales and make the papers each year. This size range, coupled with the fragile jaw structure, re-emphasizes the weakfish's role as a light tackle quarry.

Weakfish range from Labrador to Florida. They are most populous from Cape Cod to North Carolina. At the southern end of their range they are sometimes confused with Spotted Sea Trout (Cynoscion nebulosis), a cousin fish, of generally smaller size, but with much of the same habits. To further clutter the issue, a nickname for weakfish, particularly on restaurant menus, is sea trout.

Weakfish spend the months November through about March congregating off North Carolina. They arrive in our waters early to mid-May to spawn. Most spawning occurs in bays, harbors and creeks—though weakfish have been observed spawning in the ocean. I've been lucky enough to see weakfish spawn and the sight is that of hundreds (thousands?) of fish

Uncle Lenny Bednarz shows why weaks are called yellowfins.

milling and rolling on the surface at dawn. Ironically, I stumbled upon the phenomenon while returning from an all-night, early-May weakfish expedition during which I got skunked. Besides being awestruck by the sight, I learned that spawning weakfish are even tougher to catch than non-existent weakfish.

The May spawn is undertaken by the bigger fish, and following the mating ritual, it's a good time of year to target a tiderunner. A second spawn, consisting of more numerous smaller fish, occurs in June. The fish spread out across the inshore waters during summer, then school up and head for the offshore waters of North Carolina in November.

During their stay here, they inhabit the surf zone along the Ocean beaches, thriving near cuts and bars. On the Sound, look for them in boulder fields close to shore, particularly if sea grass or kelp is thick. The stretch of beach west of Dosoris Pond in Glen Cove is a good example, the boulders providing cover and the pond a ready source of bait. In the South Shore bays they can be found along channel edges bordering marshes. I remember a

Seaworms are weakfish candy.

killer trip drifting between the Zach's Bay entrance and Sanford Island. And in Peconic and Gardiners Bays, look for them where the waters run swift: the South Race, Jessup's Neck, along Long Beach. But don't neglect the flats that border these areas, particularly the sharp –edged drop-off in front of the Southampton College windmill. There is a great run of fish along the Ocean beaches in late September or October during years in which the fish are abundant. In recent years, weakfish have been around in good numbers, after many lean years. Those who study the habits of fish tell us that weakfish are among the most cyclical species. Enjoy them while they are here. If they pull a disappearing act as they have in the past, catches may be few and far between for as long as a decade.

Weakfish can tolerate a temperature range of between 45 and about 80 degrees, with temperatures above 60 degrees preferred for active feeding. Most of my catches have occurred when temps exceeded 62 degrees, according to my logbook. May fish spawning over shell and grass can be in 60 degree water, even if the reported water temps are lower, provided one of several factors is present.

First, if the bottom is muddy or dark and it's a sunny day, the water will warm appreciably in that local area. Second if the above is true AND flood tide occurred in the morning, you may have a bonanza. The cold ocean water now has time to warm in the sun over the dark mud. This warm high tide will at some point create a warm outgoing current. Weaks love moving water, hence the tide runner moniker. On the other hand, I've had early spring bites killed by a tide change that brought chilly Ocean or Sound water into a back bay and cooled things off, despite a warm sun. Water coming in from the deep Ocean or Sound doesn't warm as fast as water that's been lying over the shallows. TIP: Look for morning flood tides in MAY and plan to target weakfish midmorning as that tide drops. That way you'll be fishing in warm, moving, current.

Biological studies have shown that shrimp and other small crustaceans are the chief diet of smaller weakfish, those less than two pounds. As weaks grow, their diet changes, and the cluepids—herrings, bunkers, anchovies—become the primary food source. But these are overall figures based on random samples from net-caught fish. The truth is that weakfish are a top predator capable of feeding from the surface to the bottom and will eat what is available. As anecdotal proof, I've caught plenty of weakfish drifting sandworms, and back at the fillet table discovered snappers or squid in their bellies. They are opportunists, and in my opinion will eat the food that is present that contains the most energy that can be caught expending the least energy. As I've stated throughout this book, predators cannot afford to expend 20 calories chasing down a 10 calorie morsel. Even though a snapper bluefish may contain more protein than my drifted sandworm, the worm hook bait can be inhaled with little energy expended compared to tearing into a school of snappers or squid. Naturally, there are times when weakfish, like most predator fish, will fixate on a single bait—the one that is most prevalent in the water. The wise angler keeps both concepts in mind, fishing with a well-presented, easy-to-catch bait or lure, while remaining alert for temporary local conditions that may be skewing the fish's habits. Nature is not black and white and if we are to fulfill our role as apex predators, than we must be ready to exploit the shades of grey.

Light spinning tackle and a jig tipped with a "rubber bait" is classic weakfishing weaponry.

TACKLE AND RIGGING

You can target weakfish effectively in a variety of situations with just two rod and reel outfits: a 12 pound spinning setup and a 15 pound bait casting rig. These two will cover you for most situations. There are those sharpies, mostly denizens of the west end channels and bridges, who still practice the art of live-lining bunker for weakfish. These guys are targeting big, usually solitary fish, and the tackle choice is obviously heavier due to the size of the bait. Most weak fishing is done in the hopes of intercepting a school of fish, or at least roving packs. But I'll touch on targeting tide runners, which often means excluding the others, as well.

The first rod I grab when heading out for weakfish is a six foot conventional rod with a soft action to which is mounted a revolving spool reel loaded with 15 pound line. I prefer a true "casting" reel, one with a magnetic spool break and lots of ball bearings so that I can switch from bait fishing to tossing artificials at will. This rod bends as "part-of-a-circle" from fore grip to tip. It is a key to landing a higher percentage of the weakfish hooked. Coupled with a light drag setting, this soft action rod helps to prevent tearing out the jaw and losing a hard running weakie in the middle of battle.

To elaborate, I use a spring scale to set the drag at 40 percent of the line's breaking strength, which in this case means eight pounds of pressure. Typical drag settings are at 30 percent. Remember that's with a full spool. When line is out, as it is at the end of a cast or with a fish peeling line, the spool diameter decreases and the drag pressure increases proportionally. (It's simple physics. Think of how a bicycle is harder to pedal when the chain moves to a smaller sprocket.) To set the hook and add any additional brake that's need to slow down a fish during the fight, I use my thumb in measured amounts. Coupled with the soft action of the rod, there is enough "cushion" in this system to prevent pulling the hook on a weakfish. "Ripping lip" might be an enthusiastic colloquialism when referring to other fish, but it an unfortunate literal probability when weak fishing.

While I will cast with this rod, I use it primarily for fishing bait. If I am drift fishing, I like to use a high-low rig. Take a four foot section of 20 pound leader, mono is fine, but fluorocarbon is better, and tie in two dropper loops, the first one a foot above the bottom, the second two feet above that. (At any rate, make sure the distance between the droppers exceeds the length of the hook leaders by a few inches to avoid tangles.) Tie an overhand loop at the bottom, big enough to enable you to attach the appropriate weight bank sinker using the catspaw. That is, slip the loop through the sinker's eye, then slip the sinker through the loop. To each dropper loop, catspaw a barrel swivel. Then catspaw a leadered hook to each barrel swivel. I use a three foot leader on the bottom hook and a short, one foot leader on the high hook. The conventional reel is better than spinning gear for fishing the hi-lo rig because you can let the line out to the bottom slowly. If you just drop it fast, the bottom hook and leader is likely to wrap your main line on the way down. Fishing in current is also a key to avoiding tangles with the hi-lo, as the current helps stream the leadered hooks away from the main line. You could go to shorter leaders as well, and I do sometimes, if the bite is hot. But the longer leader presents the baits more naturally and is generally worth the extra effort required to fish it.

As often as not, I'll use wide-gap "fluke" hooks for weakfish, preferring size 4/0, and choosing black hooks over gold or silver. These provide a good hook-up ratio and hold well, although the wire they are constructed of is a little thin. I've had these bust on five and six pound fish occasionally. If I suspect larger fish, then, I'll rig up size 5/0 live bait hooks with kirbed (bent) points instead. TIP: If you can't find kirbed hooks in the size and style you want, make your own. Buy the straight-pointed hooks, put them in a vise and use locking pliers to gently nudge the hook point aside a few degrees. Live bait hooks are made from heavier wire than the Kahle, or wide gap style, and won't break as easily. The drawback is that their extra weight may not allow a sandworm or squid strip to flutter as naturally as it does on a wide-gapped hook, and the fish don't seem to set the hook themselves as much as with the wide-gaps.

Now, you will often run into bluefish while weakfishing and these short-shanked hooks increase the odds of getting bit off. Some guys like to use Carlisle hooks—the old-style, long-shanked, "fluke" hooks for this reason. It's a matter of priorities. The shorter shanked hooks are less visible and present the baits more naturally to line-shy weakfish. Bluefish are not line shy. Mixed-bag catching is a blast, but I suggest focusing on weaks when weakfishing. There's rarely a paucity of bluefish in Long Island waters, whereas the windows for catching weaks shut firmly and absolutely.

For live bait fishing, the rig I suggest is simplicity itself. Tie up five foot long, 20 pound, fluorocarbon leaders, snelling a live bait hook (smaller for snappers or "pin" porgies; larger for bunker) in size 4/0, 5/0, or 6/0 to one end. Tie a Uni-knot loop or Surgeon's Loop (double overhand knot loop) to the other end. Tie a bead-chain drail of sufficient weight to hold bottom in the conditions you are fishing to the terminal end of your main line. Use the drail's snap to attach the leader via the loop knot.

This drail rig is for fishing from a drifting boat. If you are anchored, or shore fishing, a fish-finder rig may be better, though as I've said before, when fishing live baits my belief is that the fish expects some resistance when he chases down and chomps on my bait. Therefore the fishfinder rig's advantage is nil. Also, I can better feel the actions of my bait with the drail rig than with the fishfinder.

You can buy live bunker in many locales or catch them yourself. If you want to catch your own bunker, and you don't want to learn to throw a cast net, you can snag them. A heavy duty spinning outfit, say an eight-footer, with lots of backbone, is great for snagging bunker and fishing it live right on the spot. Mount a reel capable of holding 200 yards of 20 pound line. You need this beefiness because your gonna throw a big weighted treble hook out into the school of bunker, allow it to sink, and then rip it back with sweeping snaps of the rod in hopes of snagging a bunker. You can make a leader, using 60 pound mono, using dropper loops to attach an un-weighted treble or two about a foot apart, above the weighted snag hook. This lets you snag more than one bait at a time.

If you want to use small porgies or bergalls—good baits—head for the local jetty, bulkhead, or rockpile, and fish clam-baited hooks. Or you can jig a small sabiki bait rig. One of these, fished while tied up to a local dock, usually provides me with a supply of small baits—snappers, bergalls, etc—in short order.

Snappers and especially menhaden need lots of water to stay lively. You can keep about 10 bergalls alive in a five gallon bucket if you change the water every 15 minutes or so. TIP: The easiest way to change water when a bucket is your live well is to use two buckets. Pour off most of the water from the bucket with the bait in it. Then pour the bait and remaining water into the new bucket. Top-off the new bucket with fresh seawater, using the original bucket.

I've been casting lures for weakfish since the time when Tiger Tails, Nordic Eels, and Bagley's Salty Dogs were the choices of sharpies. Now I use bucktails and leadheads dressed with the likes of Fin-S Fish, Sluggos or shad bodies. Sometimes I tip these with a sliver of squid or section of worm.

Other times I'll use a "naked" leadhead and slide on a large strip of squid or whole sandworm as the "lure." With all of these jigs and their relatives, I tie directly to the fishing line, using a Uni-knot loop. I like to work the bottom third of the water column for weaks, and these lures do it well, whether cast and bounced back to the boat or simply hopped along while drifting.

I will use hardware when diamond jigging for weakfish. Whether it's a Hopkins or Ava jig, and whether with or without a surgical tube tail, these lures twist the line. So, when I'm serving-up "heavy metal" for weaks, I always use a black ball-bearing snap swivel of about 50 pound test. TIP: It pays to use ball bearing swivels. The cheaper swivels tend to bind-up and lock, defeating the purpose of keeping twist out of the line.

Finally, let me relate a rigging tip I used to use when I fished the Babylon area extensively for weakfish, in particular, the Hecksher Flats. While drifting and casting a leadhead, I would deadstick a couple of whole sandworms three feet below a bobber. A small split shot kept the bait down, wriggling a foot or two above the bottom. Boy did that rig catch weaks! In fact, when ever I'm fishing relatively shallow water—or a channel bordered by flats—I almost always put a rod in the holder, in freespool, with the clicker on, setup with a bobber rig. Use a big bobber; the ones on your snapper pole are easy to see in the calm waters of a creek. Out in a bay or harbor there's likely to be some chop, and the bigger bobber is easier to see.

FISHING

Before discussing lures, baits and techniques, it's important to realize that time of day and boat traffic will often have the greatest affect on the success of a weakfish trip. Weakies love the night, and my most successful outings with them have occurred just before dawn and just after dusk. Fishing night tides is part of the game if you want the handle weakfisherman. But it's not just because the fish can thrive and hunt in the dark. It's also because weakfish are the most boat-shy of Long Island's inshore gamefish. Getting there early—or late—means their will be less boat traffic to disturb the fish and put them off the feed. It also means less competition from other anglers, those less motivated than you, who prefer to sleep in when they should be on the rip. You can catch weakfish at high noon, and you can catch them when a fleet of Sea Rays is running down the channel, but you'll have generally better success at the opposite extreme. On to the how-to.

My favorite way to catch weakfish is to cast bucktails or leadhead jigs dressed with plastic tails, “rubber baits” as I call them. My go to lure is a six inch Sluggo, in rainbow trout pattern, rigged on a 5/8-ounce arrow head jig tied directly to the line with an Improved Clinch knot. (While I use loop knots for bucktails, the plastic baits have good swimming action on their own, and don’t need the extra action a loop knot provides. Additionally, the Improved Clinch is stronger, in my experience, than any loop knot.) This bait is fished, as are bucktails and other leadheads, by casting either up-current, cross-current, or some angle in between, and letting the jig find the bottom. Once you think the jig is on on the sand, engage the reel and take up the slack. Twitch the rod tip as the belly comes out of your line, if you’re using appropriately light tackle, you should feel the bump telegraph back to you as the lure thuds the bottom. Now it’s simply a matter of hopping the lure back towards you and waiting for a weakie to gobble up your offering. Well, it may be not that easy.

For one thing, weakfish usually prefer a slow retrieve. My dad used to say when I think I’m reeling in slow enough, slow down some more. It takes a little practice, with a variety of lures in a variety of depth and current situations, to retrieve as slowly as possible, yet still keep the lure “working” all the time. The right balance of tackle really helps, as over-gunning with a heavy rod won’t provide you the sensitivity needed for such slow fishing. However, the light action rods described, particularly if they are constructed using graphite blanks, will aid in this matter greatly.

Secondly, while you’re reeling as slow as possible AND still providing action to the lure, you want to minimize the amount of time during each hop that there is slack in the line. Some slack is inevitable, as the lure drops after you lower the rod tip. But it can be minimized. What I do, is “follow” the lure with my rod tip.

After the first few “hops” of a retrieve with a given lure in a given set of conditions, I’ve got a feel for the down time—how much lift of the rod tip is necessary to take the slack out before the jig actually rises off the bottom again. By getting a handle on this, I can begin to bring the rod tip back up a split microsecond before I actually feel the lure hitting the bottom. If I’m on my game, the lure kisses the mud, and immediately jumps off it again with no delay. I guess it’s like the backswing in tennis or baseball: a fluid combination of motion and timing, that, with practice and concentration, eventually becomes so natural you’re not even thinking about it.

At the top of the hop, that is as the rod tip is raised, the same principle applies. Rather than simply raising the tip and then dropping the tip quickly—putting a loop of slack in the line—I try to anticipate the lure's descent and smoothly follow the dropping jig with the rod tip. That way, if a fish hits the lure on the drop, there's less slack in the line, and hence, a better chance for a hookup. Weakfish readily bite jigs, but are notorious.

This "slow and follow" retrieve is a general method. Weakfish, like other gamefish, are going to prefer a certain retrieve over others on any given day. Our job is to find that out and fill a limit. Sometimes they like the jig presented with sweeping motions of the rod tip. Other days might find them pouncing on jigs that are barely twitched and hop just inches above the bottom. Vary the style until you find what's turning them on.

Leadheads work best for weakfish when fishing waters less than 20' deep. It's not that you can't fish a bucktail deeper—you can—but you need heavier tackle to do so. Therefore, I like to use these jigs in shallower water. When doing so, I'm always looking for a dropoff, especially one that's dramatic, at least relatively speaking. A flat or shallows with eel grass or boulders bordering deeper water is ideal. In the Sound, places like the west side of Lloyd Neck, between Whitewood Point and the Sand Hole, there is a drop-off from four to 11'. Likewise, in Port Washington, the stretch between Sands Point and Barkers Point in front of the creek is real good. Further east, I've caught weaks at Herod Point Shoal, off Wildwood: fish the deep cut into the shoal, working the 12' to 24' drop on the cuts inshore edge on falling water.

On the South Shore, I like the Hecksher Flats, of course, but also the shoreline to the west of the Sailor's Haven harbor entrance, fishing the edge of the flat and deep water. Further west, the entire edge of Sloop Channel has been good to me. To the east, try Taylor Hole in Moriches, or the Quogue Canal.

All of these places have several things in common: lots of current, an abrupt transition from deep to shallow, and structure in the form of shell beds, boulders, grass or a combination of all three. Any of these places and places like them are excellent spots to tempt a tiderunner with a cast jig.

But why not hedge your bets. I do. In one of several ways. If I am drift fishing, I will dead stick a rod rigged with a three way rig and baited with a couple of whole sandworms. I cut off the worm's head, thread an inch or so of his body up the hook shank, and leave the remainder to dangle enticingly. I use a conventional reel, in free spool with the clicker on. Snappers, bergalls, porgies, searobins—they may all drive you crazy by stealing your bait or even getting hooked. Plan on bringing several dozen worms if you elect for this plan.

The second variation I use is when I'm anchored and chumming for weakfish. Chum can be ground bunker or clam logs or, if you can get them, grass shrimp are best. (You'll have to seine your own, as I don't know that tackle shops carry frozen grass shrimp like they did back in the heyday. If the weaks keep re-bounding, perhaps that practice will be resumed.) I'll anchor the boat up-current of the drop-off, get the chum overboard, and then deadstick a baited hook as described above. Then I'll start fan casting with my jig, allowing it to touch bottom and move down current with every hop, describing an arc across the face of the drop until the lure is dead downcur-

A wide-mouthed net is essential for weakfish.
A young Ryan Horowitz shows how.

rent of my location. At that point, I reel up and cast again. Sometimes the jig outfishes the bait. Other times all they want is the sandworm. On rare days, I've had the fish get so thick I had to abandon one rod completely.

Regardless of what they eat, weakfish hooked in shallow water strike with a quick viciousness. They not only bend the tip of the rod, but force you to lower your stance as they hit and run, surging line against the reel brake. Expect some sideways running and then a pause. Now pump up! Reel down…hold it…she's gone again. You gotta let these fish have their head, even with light tackle, or you will pull the hook. (Though the dead-sticked, bait-caught fish are often gut-hooked.) Stroke easy, and only when she rests. Cajole her. The drag is light, so palm the rotor or thumb the spool ever so lightly if you need a little more on the lift. Be ready though, there's always that last run at the boat.

Charles Falvey with a "spike" weak caught in the back bay.

Now, I've seen as many weakfish lost while being netted as I have seen lost in the middle of battle. The reason? The angler didn't listen when I said to keep his head in the water. There's this beautiful fish, though beaten and barely finnng, laying on its side beside the boat. The net comes down, and instead of moving the fish forward, the guy on the rod lifts and moves the fish toward the net. Even though mostly supported by water, that lifting component of the movement puts enough strain on the hole worn in the weakie's jaw to send him bye-bye. At crunch time, the angler has to keep the fish in the water. It helps of the netman is good and deep with the mesh, too.

Now in deeper water, I generally abandon the leadheads in favor of either diamond jigs or strict bait fishing. This is not blue fishing—though you will probably catch your share fishing weaks in water deeper than 20'. The jigs can be dropped to the bottom and slowly lifted and dropped about a foot at a time—just enough to keep it moving. Ideally, the flex of your rod's tip is imparting the action, the rod butt hardly moves at all. This method works very effectively if you have found fish, narrowed down where they are holding, and are "hitting them on the head."

If, however, you just started a tide's fishing trip, you may want to cast the jig diagonally across the current, let it hit bottom and work it back to the boat, again in small, slow, one foot or less hops. Once you find 'em, you can vertically jig, although the horizontal component of this retrieve imparts a more strike-inducing action to the lure, I believe.

To bait fish these deeper water areas, I like the Hi-Low rig. At least initially. I'll start off baiting one hook with a squid strip, cut into a six or seven inch pennant, and the other hook baited with a whole sandworm or two. If the fish show a preference for one bait over the other, I'll start baiting both hooks with that bait. If they start showing a preference for either the high or low hook, I'll re-rig, using a three way rig to present a single hook at the depth at which the fish are responding. The Hi-Low is great, but more cumbersome and tangle-prone than a three-way rig. Once the Hi-Low has shown me what the fish want, and at what depth, its job is done for the day.

Weakfish in deeper water don't strike with the ferocity exhibited in shallow water. Part of that is the extra line in the water; part of it is the fish feeling more comfortable with so much more water between him and deadly fresh air. With bait, it's a firm pickup and often a moment of slack—I think they swim up after swallowing for some reason—followed by another good tug. The run follows. This will be a rod-throbbing drag puller, of longer duration than I've noticed when catching in shallow water. This is followed by your carefully pumping the fish to the surface. Expect a last-ditch surge at the boat.

With slow-worked diamond jigs, I've noticed that most hits come on the drop, as slight as it is. Instead of a rod bending initial strike, you get a bump or hesitation, a thing that interferes with your jigging rhythm. At this point you need to crank the reel, drop the tip, then come up smartly and set the hook. Now she knows she's hooked and the fun begins. Go gentle, but stay in charge. Have the net ready.

Where are some of these deeper water weakfish hotspots? Great success can be had at Rose's Grove or the South Race in Peconic Bay. Further east, I've caught weaks drifting bait at South Ferry and by the Number four buoy just west of Napeague Harbor.

To the west, Sloop Creek between the Jones beach fishing piers and the bridge has produced on both tides for me. The Goose Creek Bridge seems to be an outgoing-only spot according to my logs. Just north of Island Park, near the number seven Buoy, there's a 40' hole that locals tell me is loaded with weaks on incoming water.

In the Sound, the steep drop-off near the Red number eight Buoy in Hempstead Harbor produced a lot of weaks for me and my father back in the day when we rented from Bills Boats. I also used to catch quite a few across the way, from shore, off the big jetty in Glen Cove. Further east, try the deep rift between Eaton's Neck and the 11B buoy or the drop-off paralleling Old Field Beach at Conscience Bay.

The spots for weakfish, like the spots for all of our gamefish, are really too numerous to list. So numerous that they are too general to be of real value. For instance, if I were to write: "Fish the bridges and inlets for weakfish," there is no one in the world who could dispute that. However, you have to know each inlet and each bridge with some intimacy before you can catch consistently. The fish may show at Debs at High Slack and at Fire Island an hour after Ebb starts. Ponquogue may be good on outgoing water; Smith Point on incoming water. You get the picture. Look for the environmental factors they favor, such as swift water and access to flats and structure, but with the protection of deep water near at hand. Fish those spots. Fish them on different combinations of wind and tide. Do so and you will catch fish, and you will start to see why. And unlike famous spots such as Hecksher or South Race, you won't be competing with everybody else all the time. Fish at night and you'll have the fish even more to yourself. Remember, with rare exceptions, heavy boat traffic and good weakfishing don't mix. Think like a fish and catch more fish. Fish more and you'll catch more because you'll learn more.

Weakfish Crib Sheet

Weakfish, a.k.a, Squeteague, yellowfin, tide-runner

Season: May-October, best in May, October

Location: Fast water near opposing points (bridges), inlets, rocky points, deep holes and channel edges bordering grass flats.

Baits: Live snappers, bunker, bergall, porgy, seaworms. Squid (whole or strips). Leadheaded jigs with plastic bodies, bucktails, diamond jigs, tubes.

Tackle: Light to medium spinning and baitcasting.

High Hook Tip: Use a dropper loop to attach a fly or small, unweighted, plastic bait ahead of your jig and your score will soar.

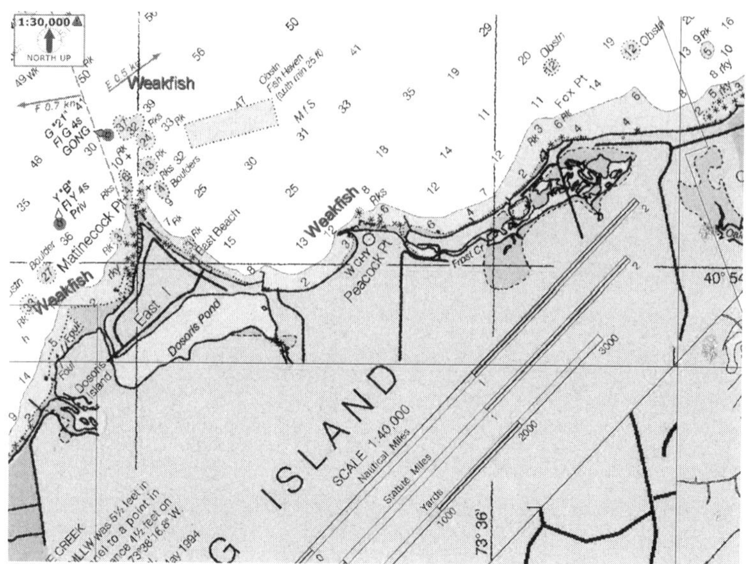

The pond outlets, on dropping water provide a means for weaks to ambush bait being flushed out with the current.

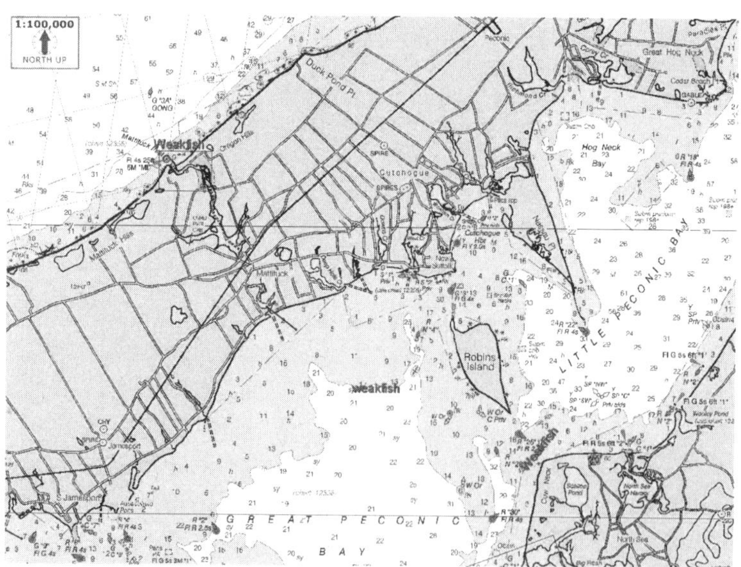

South Race can be hot. Don't neglect to try inside Mattituck Creek.

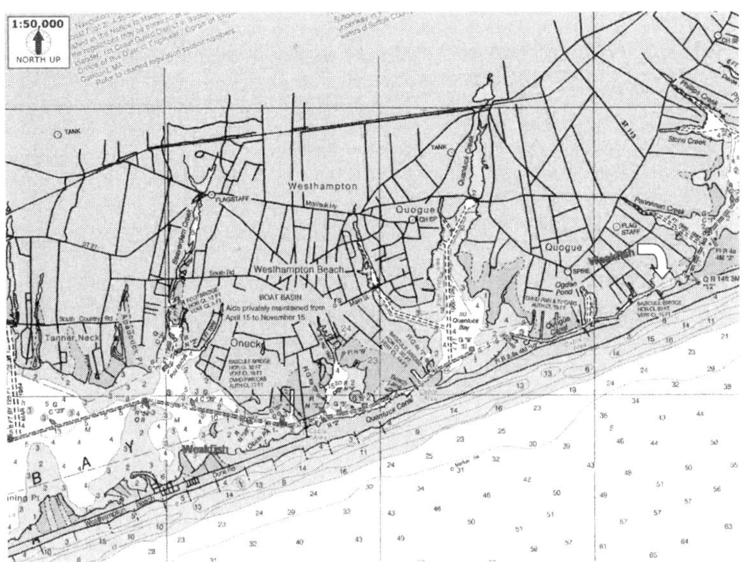

Quogue Canal can be fished from shore or boat. There's a deep hole in that Moriches Bay flat.

CHAPTER 6
Blackfish
(Tautoga Onitis)

THE TAUTOG.
Tautoga onitis (L.), Gthr. (p. 268.)
Drawing by H. L. Todd, from No. 17738, U. S. National Museum, collected at Wood's Holl, Mass., December 13, 1875, by Vinal N. Edwards.
PLATE 85.

Blackfish and football are inextricably linked in my mind. You see, the only thing my father Charlie, an inveterate bottom fisherman, liked more than blackfishing, was the New York Giants. And so, as a kid being taught the ropes, whether we were in our own boat or a rental skiff, aboard a party boat or fishing from shore, a transistor radio tuned to Giants Football was an essential part of our kit. When I think back on blackfishing as a kid, the exclamations "goin' up!," "gotcha!," and "fish-on!," reverberate as loudly as Jim Gordon shouting, "Touchdown, Giants!" Actually, the Giants didn't give Gordon much opportunity to say that in the 70's, but the radio was always tuned to WNEW nonetheless. Fishing enriches life beyond the pleasures of pursuit and capture.

Now, if you can consistently hook blackfish, you can consistently hook any other species of bottom fish. They are worth catching for that reason alone, but offer additional opportunities for personal growth as well. You'll need to rig specially for the hook-snagging environment in which they live, present your bait properly in that environment, and if boat fishing, possess the ability to find the structure and anchor over it precisely. Atop a dinner plate, they have few rivals.

TAXONOMY AND BIOLOGY

Blackfish are ideally evolved to thrive in the rough bottom and sticky structure in which they live. They possess a stout body with a near vertical forehead, small scales, and thick, tough skin. This allows them to poke into crevices, voids, and cracks in the rocks, reefs, rubble and wrecks in which

Dr. Julie Ball with a 15 pound World Record blackfish. Julie has caught record Tog to 22 lbs. (Photo Credit: Dr. Julie Ball)

they are found without self-inflicted injury. Their tail is connected to the body by a wide caudal peduncle. This, along with a one-piece, full-length dorsal fin, in concert with relatively large pectoral and anal fins, give them close-quarters maneuverability akin to that of a twin-screw powerboat—with bow and stern thrusters! It's for this reason, that you'll see sharpie 'toggers lifting their rod overhead after the hook set, and taking several quick turns of the reel. Blackfish can dart back into the cover they came from with lightening speed and the overhead reeling gets them away from the structure before they can do so.

Of particular importance to fisherman is the structure of a blackfish's mouth. Thick, protuberant lips can probe mussel clumps, barnacle clusters, and live crabs without the injury thinner-lipped species might sustain. Within the mouth, blackfish have two distinct sets of teeth. At the front are two or three rows of conical canines. These are used for picking up prey and manipulating the food within the mouth. An angler who strikes when feeling the rapid taps of a blackfish with bait in these teeth is likely to come-up empty. You see, at this point, the blackish is merely orienting the bait properly before sending it to the "crusher" teeth (pharynyeal teeth) located at the entrance to the throat. Then is the time to strike, as will be discussed in detail below.

Blackfish vary in color from gray to green to dusky brown. Smaller fish are marked by blotches of darker color, whereas larger fish tend to be a more uniform brown or even black. All of this depends largely upon the bottom in which they are caught, as blackfish have the limited ability to change color and pattern for camouflage. Larger fish also sport a white chin, which accounts for one of the several names by which the fish is called. If you want to impress your buddies, male fish generally have a white spot or blotch on the sides, just aft of the pectoral fins, near the lateral line.

The IGFA All-Tackle World Record tautog weighed 25 pounds and was caught off Ocean City, NJ, in January, 1998. The New York State record 'tog is a 19 pound 12 ounce fish caught by Jim Burgon off Riverhead in August 1992. That IGFA record 25 pounder is about as big as they get, according to biologists, and my research turned up no historical reference, either commercial or recreational, of blackfish any larger. Most fish caught by Long Island fishermen will weigh between two and four pounds. Anything over five pounds is a good fish and you'll start seeing white chins on fish of about eight pounds. Freely brag about double-digit weights. The minimum size limit at the time of this writing is 14", which translates into a fish of about a pound and a half. Blackfish are one of the longest-lived fish in our waters, with a lifespan approaching 40 years. It takes eight years to make a barely-a-keeper two pound blackfish; 10 to make a four pounder. Blackfish range from Maine to Virginia, though lucky for Long Islanders, they are most populous south of Cape Cod. Around Long Island, blackfish are present year-round, both inshore and off. Certainly the bigger fish tend to come from offshore wrecks and reefs, or areas such as the Cholera Bank. But quality fish are available to the rental boat and shore angler as well. As a younger man, I caught numerous five and six pound fish from one of several jetties at Point Lookout. The current October-May season is an attempt, I'd guess, to prevent anglers from catching fish during spawning, which occurs during the summer months according to the scientists.

In any case, blackfish will be found where there are rocks, piers, reefs, shell beds, wrecks or other obstructions, either man-made or natural. They do not school, though they will tend to congregate together in prime areas. Typically, they are active from dawn to dusk, spending the night inactive within a "home" crevice or cranny. During daylight, they leave "home" to feed. Biologists tell us that smaller fish rarely move more than several yards from home to feed. This is an important behavioral characteristic to understand: if you catch a few and the bite stops, it helps to move down the jetty or drop back on the anchor a few yards. Bigger fish tend to range further from " home." Substantiating this is my own experience of catching five pounders in the inter-tidal zone at Plum Island. At high tide, these fish would move up onto the ledge and flats to feed (I'm guessing) on the abundant and otherwise inaccessible mussel beds there.

The same behavioral difference between small and large fish applies to migratory habits. Fish less than three pounds or so tend to over-winter inshore at their home area, remaining in a torpid, inactive state during which they feed little if at all. Larger fish move to offshore wrecks and rough bottom as the water temperature drops below 50 degrees returning to the shallow boulder fields when inshore waters once again rise above 50 degrees in spring. Fatal temperatures are close to 90 degrees, a temperature not found in Long Island's waters. Legal seasons permitting, warm water shouldn't impede your efforts. Remember that the New York state record was caught in August. Finally, you will lose rigs to the bottom when blackfishing. As the saying goes, if you're not hanging-up, you're not fishing in the right spot.

Blue mussels are the main component of the blackfish's diet according to scientific studies and the observations of divers I've interviewed in researching this book. These sources told me the blackfish tears a clump from the bed, targeting small mussels, and ingests the whole clump. (Perhaps clumps will become the new hot bait if I can figure how to hook them.) Other foods include barnacles, sand fleas, seaworms, crabs, soft clams and lobster. For lobster, one diver said that immature ones were swallowed whole but that larger ones were cracked by grabbing them, apparently using the crusher teeth to crack the shell, and spitting them back out several times before actually eating. At any rate, all of these will work as blackfish bait, but as I'll detail, keeping bait on the hook, especially in the presence of the bergalls that live alongside blackfish, limits your practical choices to a select few.

Tautog are preyed upon by several desirable species, including whiting and striped bass. While filleting fluke, I've occasionally found juveniles in the bellies. However, size limits at the time of writing mean you can only legally fish a very large bait. Hey, big stripers eat large baits. Hmmm. Might be that's one more reason for you to go 'togging!

TACKLE AND RIGGING

Spinning tackle has little place in the hands of a tog fisherman. The rods aren't stiff enough to handle the weight often needed and the bail, too, just won't hold up to sinker bouncing with eight, 10, or 12 ounces of lead. Get yourself a seven to eight foot long conventional rod capable of handling up to 12 ounces of lead. You want the extra length so that you can lift the fish further away from the structure after the strike. A six foot boat rod will work, but leave you at some disadvantage in this respect.

The rod must have a stiff backbone, yet have enough sensitivity to feel the distinction between the rat-a-tat-tat raps of the inevitable bergalls and porgies and the solid tug-tug of a 'tog that's swallowed your bait and begun to move off. Mount a reel to a prospective rod and tie on a 10 ounce sinker. Feel the action. If, when you lift the rod, the first foot or so of the tip bends, but the backbone remains apparently straight, you're probably making a good choice. I've found that stock rods labeled as Muskie models work well, as a rule of thumb. An example is the St. Croix " Big Dawg" Legend Tournament. You can find this action in fiberglass, composite and graphite blanks. The choice is yours. But remember you may be holding eight ounces at the end of a seven foot long lever all day, so that a lighter rod that'll do the same job will be more comfortable to use.

Though most blackfishing is done in deep waters and swift tides, there are times and places that you can crush the 'tog when the water's not so deep and the current isn't screaming. Slack tide, in fact, is prime time for blackfish, no matter where you find them. If you are fishing water under 20' deep and the current isn't so bad, you can drop down to a lighter rod. In this case, a six and a half to seven foot fast action conventional stick will serve you well, provided it doesn't collapse under the anticipated sinker weights. It can also be pressed in to service as your primary 'tog stick should you get a backlash during a hot bite. Often, the window in which blackfish go on the feed is a short one. Re-tying after hanging the wreck or fighting a tangle with frozen fingers is no way to spend your time productively. I always carry a backup rod, rigged and ready, when blackfishing.

To either of these rods, mount a high-speed conventional reel capable of holding 200 yards of 30 pound mono (you'll load it with braid,

You may have to fish through an army of bergall to get your 'Tog.

though). You want the high gear ratio—minimum 4:1—so that you can gain line and get the fish off the bottom after the strike. The large line capacity helps as well: since it's a bigger spool, you retrieve more line with each revolution. TIP: Check the reel's specs and leave any with brass gears at home. The demands of 'togging necessitate steel or bronze gears.

In addition to their line capacity and retrieve speed, these have an infinite anti-reverse, meaning there is no slop in the handle. You want to move that blackfish with every turn of the reel, especially at the beginning of the fight, so this feature is nice. I load my blackfish reels with 50 pound braid, and tie on a 50' top-shot of 40 pound mono using a 20 turn Albright Knot. The mono is more abrasion resistant—and your line will get abraded while blackfishing—and provides the necessary cushion against a bulldog black's last-ditch run during the end-game of the battle. Blackfish are very powerful swimmers.

One exception regarding the use of spinning tackle comes into play for the jetty fisherman. Sometimes it is necessary to lob your bait out to the "foot" of the jetty to get into prime 'tog territory. The foot, or base of the jetty on the inlet bottom, may be 20 or more feet further out than where you are standing. Also, many jetties place you in a position where you have to lift the fish 10 or more feet from the water's surface to land them. Morgan Park jetty in Glen Cove comes to mind. In these cases stiff, 10' or 11' long surfcasting rod with a beefy reel fills the bill. I know of more than one striper hound that blackfishes while waiting for the linesiders to show in the suds.

Terminal rigging for blackfish is very straightforward and simple. Use no hardware, as doing so will only increase the number of snags you have to deal with—and you will deal with snags while blackfishing. The old adage is true: If you are not hanging up once in a while, you are probably not fishing over productive blackfish structure. Instead of hardware, you'll use three knots, maybe four. These are the hook snell, the dropper loop, the perfection loop and the overhand loop. If you buy pre-snelled "blackfish" hooks, which work fine, you won't have to snell. However, these pre-packaged hooks are generally Virginia style, in size four or five, which I prefer. Some sharpies like Octopus pattern hooks. TIP: The Virginia Hook's heavy wire is strong enough to withstand the bulldogging tugs of an out-sized blackfish. However, my dad always preferred the Sproat hook. Made of finer wire, it can be "sprung" loose of the wreck at lot easier, you just have to play a big fish with more finesse. Snag your Virginia, however, and it will become part of the wreck.

The simplest rig, the one that has accounted for the most blackfish over the years is a single-hook job. Clinch knot a 50 pound ball-bearing barrel swivel to the end of your fishing line. Take a 20" section of 50 pound leader material—fluorocarbon isn't necessary for blackfish, in my experience; we used to catch 'em as a kid with black leaders and dacron running line—and tie a Dropper Loop about 10" from one end. Next, tie an overhand loop knot, large enough to cat's paw the sinker size you're using, at the bitter end. At the top of the leader, tie a Perfection Loop. Use a loop-to-loop connection to cat's paw your leadered hook to the Dropper Loop. The entire rig gets loop-to-looped to the barrel swivel via the Perfection Loop.

You use an overhand loop for the sinker connection because it's easier to break-off WHEN you get snagged. And snag you will. Another breakaway sinker rig is to use a heavy rubber band to connect the sinker to the leader. If you get snagged, reel down to take out the slack, then come up and break the rubber band. TIP: Slab-sided diamond sinkers (not pyramid) tend to snag less than bank sinkers.

Now there's been lots of hullabaloo in recent years about using a double hook rig called the Snafu. Simply, a Snafu rig is a 15" long leader with a loop tied in its middle. That's where you attach to the main leader's dropper loop as described above. The two resulting arms each get a snelled hook, each of which is placed into a single large crab bait, one through each side of the crab, so that the whole crab lies flat. It works well, especially with hermit crabs or big greens, as once the blackfish starts to chew up the bait, one of the hooks invariably become detached from the crab bait and acts as a free swinging stinger. I like the idea, but the two arms of the Snafu rig's enhanced hook-up ration is negated by its increased chance of snagging the wreck. Visualize each arm hooked into the crab and you will see that, essentially, a loop of heavy line, about a foot in diameter, has been created. Do you really want to scrape a wreck with a lasso? In my experience, there is a better two-hook rig for fishing whole greens, hermits or other large baits.

Take a two foot section of 50 pound leader material and snell two hooks in tandem, about four inches apart. One hook is at the bitter end, and the other is just above it, sort of like the big strip bait rig some fluke sharpies use. Tie a Perfection Loop at the other end to attach to the dropper loop of the basic leader described above. Now you can double-hook large, bulldog-sized bait, and everything is neat and in-line. One hook goes in each side, or end, of your bait.

As always, be prepared to adjust. For instance, the fish may want the bait higher, in which case it pays to have some leaders tied with the dropper loop a little higher. Or maybe you are mixed bag fishing and want a second dropper loop and hook two feet above the bottom to tempt sea bass or porgy. If what you're doing isn't working, tweaking the terminal rig can make a difference. It's certainly easier than moving the boat. Of course, you'll do plenty of that while fishing blackfish anyway.

A final note on rigging, or at least, the use of your tackle. Do not try to free a rig that's stuck solid in the bottom by high-sticking the rod. You're fighting the bend in the rod for one thing and for another, you may break the tip or tip-top guide. Also, grabbing the line by hand is a sure way to get cut, especially with braid. TIP: When you get stuck in the wreck, take a little slack off the spool and wrap it around the reel a few times. Then invert the rod, holding it like a butter churn, and pull up, directly in line with the direction of your fishing line through the guides so that there is no bend in the rod and the line becomes bowstring-tight. Wait for the boat to drop into the trough of a wave and then quickly take up more slack and wrap it around the reel. As the boat rises with the next wave, you'll pop free with no cuts and without grunting and groaning.

FISHING

Besides, you'll need those grunts for the fight. Blackfish richly deserve the bulldog moniker. But before you get to say, "Gotcha!" you have some work to do. If you are a private boater, your blackfish success is directly related to your ability to find productive bottom and anchor your boat over it, precisely and exactly. The difference between a leap job and flying the skunk flag is a matter of several yards. Standard nautical charts show plenty of wrecks and bottom composition suitable for 'tog, so long as you learn to read the symbols. "Chart No. 1" is not a chart at all, but actually a list of those symbols and available from NOAA. Chart Number 1 is no longer available in print, but can be downloaded free at: www.nauticalcharts.noaa.gov. Learn to discern Wrk(wrecks), P (pebbles), G (gravel), stones(St), shell (Sh) and Cb (cobbles) for starters. This same website has a "wreck finder" feature that any computer literate bottom fisherman should familiarize himself with. There's even a link where you can print out a fishing chart for a given area. You can also get "numbers" from other fisherman, the DEC (for artificial reefs) and by using computerized chart programs such as those from Maptech, which I use. Get your numbers, plug them in, and fish them hard.

This is a fishing book, not one on boat handling, but suffice to say, those wishing to slam blackfish need to know more than just how to follow the rhumb line their GPS gives them. Sharpies know how to rig a bridle to double anchor. They know how to judge the current and wind once they find a spot and drop the hook at the right time. They know they might have to make three, four, or more attempts at dropping the hook, laying back on it and seeing where they're at. About the third try, the anchor starts to get real heavy, let me tell you. But to just anchor and hope for the best is a fool's game. Once on the piece, current and wind can change, or the bite can slow. In theses cases the pro knows to slide back on his anchor to re-position, how to belay the anchor line to veer off sideways, and yes, when its time, to pick-up and a re-set on the same piece all over again. And perhaps again.

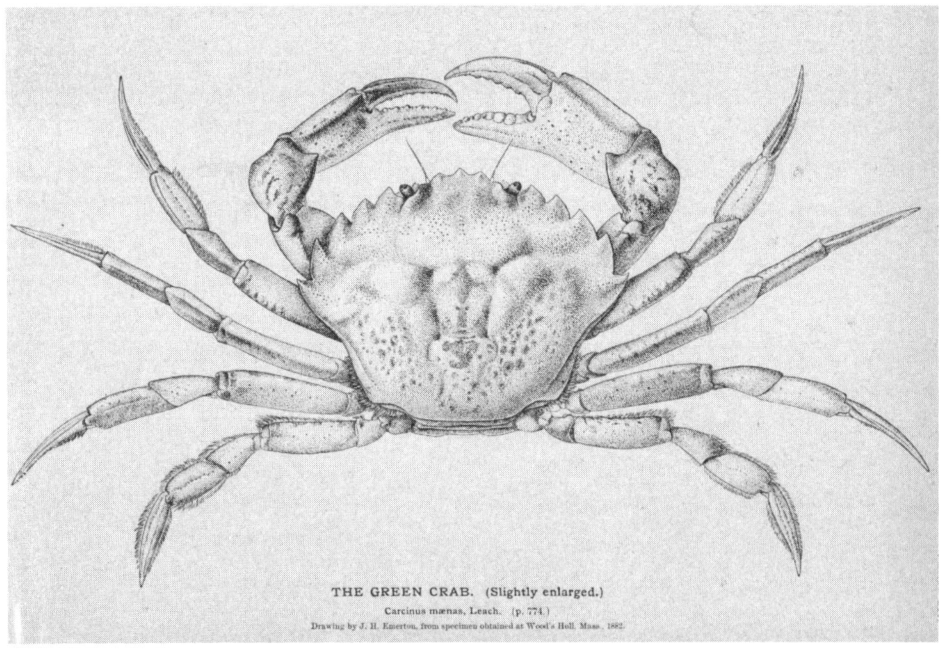

Green crabs are a proven bait and readily purchased.

The blackfish sharpie is also a master of currents. Slack water is prime time for blackfish—they really put on the feedbag when the current slows. But when is slack tide? How do you plan for it? Sure the papers print a time. But that's usually for an inlet, harbor, or other point of land. What time is slack water six miles from the spot in the paper? Will the wind or moon phase affect that time? The approach of a front? These skills are less science, than the artistry of a dedicated blackfisherman at work. You can't swipe your credit card to get it, you have to put in your time and even then, sharpened instincts come into play. It is the most challenging aspect of the game. I'm not lambasting party and charter boat anglers. I grew up a party boat fisherman, usually tying my rods to the stern rail of the Capt Al, back when he sailed from Freeport. This book is written for all anglers and private boaters seeking blackfish need to know: the view from the wheelhouse is different. 'Nuff said.

Bait for blackfish is primarily crab, of various types. You remember from the start of this chapter that blue mussels are the number one food of blackfish. You can use them for bait, as well as clams strips or worms. Blackfish will eat them heartily. Problem is, they aren't likely get to the bait before the ever-present bergalls, and a bergall can clean a hook faster than a trophy wife can clean out your savings. They aren't called cunners for nothing. So you'll use crabs (plus a couple other lesser-known baits, that I'll reveal below), the shells of which inhibit your bait's being stolen before a bulldog black can gobble it.

The standby bait for blackfish is the Green Crab (Carcinus maenas). They are readily available in tackle shops and bait stations and are usually what's provided for bait on party boats. I've used Rock Crab (Cancer irroratus) with equal success. They fish the same and you can pot both yourself at most any rocky shoreline, bridge rip-rap, etc., where a baited trap can be set for a day or two.

These crabs can be fished in a number of ways, including: halved or quartered; the back shell peeled off; with legs removed; with tail flippers removed; etc., etc., etc. It pays to experiment and there is no absolutely right way. Personally, I like to fish halved green crabs.

I'll take a sharp, stiff knife and placing it squarely on the back of a splayed-out crab, lean down with my palm on the back of the blade. No chopping, please. TIP: Heavy-duty garden shears also work well to cut green crabs. Then, I'll compare the positions of the legs on each half of crab to the width of my hook's bend, let's say 5/8" for a size five Virginia hook. I will remove only one claw and one leg, by pulling them out, so that I can place my hook into one now empty leg socket and out the other. Typically I insert the hook from the back leg socket and come out the front, believing that my hook more closely resembles the now removed pincher claw than one of the legs. If the crab is big enough, I will leave the claws, remove two legs and insert my hook through leg sockets only. TIP: In all cases of baiting blackfish hooks, leave the point, barb, and part of the bend exposed.

Instead of being halved or quartered, smaller green crabs can be fished whole. Use either the Snafu or two-hook rig, both of which were previously described. Place each hook of these rigs through leg or claw sockets so that the crab has a natural "lie" about it. I leave every appendage on, except those that have to come off to insert my hooks. TIP: Take care placing the hook through the crab. You can dull the point on the hard shell if you're not careful. Sharp hooks are a must in all fishing, but especially when blackfishing.

If the green crabs are small, say, smaller than a silver dollar, or at any rate, not so big that my hook's bend won't span both rear leg sockets, I will leave the crab whole and remove the two back legs, one each side. Then, I place the hook through the aft leg socket on one side and out the aft socket on the other. Before I send it down, I use my sinker to tap the crab's shell, not hard enough to kill it, but hard enough to get some "spider cracks" going. I have noticed, and have the logbook to verify, a very good hook-up ratio when fishing small green crabs in this fashion.

Fiddler Crabs (genus, Unca) are another common bait. Its easier to catch blackfish on fiddlers, as the blackfish seem to just inhale them, there's rarely any "foreplay" before the bait is passed to the crusher teeth as there is with greens. However, I've always caught bigger fish on green crabs.

You can buy or trap fiddlers. Bury a bucket up to its rim at the edge of a marsh at low water and place some bait in the bucket. Walk away. Come back later, before the tide covers the bucket, and the fiddlers will have fallen into the bucket.

If trapping your own fiddlers you want the white, "china-back," fiddlers, rather than the darker "mud" fiddlers. The former inhabit sand, the latter, mud. These work well, though another reason I prefer greens to fiddlers is for their better resistance to the bait-robbing efforts of bergalls and porgies. (TIP: If you do catch a big bergall, as sometimes happens, keep it. They are delicious, their rep as a "trash fish" notwithstanding. They are small, so a single-hook rig is fine.) Remove a claw and place the hook in the socket, pass it through to the back of the crab and gently poke the point out through the side near the rear. The crab will be hooked through the side, essentially, and there's little worry of dulling hooks on the brittle shell of a fiddler crab.

Now, my very favorite blackfish bait, the one I suggest you take efforts to procure if you want the best shot at the most, and biggest, blackfish, is not generally found in tackle stores and bait stations. Nor are they easily trapped by the industrious. This bait is the flat-clawed hermit crab (Pagurus longicarpas). They are the big ones, caught by lobstermen as by-catch. They inhabit whelk shells or other large discarded shells, and are not to be confused with the tiny long-clawed hermits found along the beach. Bait stations do sometimes offer these, but I usually get mine from a losterman. If I see a waterman pulling traps, I'll idle over and ask if he wants to sell me some hermits. More often then not, these gentlemen give me crabs and refuse payment. Still, be advised that they are fishing to pay the mortgage and we

Hermit crabs are the best blackfish bait, but not so easy to get.

are simply out for fun, so be insistent, without being insulting, about payment. As an alternative, hermit crabs can be ordered over the internet. Apparently several species of land hermit crabs are popular as pets. I haven't tried them yet, but it's on my to-do list.

You can rig hermits using a single or double hook rig described above. First, place the crab on your bait board and crack the shell using gentle taps and/or steady pressure until enough of the innards are revealed to remove the animal without damage. The visible part of the hermit, its face, claws and part of its back, are armored with shell. But within, its long, soft, succulent tail will be coiled around the spiraled, "reticulate sculpture." If you try pulling him out without cracking the shell, you'll just rip the crab in half. For a single hook presentation, insert the hook point into the soft body and thread the shank through towards the armored shell of the hermit's shoulders and bring the point through just inside that armor.

For twin hook presentation of a hermit crab, insert the hook point just aft of the shoulder armor and thread the shank aft towards the tail. Place the second hook through the joint where the big claw joins the body. This rig provides better protection from bait stealers and will up your hook-up ratio. It's worth the time to tie 'em up when fishing with hermits. Its one thing to go through six or seven baits when using something as easy to get as green crabs. But when using a rare commodity like hermits, getting a bushel of which is a rarity, you have to protect your investment.

TIP: I have used crawfish for blackfish bait and their performance rivals that of hermit crabs. Crawfish can be purchased at gourmet fish markets, or shipped live when ordered over the internet.

FISHING

You've got the numbers for a secret rockpile, the boat is anchored over it, and you're locked and loaded with baits and rigs. First thing is to focus. As soon as your baited hook hits the bottom, it is going to be assaulted. This may not be by a blackfish—hopefully it is—but rest assured that plenty of by-catch species are ever-present on the blackfish grounds. Therefore, it is imperative that you engage the reel, take-up any slack, orient the rod in a down-pointed position and be ready the second you feel the sinker thud bottom. This ain't flukin'. If you are not on your toes, you are going to have a high percentage of stolen baits and missed fish.

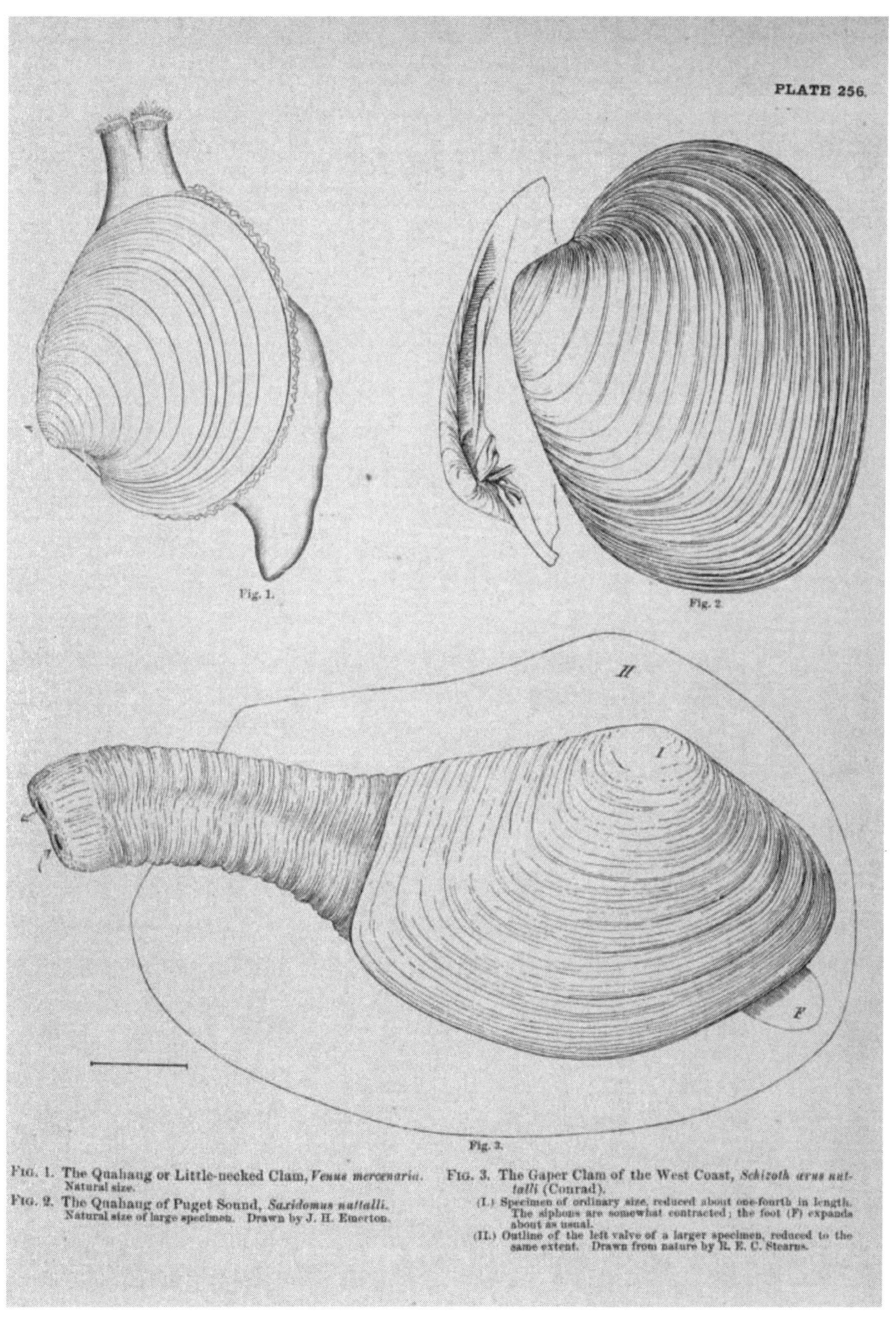

Soft clams (steamers) are fished shell-on for blackfish.

Second, be attentive to how your line lays. Often it will belly, but still be tight. In fact, in any bottom fishing, in relatively deep water, where there's current, your line is gonna belly. It takes a feel to know when the sinker has hit bottom and is holding. Some guys just keep letting out line, thinking they haven't hit bottom. What's happening is, the sinker is planted, but the current is taking the belly downcurrent somewhere between there and the rod tip. Learn to know your line belly.

Third, keep that sinker still. Don't move the tip up and down, place it in a holder than pick it up again. Blackfish are wary and a pounding sinker doesn't attract them like it does flounder. Sharpies don't move, or move their rod, when blackfishing.

Fourth, remember the description of how a blackfish eats. It picks up a bait with its front teeth and moves it to the rear, or crusher, teeth. Until you

A brace of blackfish from a near-shore wreck. Note the stout tackle.

get used to it, you'll need nerves of steel to resist setting the hook when you feel the tap-tap-tappity-tap of the front teeth. Swing on 'em now, and you're going to lose your bait and miss the fish. You must wait through these taps until you feel a solid tug-tug-tuuug, indicating the bait is in the crusher teeth. (Although with fiddler crabs this isn't always true—see below.) When that happens, reel down a turn, and then come-up smartly, taking up slack again, and raising the rod and reel above your head. That blackfish is going to be hell-bent on getting into a crevice in the wreck. You must get her off the bottom as quickly as possible. Allow no drag at this stage, using your thumb to prevent slip, and relying instead on the stretch in the line and bend of the rod. Sinker weights aside, it's the main reason you need a beefy rod for 'tog. Going light in an effort to be sporty will see your cooler clean and your freezer empty.

Once you've got the fish safely off of the bottom and solidly hooked, you can return the rod to the normal attitude. But don't let-up on 'em. Blackfish, even one of four pounds, will arc your rod and stop the reel handle in your hands with their powerful lunges. Be ready with steady pressure when this happens, allowing the drag to do its job this time. Then begin reeling again the instant you see the bend in your tip flatten out a bit. Notice I didn't say pump and reel. For blackfish, a smoother, slower, lift and reel technique will see more fish come to net. You can swing blackfish over the rail, because they are often deeply hooked. But I still use a net, especially on larger ones. Be prepared for a final lunge at the surface. In fact, backing off the drag a bit is a good idea at this time, again using your thumb for finer control.

If, after the hook-up, your 'tog gets herself wedged into the bottom, try dropping the tip and giving the fish some slack. Wait a few seconds. Sometimes a blackfish, feeling the release of pressure, will think all is well and swim out of its hidey hole to resume feeding. When to re-engage is a matter of instinct, but I suppose I'd give it a five-Mississippi count at least. Then come tight again. If the fish hasn't left on its own, you can try this slack line sneak a few times, and she may come out. If not, you'll thank me for recommending you have extra rigs and a back-up rod on hand. Go get 'em.

Blackfish Crib Sheet

Blackfish, a.k.a, Tautog, 'Tog, Bulldog,White-chin.

Season: April, May, September-January

Location: Rough, rocky, shelly bottom from shore to deep water. Wrecks. Deep bay channels and holes, especially near sedge edges.

Baits: Crabs: Fiddler, Green, Hermit, Rock.

Tackle: Stiff-backboned conventional.

High-hook tip: Soft Clams (Mya arenaria), a.k.a., steamers, make an excellent tog bait. Thread hook through siphon and into shell, then lightly crack shell, but leave intact.

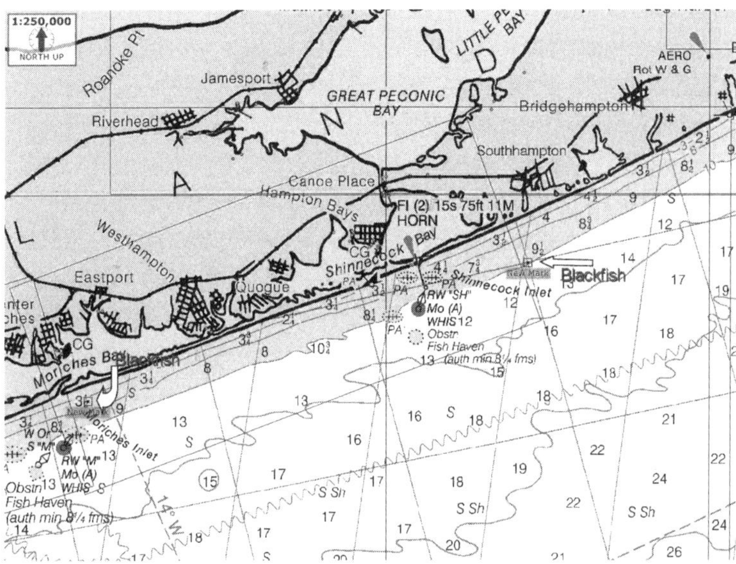

Use your sounder—there are lots of "pieces" here you'll need to find.

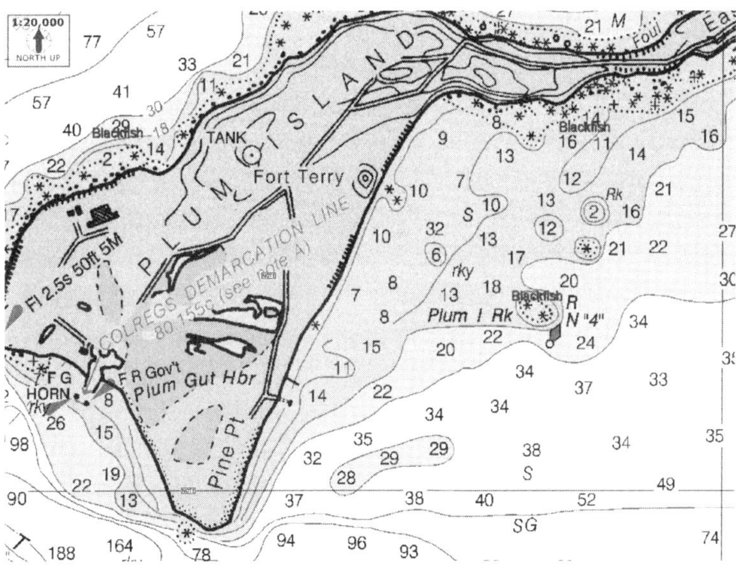

Drop anchor in the light blue water either side of Plum Island Rock and then drop back over the boulders. Blacks are numerous along shore at high water, but use caution as many rocks are uncharted.

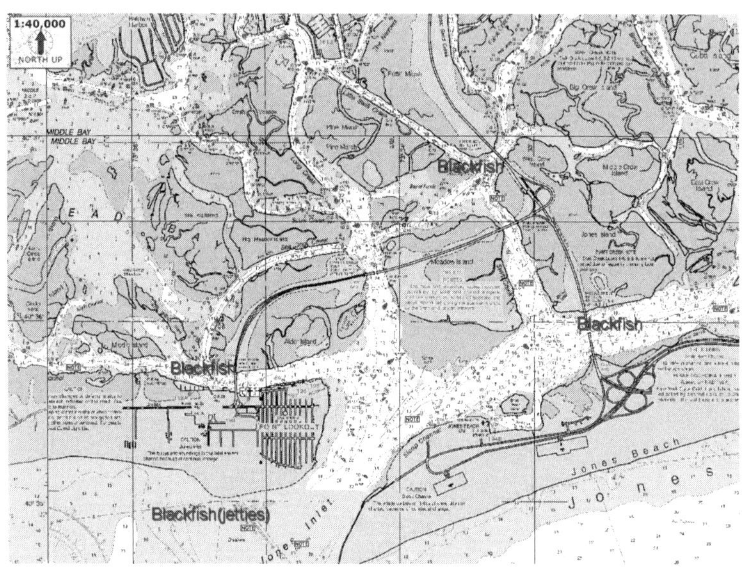

Bay Bridges are a great bet. Numerous jetties are accessible from shore at Pt. Lookout.

CHAPTER 7
Black Sea Bass
(Centropristis striata)

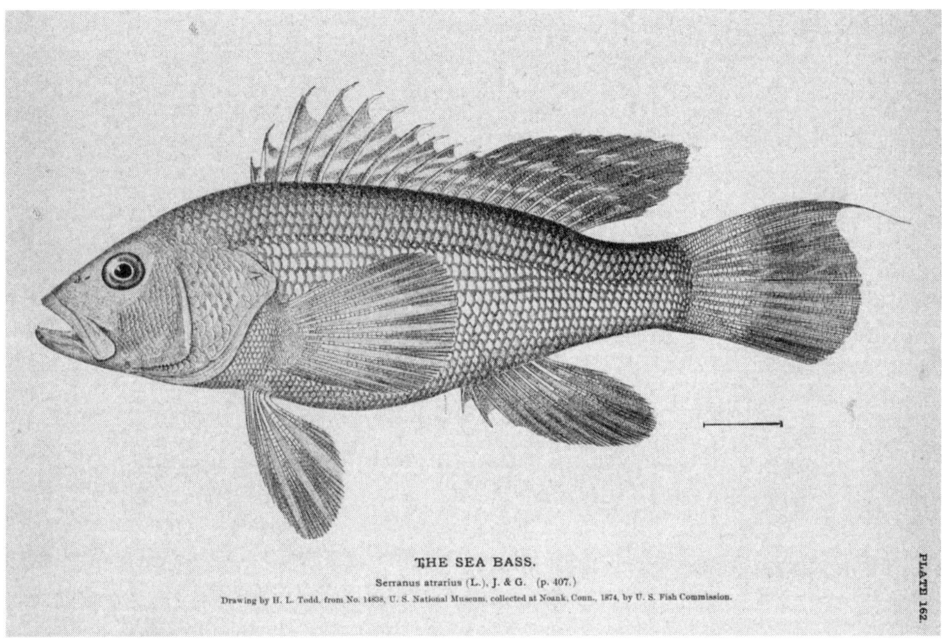

THE SEA BASS.
Serranus atrarius (L.), J. & G. (p. 407.)
Drawing by H. L. Todd, from No. 14838, U. S. National Museum, collected at Noank, Conn., 1874, by U. S. Fish Commission.
PLATE 162.

There are those who blame commercial fisherman and the live fish market for the decline in black sea bass numbers. I disagree. If anything is to blame, it's technology.

Prior to the 1980's, there were a relatively small number of wrecks, rock piles, and "live bottom," that recreational anglers knew about (The *Iberia,* the *Black Warrior,* the *Coimbra,* some state-funded reefs, etc.). Prior to that time, commercial fisherman using bottom gear would tangle their nets in multitudes of lesser know obstructions. They would note the location of these, either by manual navigation plotting, or with the help of what was called LORAN-A, an expensive device used basically by those who needed it. Then LORAN-C went online and by the 80's, prices plummeted. A couple hundred dollars bought anyone with a boat the ability to navigate to within 100' of a wreck.

Meanwhile, the lists of "hangs" that the draggers recorded got passed around, borrowed, and stolen by other commercial fishermen, charter and party boat operators, and finally, guys like you and me. I can remember party-boat fishing in the mid-80's, when much to-do was made prohibiting fares from using the suddenly available portable LORAN-C units. I plead guilty: My portable loran looked like a WWII walkie-talkie, complete with telescopic antenna. Today, numbers thieves can work remotely. A modestly-priced radar lets you store the exact position of a "sharpie," party boat, or charter boat working a "secret" wreck simply by identifying him on the screen and pushing a button. Technology has made it possible for increasingly more fishermen to accurately position the boat over productive bottom.

Since the horses are already out of the barn, you might as well ride them. Numbers for reefs, wrecks and obstructions can be found in books, online and in magazines. Another way is to use software, such as that published by MAPTECH, which allows you to scan for, and zoom in on, interesting bottom, over any swath of ocean or sound you choose from the comfort of your home. However you get your numbers, get them. Then plug them into your GPS, mind the bottom machine, and start sea bass fishing. These scrappy fish bite readily, often in great numbers, and are delectable table fare. The demand for them in China town isn't without merit.

TAXONOMY AND BIOLOGY

Sea Bass are an elegant fish in form and color. They are broad-shouldered, tapering back to a flowing, soft-rayed tail. The tail is accented by a longer, trailing ray on top, and in larger fish can be three-lobed. They posses a combination of fins; some are stiff and spiny, others are soft and fluid. The pectoral fins are especially long. Tough, largish scales, provide them the armor required for life in rough bottom, their preferred habitat, though they are "bald" on top of their heads. The scales appear outlined in white and when looked at obliquely, a sheen of purplish-green is apparent in fresh caught fish. This coloration is most prominent about the head, with its large eyes, and results in the nickname "green head" down south. I've noticed that fish caught while migrating, either early or late in the year, tend to be a lighter blue, while the darker blue and purple hue is more common in summer-caught fish, those that have been living at one spot for a period of time. Background color can vary from brown to black to a mottled combination of the two, depending upon the depth and bottom composition over which they are caught. Unlike most fishes, the belly of a black sea bass is not noticeably lighter than the sides and back. In larger males a pronounced bulge aft of the head develops, resulting in the more common nickname: humpback.

The New York State record black sea bass weighed nine pounds even and was caught in the Atlantic Ocean in October, 1993, by one Sal Vicari. The IGFA All-Tackle World record weighed 10 pounds, four ounces, and was caught in 2000 off Virginia Beach, Virginia. Most fish will weigh between a half-pound and three pounds. A four pounder is a good fish and anything over five pounds wins lots of respect back at the dock. At the time of this writing, the minimum size for black sea bass is 12", or a fish of about a half-pound. Fishing is open year-round.

Black sea bass range from coastal waters out to the deep ocean, from about Cape Cod down the coast to Florida. They can be caught from bridges and jetties, though they cannot tolerate the lower salinity levels that, say, striped bass can. Concentrating shore fishing efforts closer to inlets and harbor mouths is more productive. While scientists say they can tolerate water

Sea bass inhabit rocks and wrecks

as cold as 42 degrees, 50 degrees is a better starting point. That coincides with the arrival of the fish inshore on or about the first of May. At the upper end, 85 degrees is the maximum water temperature they can tolerate, and is of little concern to Long Island anglers.

Black sea bass winter in the deep waters offshore and south of Long Island. The bulk of the biomass spends the cold months off of the Chesapeake Bay. In spring, the fish migrate inshore and North, arriving in our waters late April or early May. Here the fish stay, spawing in June and taking up residence for the summer, until colder temps send them back offshore in late October or early November.

TIP: Black sea bass travel in constant waves of small schools when migrating during spring and fall. As a result, it's harder to fish-out a spot at these times, as fish are constantly being replaced by new arrivals. In midsummer, when fish have taken up residence, however, making multiple drops on different pieces is usually necessary to put together a limit catch. Black sea bass are unfussy eaters, feasting on a variety of crustaceans, fishes and mollusks. The rock crab (Cancer irroratus) and the Northern Krill (Megabycytiphanes norvegica) make up the bulk of the diet of smaller fish, according to trawl surveys conducted by biologists. Crabs make a decent sea bass bait, hence they are sometimes caught while blackfishing. Krill are too small to use as bait, but can often be seen squirming on deck after a caught sea bass spits them out. By the time the fish reach 16", these same studies show that fishes such as sand eel and mollusks such as squid become a larger part of the diet. That they can catch such speedy and elusive prey is one reason not to discount using lures for sea bass. Certainly, plenty are caught as by-catch when jigging bluefish at places like Cholera Bank or the Gravel Grounds off Long Beach. Seahorse, scup and windowpane were other species found in black sea bass stomach contents.

Black sea bass are preyed upon by bluefish, fluke and mostly dogfish, the bane of Long Island bottom fisherman. If you are seabassing, and plagued by 'doggies, use the tips on jig-fishing for sea bass in the sections that follow. Dogfish are less likely to eat jigs, and so using lures is a way to fish around them while still targeting the tasty, feisty, black sea bass.

TACKLE AND RIGGING

Conventional gear, rated at 15 to 30 pounds, at least six feet long, and with the capability to handle sinkers weighing up to eight ounces, are a good bet for all-around sea bass fishing. Shimano's Tekora is one of my favorite reels and this I load with either 30 pound braid or 20 pound mono. Of course there are times, such as when fishing the deep regions of the Sound, like Stratford Shoal, or over deeper ocean wrecks, or when the current is screaming due to a full moon, that heavier tackle may be required. In this case I revert to a stiffer-tipped rod, say six and a half foot long and capable of handling up to 12 ounces of lead. And of course, a lighter setup, similar to what you might use for bay fluking, can be utilized in shallower spots or areas with less current.

TIP: Short, five foot "bay" or "boat" rods may handicap you. You often want the hook several feet above the bottom for sea bass. A too-short rod may not allow you to swing a fish aboard once you reel up to the leader.

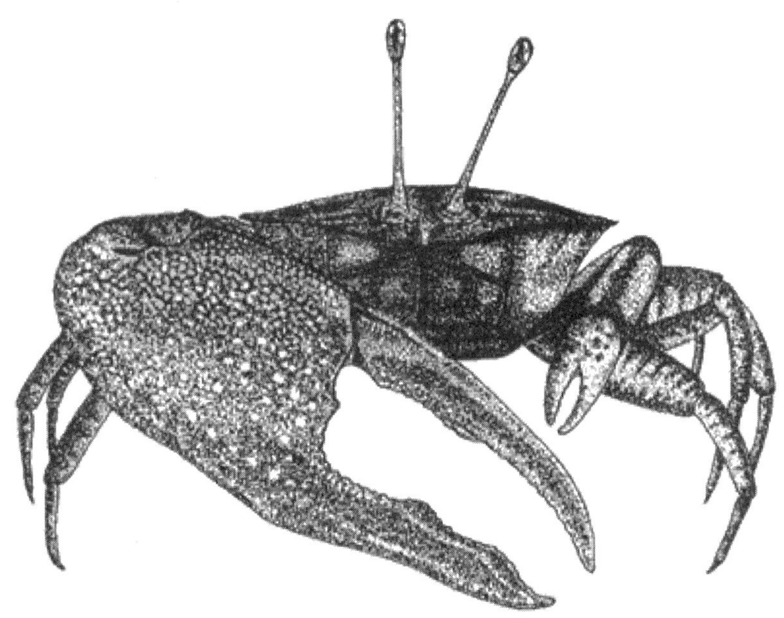

Seabass will greedily attack fiddler crabs, though I prefer soft baits.

I usually pack at least the first two outfits with me, primarily because it's easier to have a backup rigged and ready if I have a break-off during a hot bite. Secondly, I can adjust to changing conditions, using the heavier setup at the height of current speed, and using the lighter rod when the current slows. Note that you'll likely need a heavier outfit to drift the same water, compared to anchoring, as the motion of the boat requires a heavier weight than static bottom fishing.

At the terminal end, a single-hook rig is simplest and easiest to rig and use, as its chances of snagging the bottom structure are minimized. Use as little hardware as possible for the same reason. Therefore, connect a four foot length 30 or 40 pound mono leader to your main line, using a barrel swivel, or, a 20 turn Albright knot. TIP: use a ball-bearing swivel, not a cheap barrel swivel, to avoid line twist. Tie an overhand knot at the leader's bitter end, the loop of which is big enough to allow the largest sinker you expect to use to be passed-through and drawn tight. (catspawed).

Seabass, unlike blackfish, don't usually live actually in the wreck, preferring to suspend around and above the structure. Therefore, use a dropper loop, or one of the new stand-off gizmos (Bear Claw Tackle makes a nice one) to connect your leadered hook two feet above the sinker. I prefer a 5/0 Sproat hook on a 12" leader, though a short-shanked O'Shaugnessy or bait holder will work. The Sproat's advantage is that it's made from finer wire and therefore can be "sprung" out of the wreck or rock pile easier and with less chance of losing your entire rig. The hook size may appear large, but sea bass have a big mouth and I have found that "bigger fish like bigger baits" definitely applies to them. The use of bigger baits, of course, requires a larger hook to present properly.

The Hi-low rig is the most popular and productive rig for black sea bass. As above, tie a loop knot at the bottom of the main leader, which is connected to the running line with a ball-bearing barrel swivel. Then tie two dropper loops—spaced farther apart than the length of your hook leaders, to prevent tangling—the lower one at least 18" above the sinker. Hook leaders are attached to the dropper loops, or stand-offs, by a loop-to-loop connection, the venerable catspaw. TIP: Buy "stick" leader material, rather than coils. It's easier to work with and being stiffer, helps to prevent tangles with dropper loop rigs.

A final variation on the high low rig I sometime use when fishing snag-less, broken bottom, or the area surrounding a wreck and not the wreck itself, produces some big fluke along with the sea bass. Tie the bottom dropper six inches above the sinker loop. Connect a wide-gap hook on a two foot leader here. Above this—a bit longer than the length of the lower leader plus the length of the seabass hook leader, to prevent tangles—add a 5/0 Sproat directly to the dropper. The bottom hook will catch sea bass, but will add more flutter, and likely attract any fluke. The downside of this rig is that the length of the lower fluke leader, combined with the total length of the main leader, increases tangles and requires, generally, a longer rod to facilitate landing fish due to that leader length. Use it during slow periods of sea bass fishing.

Although I'm a long-time advocate of tying one's own bottom rigs and minimizing the use of hardware by using knots, a new pre-packaged rig that has come to my attention works great. It's called the Aqua-Clear, and uses clear tubing to create tangle-free standoffs for high-low rigging.

Grandpa Jim holds a keeper while grand-daughter Keira looks on.

If you'd like to try jigging black sea bass, tie a black, ball-bearing barrel swivel to the end of your line and connect a three foot, 30 pound leader to the swivel's other ring. To the end of the leader, tie on a two to three ounce diamond jig, Hopkins (I like the " Shorty" for Sea Bass) or bucktail jig (SPRO is a good brand) and have at 'em. As a variation, you can tie a dropper a foot above the jig and connect a shad body, grub, or saltwater fly, such as a Deceiver, directly to the Dropper Loop, no leader required. Double-headers can be had, and don't be surprised if a fluke or bluefish also jumps the rig. But the main reason for using jigs for black sea bass—other than running out of bait, of course—is to avoid dogfish. Doggies can inundate the sea bass grounds. Fishing bait at those times is an exercise in frustration, while lures, more than bait anyway, will be ignored by these pests.

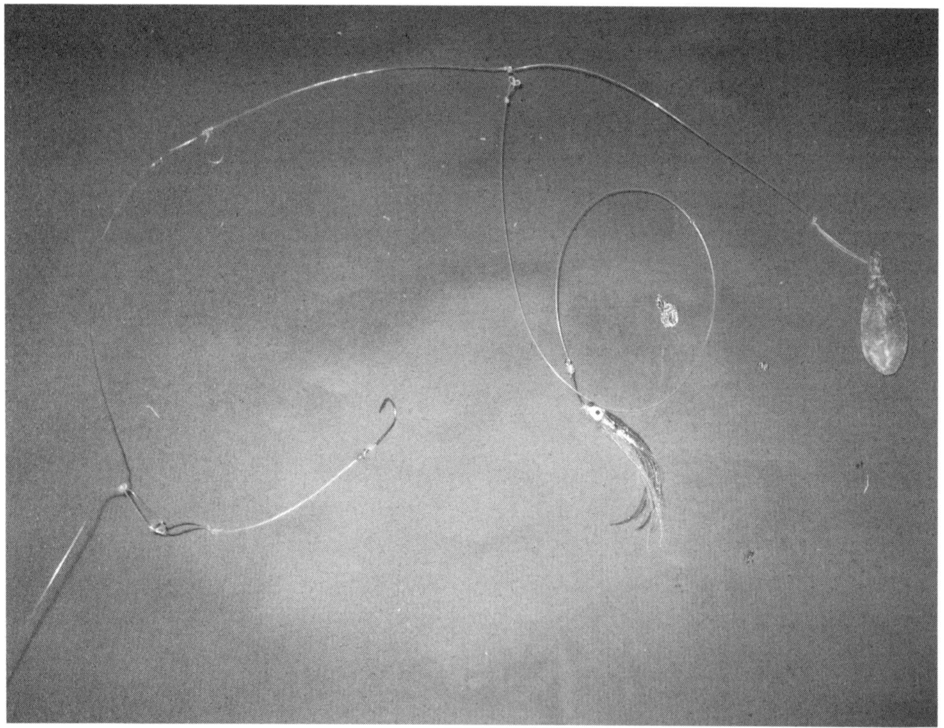

Seabass/Fluke combo rig features auxiliary dropper loop for quick presentation change.

BAIT

Crabs, whether, greens, fiddlers, or rock crabs, make excellent bait for black sea bass, particularly when fishing heavy structure as the chances of by-catching a blackfish are great. Of course blackfish have a closed season and crabs aren't generally available in tackle stores when that season is closed. At any rate, use heavy duty shears or a stiff-bladed knife to halve or quarter green and rock crabs. Fiddlers can be fished whole. With any crab, remove some legs and insert the hook through the open sockets.

Yup, crabs are great, but the most popular bait for black sea bass is squid. It's readily available, easy to prepare, and they eat it with relish. I prepare squid as I do fluke, cutting them into strips, but I place those strips on the hook a bit differently, as I'll explain.

To prepare a squid for bait, cut the head off, leaving the tentacles intact, right at the mantle. Actually, you can often pull the head off, pulling out the clear, plastic-looking cartilage with it. Do not discard the head, as I see too many fisherman do, it makes a great bait.

Once the cartilage is removed from the interior, make a lengthwise cut through one side of the mantle and spread the mantle open like a sheet on your cutting board. Next, make a series of neat pennant-shaped strips out the sheet of mantle.

Now, reach for that head before using the strips. Trim off the two longest tentacles. Insert your hook between the eyes, in the back of the head and out the front. This is a big bait, and any humpbacks below the boat will shoulder the smaller fish out of the way to get at it. Just make sure the hook you're using is large enough so that a portion of its bend along with the point and barb are exposed. Don't bury the point.

To hook the strips, thread the hook through the broad end of the pennant, folding the strip alternately back and forth on the hook until several layers are bunched up, leaving an inch or so trailing. This differs from baiting fluke, in that when placing the strip on the hook for flatfish, it's best to place the hook through the strip just once to maximize flutter. For Sea Bass, some bait flutter is good, but you'll catch more and bigger fish using the "glob for a slob" theory.

Globs work when using clams for bait as well. I prefer to start with whole clams, either fresh or frozen, and eschew pre-cut, pre-frozen clam strips. TIP: Fresh shucked skimmer, as always, is superior to frozen clam.

Cut your clam into strips so that each one has both a portion of the tough "foot" as well as part of the juicy, snotty, "belly." Thread the foot portion on the hook and then bury the point in the belly with several wraps. Clam is soft enough so that having an exposed hook point matters not.

Worms, both sands and bloods, are excellent baits for black sea bass. They are expensive, however, and so I rarely use them. When black sea bass are present they greedily take cheaper clam or squid. Still, it's wise to carry a variety of baits when sea bass fishing, as it is when fishing any species. After all, only the fish really know what they want. Towards that end, spearing, live killies, strips cut from fluke belly or sea robin, mackerel, bunker… all serve well as backup baits for the voracious black sea bass.

FISHING

You want to catch black sea bass? You gotta find some rough bottom, wrecks, reefs, and rockpiles, The charts included here are examples of places I've caught them, but represent just a fraction of the total available black sea bass habitat available to Long Island fishermen. Numerous sources for these spots are available. The DEC lists the location of artificial reefs. Standard nautical charts show plenty of wrecks and bottom composition suitable for Sea Bass, so long as you learn to read the symbols.

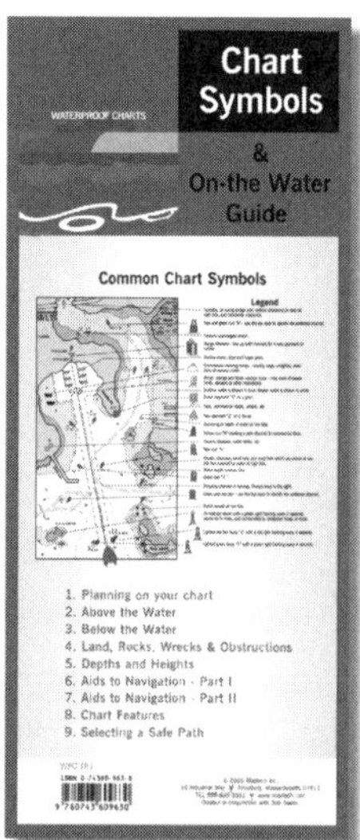

This booklet, or one like it, will help you find the structure that holds Sea bass.

Of course fishing charts, highlighting these areas are available, at more expense than standard charts. TIP: Use standard charts and go over them with a keen eye. Then use high-lighter markers to make potential areas jump out at you. I've become used to using digital charts, such as those produced by MAPTECH, in order to "search" for potential fishing spots in off-hours and during the off season. These programs allow you to mark and save chart images for later reference.

Once you select a spot and derive its numbers, you need the ability to navigate to it accurately and then find it, either with your bottom machine, or by what I call "test dropping." Test dropping means to hover over the numbers and drop baited hooks to see if there's life. If yes, you can choose to anchor, or drift, and start fishing in earnest.

Anchoring makes the most sense when fishing a wreck or other solitary structure for black sea bass. Though many wrecks and such are silted over, or have been flattened by repeated bulldozing from commercial fishing gear over the last three centuries, they still remain as a foundation for marine life. Therefore, you might have shell colonies, kelp, anemones, corals (yes, both live in Long Island waters) growing on top of this foundation and sometimes, thickly. Drifting through these areas is asking for lots of break-offs, unless you know the bottom well enough to drift past the structure. That is, right alongside it. It takes concentration in starting each drift and a feel for wind and current to do drift-bys. It can be very productive, but it's often at least as much work as dropping the hook. That's not counting the times you misjudge, drift too far from the piece to catch, and waste time. Been there, and suffered the heckling of my crew as a result.

Anchoring over wrecks is another art the Sea Bass angler, or those seeking cod, blackfish, porgies, must master to become a sharpie. What I do, after finding the wreck and confirming its position with my bottom machine, is to make a drift or two. Run upwind/upcurrent and see how the boat drifts back over the wreck. This allows me to figuring the depth of water and speed of drift, to know where to drop the hook. You don't want to put the anchor in the wreck. Instead, drop it in clear bottom upwind, set it, and then drop back over the wreck. If the wind and current are mercifully helpful, that's all you gotta do. Of course, the wind and sea will normally be at odds with your goals, causing you to veer on and off the wreck. This veering can cause as many snags as drifting. I have two approaches to thwart Mother Nature's reluctance to give me a break.

Option one is to double anchor. Run up to your "starting point" as described above, but this time run several yards to windward of that spot. Drop and set the hook. Now run up again, this time to leeward (downwind) of the spot, being careful not over-run the first anchor rode. You should be at about a 45 degree angle to the first anchor line. Drop and set the second hook. Now drop back on both until you're over the wreck. If you've wreck fished on a party boat, you've likely seen this done. The boat might pivot a bit, but it won't careen in wide swings across the wreck and back again. This is sometimes called a "Bahamian Moor," and indeed, I've been guided

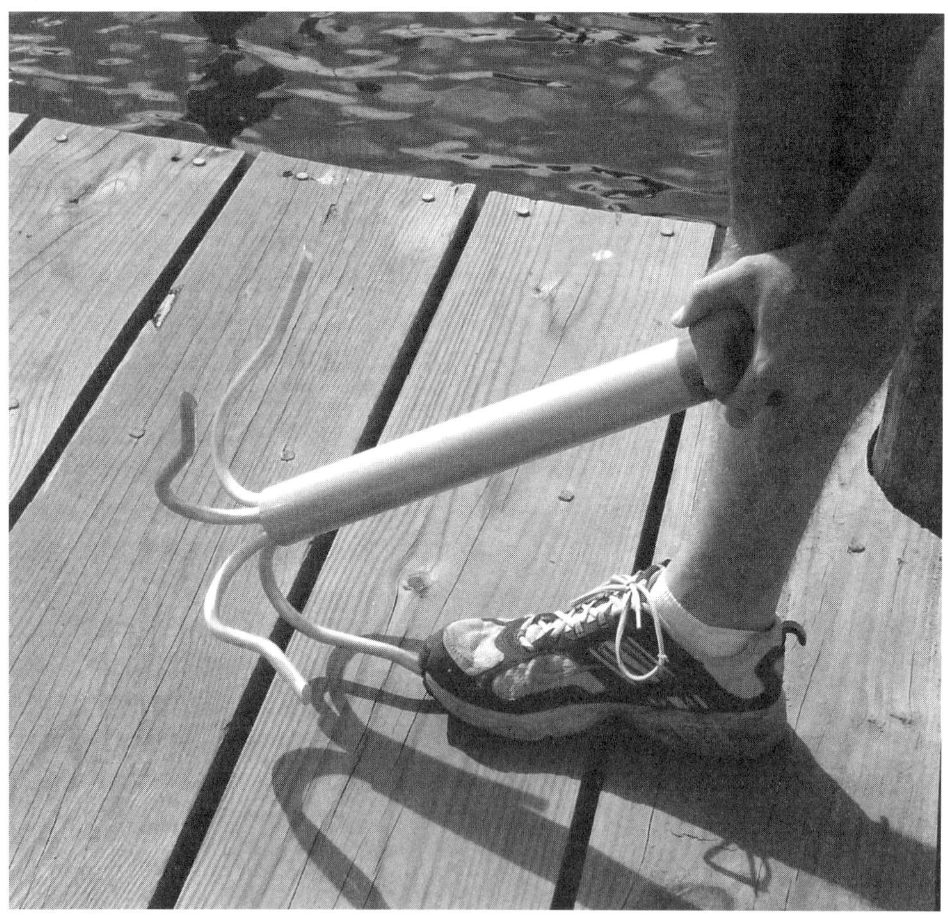

You can buy a wreck anchor like this Mighty Mite, or build your own.

to some tremendous snapper and grouper fishing off Great Isaac light by my good friend and Miami charter boat skipper, Capt. David Parsons of the *Hakuna Matata,* using this anchoring technique.

The second method is to use a grapple, a.k.a., a wreck anchor. These can be made by welding some re-bar to a pipe, or can be purchased at marine supply. The idea is to actually snag the wreck with the grapple. When its time to go home, you simply put the boat in gear and, with the rode cleated off, the stress bends the tines and the anchor frees itself. Tying a line with a float to the head of these also lets you pull them out backwards, should it be stubborn. TIP: You can drill a hole in the head of your Danforth anchor and attach a poly line and float to it as well. Even though you try to place that anchor up-current of the wreck in clear bottom, if it does get snagged, you can often retrieve it by pulling it out backwards by the float line.

Now, many guys deploy the grapple off the bow, snag the wreck and start fishing. This works OK if the current and wind are inline with the wreck and the wreck or obstruction is big enough to allow you to still be over it when an appropriate amount of scope is let out. Most times neither is the case. So, what I'll do is drop the main anchor ahead of the piece, drop back over it—using the motor if the wind isn't helping—until I'm past it. Now, while a crewmember tends the main anchor line, I drop the grapple off the stern and motor forward over the wreck again, trying to snag it as far down-current as I can. This done, I cleat off both anchor lines and adjust as necessary. With this method, I can "clothesline" myself up and down the length of the structure to follow a bite. Of course, with an anchor astern, a sharp weather eye is required for changing wind and sea conditions! Take care.

Now you are ready to fish. As with many endeavors, the preparation and satellite skills necessary to get you to the actual point of wetting your line take the most time and are at least as important. So it is with black sea bass, for once you are anchored over them, and they are home, they are ready biters. In fact, the first time I send my rig into the depths, I begin reeling up the instant it hits bottom. Quite often a self-hooked sea bass is tugging at the line before I can engage the reel. That's the way it goes—sometimes—for these fish.

Of course, there's more than the greedy hunger of sea bass at work when using the "hit 'em on the head" theory. I begin reeling up right away, even during a slow pick, so that I can get the slack out of my line. After a few turns, enough to bend the tip against the sinker's weight, I fish with a down-tipped rod and utmost attention. Black sea bass do tend to hook themselves, gobbling the bait, rather than nibbling. However, you still want to set the hook.

When fishing a double-hook rig, and after getting a bite, set the hook and reel up a turn or two. Then wait a beat before reeling in your prize. The competitive nature of these fish often sees a second fish, perhaps the one a bit too slow to your first bait, jumping on the second hook. You can always tell a guy who's sharp because he'll catch more double-headers than anyone else aboard.

Also, pay attention to which hook is getting the action. If it's the top hook, perhaps the fish are suspending higher in the water column. It pays, when several are aboard, to fish hooks at different heights on the leader until you zero in on the fish. Hell, sometimes you catch them halfway between the boat and the wreck. Don't "wait out" slow spells. Use the time to try something different.

One thing that's different, at least judging by the surprised look of some fishermen I've mentioned it to, is the use of jigs for black sea bass. Jigs are an excellent way to prospect for fish holding above the bottom. They are also excellent for when dogfish are around, and you'd prefer not to deal with them. Here's the drill.

Drop down and immediately reel up a few turns, not giving the lure as much chance to snag the structure. Next, work the jig—bucktail, Crippled Herring, Hopkins Shorty, whatever—in short twitches at a given depth. No takers? Reel up 10' and try again. Patience. Persistence. Believe.

If you do find the fish above the structure and willing to take lures, you can break out a light baitcaster or spinning outfit and have a ball. Black sea bass give a good account of themselves, even on the heavier stuff. The strike is a solid double thump, followed by a quick-circling, down-spiraling run that will bend the rod. Might even pull a little drag. Following that, it's a steady, standard pump and reel to the boat. You can net black sea bass, but they are usually solidly hooked, and rarely weigh more than three or four pounds. Over the rail and in the pail!

Black Sea Bass Crib Sheet

Black sea bass, a.k.a, Seabass, humpback, greenhead

Season: May-November

Location: Near shore to deep Sound and Ocean. Prefers rough bottom, shell beds, piers, wharves, wrecks and rockpiles.

Baits: Squid, clams, crabs, spearing, sandeel, live killies, fish strips, jigs.

Tackle: Medium to Medium-Heavy conventional

High-Hook Tip: Cloudy days, even during rain, are great fishing days because the fish don't see the shadow of the boat.

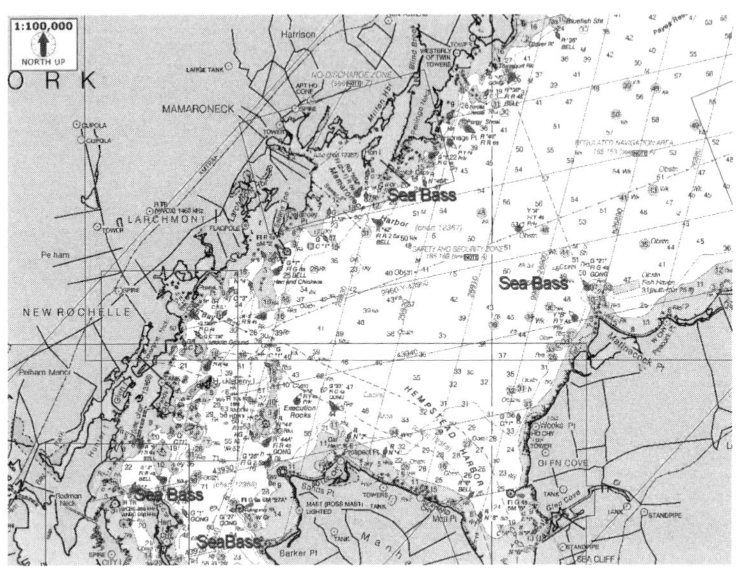

If porgies mug you at these spots, use clam baits instead of worms.

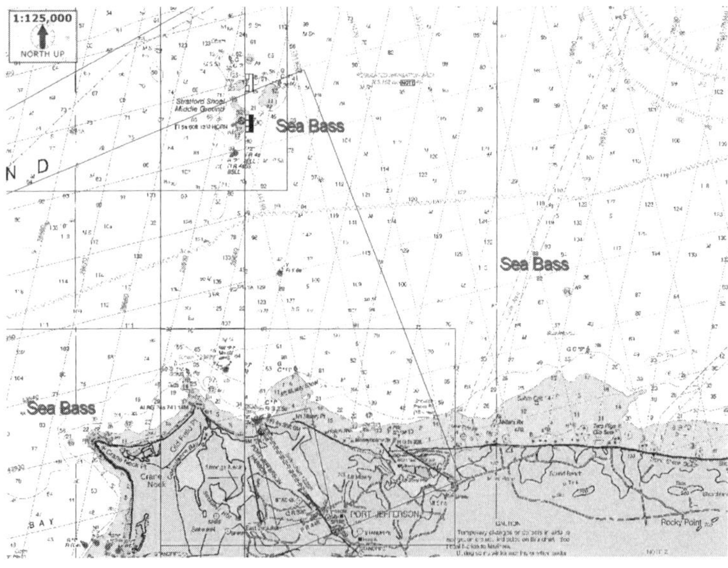

These sea bass spots turn on in September. Try the jigging technique described in the text.

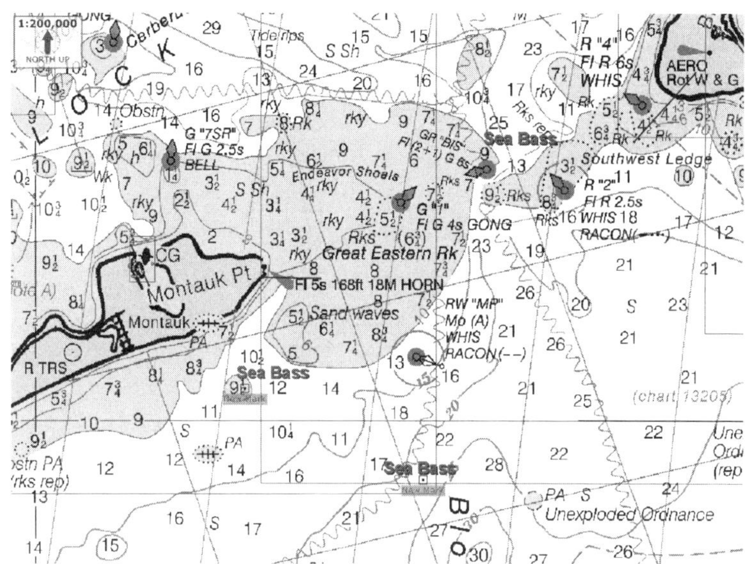

Frisbees, Cartwright and Southwest Ledge are home to large sea bass.

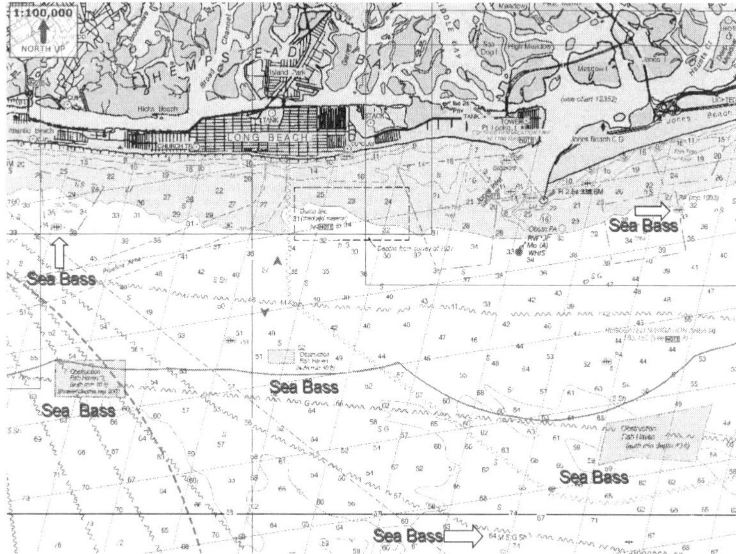

Artificial reefs, wrecks abound within five miles of the South Shore inlets and are prime sea bass haunts; subtler structure, such as the gravel/shell bottom at bottom of screen is less heavily fished.

CHAPTER 8
Porgy
(Stenotomus chrysops)

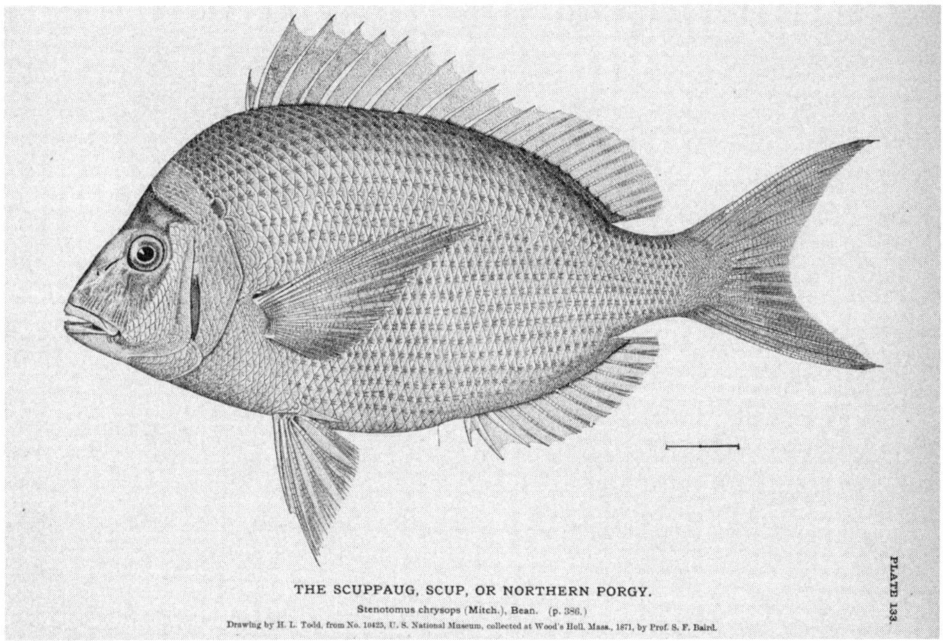

THE SCUPPAUG, SCUP, OR NORTHERN PORGY.
Stenotomus chrysops (Mitch.), Bean. (p. 386.)
Drawing by H. L. Todd, from No. 10425, U. S. National Museum, collected at Wood's Holl, Mass., 1871, by Prof. S. F. Baird.
PLATE 133.

If porgies grew to 10 pounds, I'd hardly fish for anything else. For a fish that averages about a pound, the power they display at the end of a line is awesome, despite dragging around a sinker that might weigh half as much as they do! There are those who look down their noses at the porgy, or scup, but on a weight-to-strength basis they are as hard-fighting a fish as you will find in Long Island waters.

They are also exceedingly easy to catch, and usually in good numbers. Double- and triple-headers, with all rods aboard bent, is a common occurrence when porgy fishing. That makes them the perfect target if you've got kids, or friends who aren't really fisherman, and want to put them on some fast action. Porgies are always on top when the in-laws come out for a boat ride. They taste great to boot. In fact their only downside is related to their case of capture. Back at the dock, it's you who will be cleaning that cooler full of scup. If you haven't had the pleasure, handling the spiny-finned porgy is kind of like trying to grab a greased porcupine. Just remember that the two-fold payoff for your punctured, and subsequently swollen, hands: A smiling crew and a delicious meal.

TAXONOMY AND BIOLOGY

Porgies are slab-sided, fish, about half as deep as they are long. They are pug headed, and have a tall, stiff, spiny dorsal fin running the length of their back. Their pectoral fins are very long and very sharp. The caudal peduncle—the tail connector—is narrow and muscular. The tail itself is stiff, narrow-rayed, and deeply Vee'd.

If you ignore the part about porgies being slab-sided, you'll see that their physical description—the long, tall dorsal; the long pectorals; and the V-shaped tail—includes many features associated with billfish and tuna. It is these qualities, along with their elliptical shape, that I believe grants these diminutive fish the strength to sometimes double over a medium-weight rod. Porgies come to the boat sideways, head toward the bottom, their tails hammering like a paint shaker. The biologists tell us that porgies possess both red and pink muscle tissue, the pink kicking in for added and sustained power in times of stress, such as avoiding capture. The porgies pink muscle tissue, it is said, produces higher kinetic energy than the red.

Porgy have a small, almost beak-like mouth, requiring the use of small hooks. The mouth is lined with small teeth, powerful enough to crush sand shrimp, or tear up a squid, but not strong enough or big enough to do any real damage if you get nipped. Their spiny fins handle any bloodletting.

Porgy have large tough scales that you'll need to remove if you want to cook them skin-on. They are attractively colored, sporting a silvery head and silver grey sides, often tinged with pink. A vivid blue line starts at the eye and follows the contour of their backs. After capture, and as their iridescence begins to fade, a series of dark, irregular, vertical bars sometimes appears.

Scientific studies claim that porgies reach a maximum length of about 16". However, the IGFA All-Tackle World's record Scup was 18" long, 16" in girth, and weighed four pounds, nine ounces. That fish was caught off Nantucket in June, 1992. The New York State record Scup weighed a whopping six pounds, four ounces, and was caught in October of 1978 by a Mr. Samuel Warren. No girth or length information is available. As far as my research revealed, the porgy holds the distinction of being the only Long Island saltwater fish for which the state record is bigger than the world record. Long Island is porgy country.

For all of that, the average porgy you catch will weigh between a half-pound and two pounds. Bigger fish will generally be caught in the fall, and in deeper Sound and Ocean waters. Inshore bays and harbors, while they do hold big porgies, most often host schools of "pin" porgies, comparable to snapper bluefish in size. The minimum size limit for porgy at the time of this writing is 10.5" long, which means a fish weighing approximately three-quarters of a pound.

Porgy range from Maine to North Carolina, with the bulk of the fish occurring south of Cape Cod. They spend the winter offshore and mi-

Porgy and bergall swarm a rockpile.

grate with warmer water temperatures. Porgy show up in our inshore waters around mid-April, give or take, and provide action through the summer months and into the fall. By mid-November, inshore porgy fishing is done, although they can be caught well offshore year-round. They can tolerate water temperatures ranging from 40 degrees to 95 degrees. My logbooks indicate that fishing doesn't start in earnest until water surface temps approach 50 degrees.The action gets hot once the water hits the mid-50's. Some of this is academic, as at the time of this writing, the open season for porgy in New York is June 1 to Halloween.

Porgy prefer hard bottom but not just rocks and reefs. Hard sand will hold them, as will gravel or cobble bottom. If you're occasionally snagging kelp, you are in the right place, likely enough. Areas like this abound in Long Island waters, from the 70' depths of the Sound off Mattituck to the area near the Coal Barge off the western South Shore.

Fluke and sea bass are common by-catch when porgy fishing. And I can't tell you how many times I've caught a bluefish while reeling in a porgy—sometimes half a porgy. Often, the blues make their presence known when the porgy bite suddenly stops.

You can catch porgies on wrecks and rock piles, but I've found that the bulk of the fish will hang down-current of an obstruction. This differs from blackfish, which prefer to live right in the wreck. However, porgy can be a bait-stealing nuisance to October blackfishermen. Hey, if you can catch them off the piece, you won't snag bottom as much. 'Nuff said.

What rings the dinner bell for porgy? A strict bottom feeder, porgy eat a variety of small shrimps, crustaceans and fish eggs when young. As they mature—at approximately 8" inches in length—the diet shifts to include more small fishes and squid. By the time they reach 10" or 11" keeper size, porgy are feasting with relish on primarily sand eel (Ammodytes dubius), butterfish (Peprilis triacanthus) and squid (Ilex and Loligo). All of these make good baits for porgy, when cut into smaller strips or chunks. Clam is also excellent bait—it's the one I prefer—and sea worms sometimes stow aboard the porgy angler's boat. In truth, if the bite is on, I'd bet these fish would eat anything you hit them with. Worms are kinda costly for a fish that'll eat dried-up clam sputem stuck under the gunnel from yesterday's trip.

Tackle and Rigging

Porgy are a small fish, but powerful. They also like deeper water and that often means stiff current. Finally you should fish a double-hook rig, even a triple-hook rig, to maximize your catch. (Porgy fishing is unabashed meat-fishing, don't let anyone tell you different.) Based on these parameters, the go-to porgy set-up is a medium weight conventional outfit, capable of handling weights up to eight ounces without losing the sensitivity in the rod's tip due to "overbend," more accurately known as overload. As I like to fish multiple hook rigs on a four-foot leader, I recommend the rod be no shorter than six feet in length. You don't need a fancy reel for porgy fishing. An old Squidder, provided it's in good working order, and

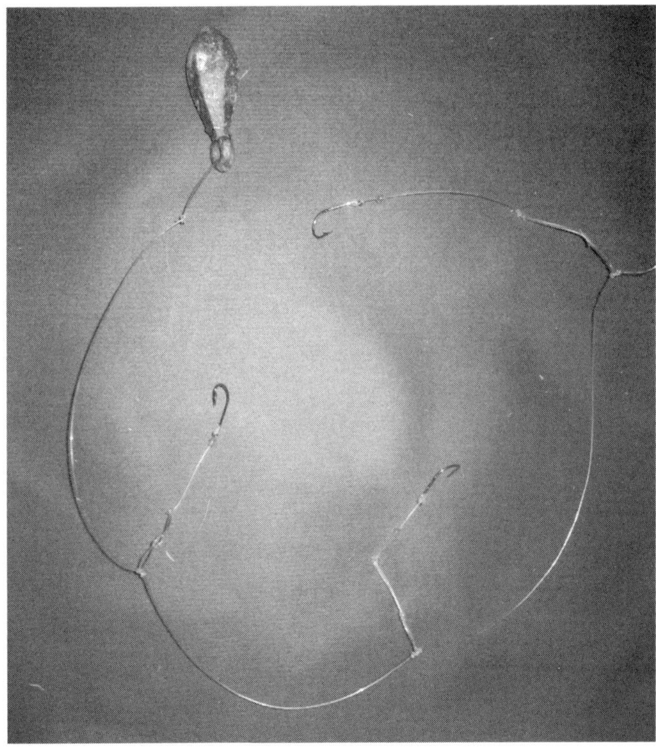

Multi-hook meat rig. Note spacing and leader lengths don't allow hooks to tangle. It takes 12 knots to make this rig.

loaded with fresh, 20 pound test monofilament, will get the job done. My preference, however, would be on the order of a Penn 940, loaded with 30 pound braid. Thus equipped, you'll be able to use lighter sinkers and still hold bottom. Plus the no-stretch quality of braid, coupled with a rod tip that's not overloaded, will provide you with the utmost sensitivity. You'll need that sensitivity, for porgies are the champion bait stealers of Long Island waters, capable of stripping your hooks before you have a chance to engage the reel after dropping down. That's another nice feature of the Penn 940, or other reel that engages by a quarter-turn of the handle. These give you the ability to set up on fish the instant the sinker bounces bottom. Reels that require a clutch lever be thrown, cost you the second-and-a-half it takes to get robbed. For all that I've said about the porgies willingness to strike and multiple hook-ups, porgy fishing is still fishing. And if you're like me, you hate missing a fish more than you hate not having any action at all.

Terminal rigging is simplicity itself. Take a four foot stick of 30 pound mono leader and tie two or three Dropper Loops in it. Tie one a few inches from each end, and if you like, tie a third in the middle of the other two. Use a loop-to-loop catspaw to attach either, depending upon the size fish expected, a number eight 1/0, or 2/0 Beak baitholder or O'Shaugnessy hook. I like the baitholder because it helps hold clam snot on the hook. But I like the O'Shaugnessy because I can grab its longer shank and shake a porgy into a bucket instead of having to handle the spiny thing. Take your pick. Tie an overhand loop for sinker attachment to the bitter and clinch knot the top end of the leader to a ball-bearing barrel swivel. The other loop of the swivel is clinch-knotted to your main line. Sliding a green or red bead over the dropper loops prior to catspawing on the hooks doesn't hurt the rigs attractiveness to porgies. Let's go get'em.

FISHING

You've baited your multi-hook rig with pieces of clam, probably, and sent it to the bottom. You engage the reel, take out the slack so that there is just the slightest bend in your rod. Suddenly, your rod tip jumps in manic fashion... ratta-tatta-tatta. Now it bends over in earnest and you start to lift against the strain. No drag is being pulled, yet the line which was vertical a moment before, suddenly angles off to one side and gets active, slicing through a foot-wide arc in the water's surface. You set the hook with a sharp lift. Just as you begin to reel up, BANG! another porgy hits. Doubleheader! If your fishing three hooks, the trick now is to set the hook on the second fish, wait a beat, and chances are good you'll get a shot at a third. More than likely though, you missed the third bait being stolen while the first two fish were causing a commotion. Over the rail and in the pail! This is porgy fishing at its finest. TIP: It pays to be attentive to your line on the drop. Porgies will often hit the bait in the way down before you know what "hit" you. I use heavy thumb-pressure and keep my rod tip elevated when dropping down a porgy bait. That keeps me at the ready for these bait stealing pros. It's also a technique you can't utilize with spinning tackle. A word to the wise.

Of course it's not always that easy. First thing, you have to put the boat over the fish. That's not so hard as when the porgy are running, any piece of rough bottom is likely to hold some fish. From Execution Rocks, to Stratford Shoal, on into Gardiners Island and around Montauk; from the Artificial Reefs just outside the South Shore inlets, the multitude of shipwrecks and the rugged bottom of the Tin Can Grounds, all these hold porgy. Personally, I like to find a rock or boulder, and anchor near it. This gets me away from the fleet, and keeps my blackfish numbers up to date. Some favorite "stones" I've porgied over the years include: the north eastern most of the Stepping Stones off Kings Point; the one off Fox Point, Bayville, in 20'; 70" depth rock off Crane Neck; Parker Rock, Southold; Plum Island Rock; and Roger's Rock in Peconic Bay. I don't have to be as precise in anchoring over these rocks as I do when blackfishing because porgies respond to chum. Close enough for rock and roll is good enough.

For open bottom drifting on the North Shore, try the "sand waves" area in 85' off Horton's Point. You can hold a school of porgies to a drifting boat with lots of chum and provided you have at least four rods in the water. TIP: "Bail" porgies by always keeping a hooked fish in the water until another crewman hooks up.

On the South Shore, any of the artificial reefs will hold porgy, but better success is to be had over shelly, gravelly, hard bottom or wrecks. Some proven favorites: the charted rocks in 44' off Napeague; the Panther wreck; Shell Bottom in 17 fathoms, SW of Shinnecock Inlet; The Gates City Wreck, off Moriches; and both Angler and Cholera banks. Anchor at the wrecks—or do "drift-bys" and drift the banks and shell bottom.

Chumming is imperative when porgy fishing. These fish can get skittish, and while you might drop in and hit a few on the head, the schools wander around. A steady dose of chum will keep the fish near the boat—and bring them if you are even close to good porgy bottom.

I recommend a gallon size chumpot and at least two gallons of clam chum. Of course this depends on water temperature, sea conditions, and current strength—more of each will melt your chum quicker. I go through about a gallon of chum per two hours of fishing on a nice summer day. Hang the chum pot amidship, or even at the bow, so that all baited hooks are in the chum stream. Sometimes you have to add some weight to the pot—like a brick—to keep it from "blowing back" and getting tangled with your lines. You can use chum whether drifting or anchored, but it has the best effect when anchored up-current of good structure. Porgies will respond to the chum. Just give them some time. When they do, you may find yourself too busy unhooking others fish and preparing bait to fish yourself. The action can be that fast.

Along those lines, have plenty of bait defrosted and ready. Nothing's worse than trying to jam frozen chunks of clam onto a hook. They fall off the minute they hit the water. Instead, have some bait out and sliced, some more defrosting in a bucket of water, and still more on ice where it can be kept frozen. Then just keep rotating your stock through the trip, or assign a crewmember to do so.

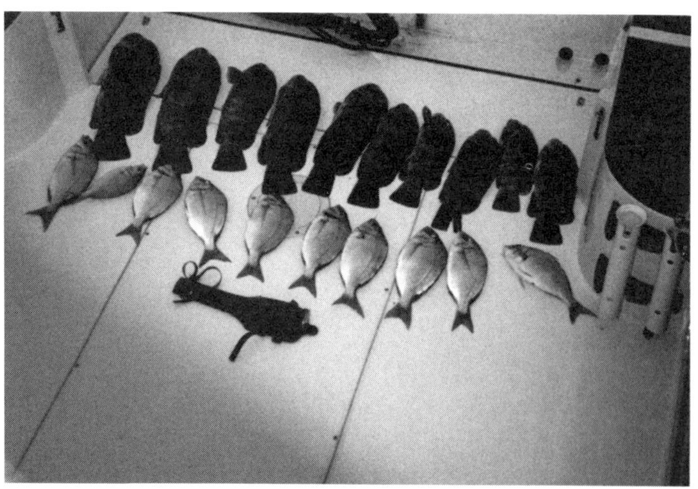

A mixed bag caught at a bay bridge.

Which bait to use? Bring clams and squid. In a pinch you can use worms, crabs, fish strips, etc. But clam and squid get the job done.

Prepare clam by cutting small, dime-sized pieces, being sure to include part of the tough foot and part of the juicy belly. Sometimes this is hard to accomplish, given the small size of the hooks used and thus the small size of the bait. You end up with all squishy belly. So, often as not, I find myself attentively winding clam entrails over and around the hook, over and again, penetrating the belly meat several times to ensure a solidly baited hook. Porgies will make a fool out of a guy fishing a hook not baited with careful, firm implantation. In fact, I like to use the connecting tissue of a skimmer clam, that tough, stringy stuff around the meat's perimeter. It takes patience to weave this on your hook, but it resists thievery very well and the porgy eat it with as much relish as anything else.

TIP: If the porgy are thick, just use barley enough bait to cover the hook point—you'll catch 'em every time.

Aggressive? This humpback committed suicide on a worm and tube trolled over a boulder field for stripers.

For squid, I cut little inch and a half by half-inch strips and bunch them over the hook point several times, leaving perhaps a quarter-inch "tail" protruding. Squid is tougher than clam, and so harder for porgy to steal. But clam usually out-catches squid by a lot. Always carry more than one bait, and more than you think you'll need, whenever you go fishing.

Get the corn meal ready and heat the skillet, we're going porgy fishing!

Porgy Crib Sheet

Porgy, a.k.a, Scup, Scuppaug, Humpback

Season: June through October

Location: Hard sand bottom; shell beds, wrecks, reefs, rock piles. Bridges, piers, jetties, deep bay holes.

Baits: Clams, squid. Also worms, sandeel and cut fish.

Tackle: Medium weight conventional.

High-hook tip: Porgy feed voraciously at night. Set up in a good spot and let the good times roll. As a bonus, by-catch weakfish are a distinct possibility.

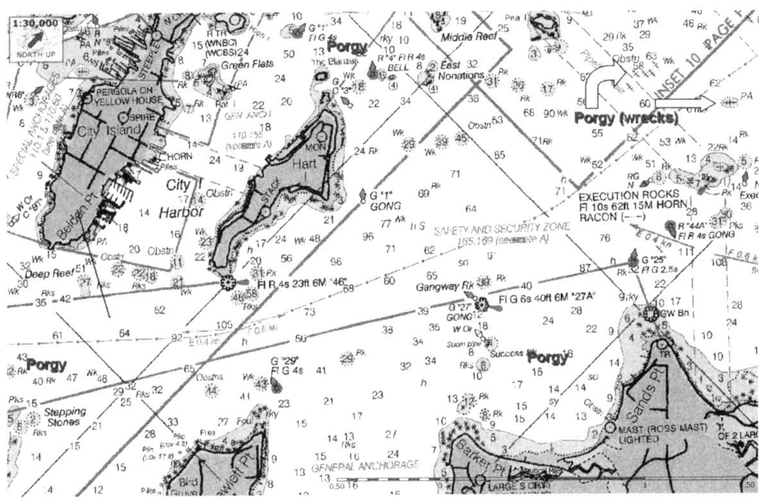

The Sound is bottom-fishing heaven.

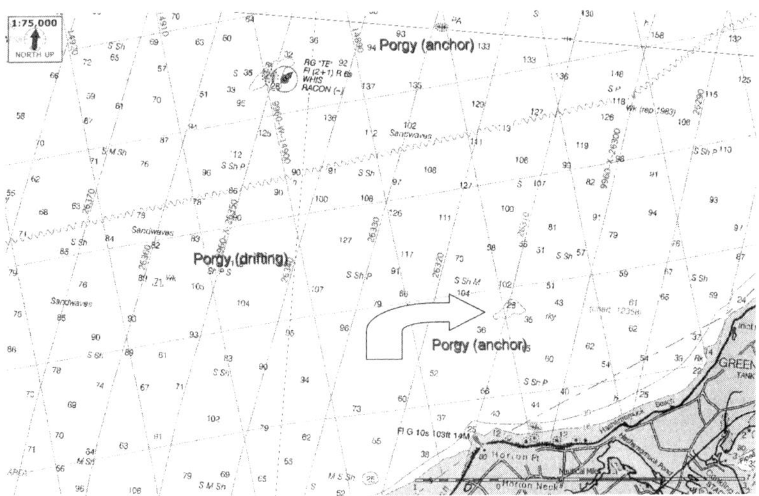

Horton's Point: The arrow indicates shallow spot to set the anchor—then drop back over deep water.

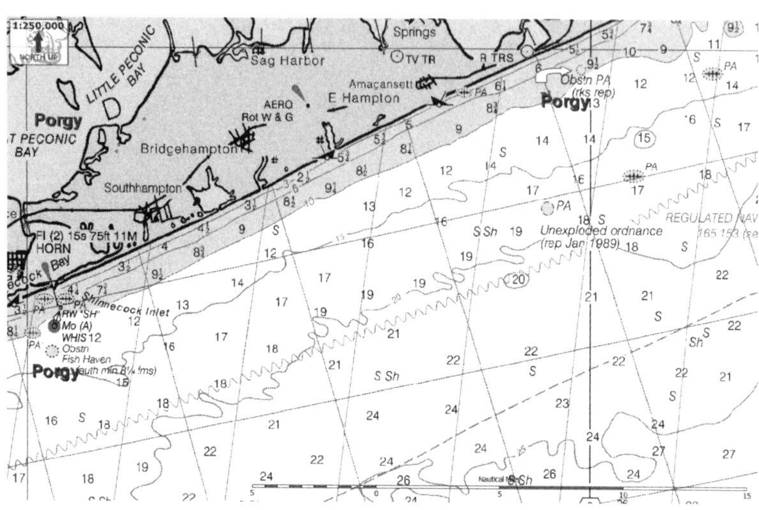

Rockpile at (40.59.27/ 072.00.52); Peconic Bay's Rogers Rock is great; Shinnecock Reef holds fish.

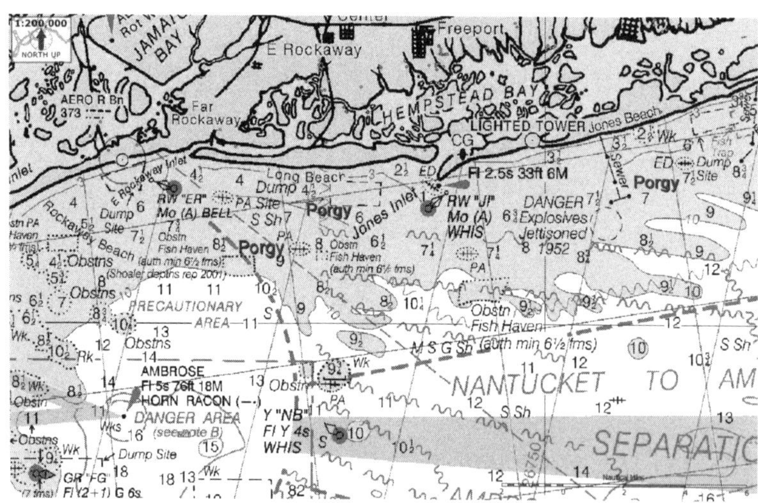

Porgy spots are varied, and there are plenty of them.

CHAPTER 9
Speedsters, a Migrant, and Bait
False Albacore, Triggerfish, Herring, Mackerel, and Squid

I was going to title this chapter "Odd Fellows," on the basis that these fish are hardly Long Island's most sought after species. Some, like the mackerel, take up such fleeting residence that even those dedicated to their capture often skip several seasons between catches. Being able to jump through so narrow a window in these busy times is tough. Others, like the false albacore, have an ardent following, but a small one in comparison to those pursuing blues, bass, fluke, and a host of big pelagic species, all of which are at the height of their runs when the little tunny show up. Squid and herring too, have a very dedicated following, but these also comprise niches. Striped bass live-liners, pier fisherman in the know, and those with pickling and calamari recipes are a few of the subsets. Triggerfish? What's a triggerfish? I've heard that one all too much in reference to this tasty, hard-fighting, and under-pursued late summer visitor. That these fish exist in the back eddies of Long Island's fishing mainstream is no fault of the fish themselves. All have given me enjoyment over the years, and for some very different reasons. At the least, an awareness of their presence will see you more keenly attuned to the workings of the environment in which we pursue our passion, our playground, the marine waters of Long Island. In the end, that is this book's mission.

False Albacore (Little Tunny)
Euthynnus Alletteratus

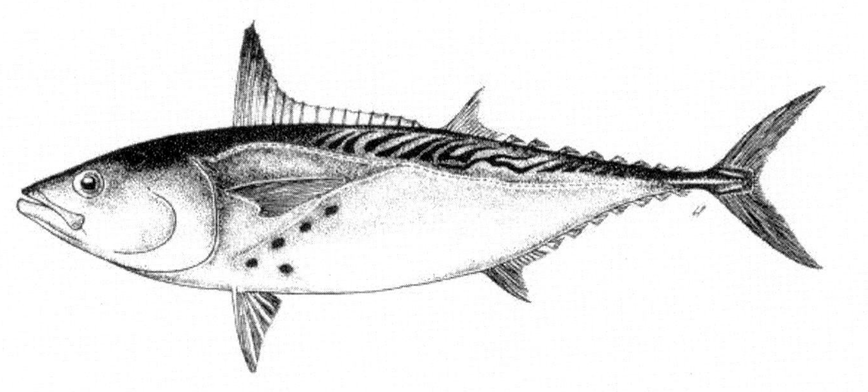

Also known as "Fat Albert," the false albacore shows up in local waters for a brief run in late summer and early fall. False albacore are often confused with the oceanic bonito (sarda sarda), but distinguishing between the two is relatively easy. The false albacore has wavy stripes along its sides and back, all of which are above the lateral line. The bonito's stripes are dead straight and start below the lateral line near the pectoral fins. Were you to fillet them out and cook them, you'd also tell them apart with ease: the bonito's meat is firm and flavorful; the false albacore is cat food, or shark bait.

The current IGFA All-tackle World Record false albacore weighed 35 pounds and was caught off Algeria. A 36 pounder, caught off North Carolina in 2006 is pending. There is no New York State record for false albacore.

There's no denigrating this fish on the end of a line. False albacore give Long Island's inshore anglers a shot at the tuna clan, and all that those fish are respected for. Hook-up little tunny and you will be rewarded with blistering speed and a seemingly inexhaustible power that will tax your skills and your tackle to the max.

False albacore are very keen-eyed and line-shy. Additionally, they feed on small baits, mostly bay anchovies while in our waters. Both of these facts require the use of light tackle. The first demands the low visibility of gossamer lines and fluorocarbon leaders (leave the braided line home for these fish, or else fish with a 50' top-shot of mono ahead of your fluoro leader). The second requires casting tiny lures. Fly tackle is ideally suited to presenting a lure to these fish. An eight-weight setup, with an eight or 10

Pete McDonald of Garden City with a little tunny caught off Shinnecock on a fly.

pound tippet to throw epoxy flies or Bonito Bunnies, is good. My little tunny setup is an ultra-light spin setup loaded with 10 pound mono. This gives me good casting distance with the tiny lures required for hook-up. Small Hopkins, Kastmasters, and Crippled Herrings in weights of a half-ounce or so work good, with the nod going to the smallest you can cast efficiently. The BEST jig is a Deadly Dick, and regardless of the metal at the end, I tie a dropper loop in my 20 pound fluorocarbon leader and attach a Deceiver, or one of the flies listed above, as a teaser. Usually, the teaser is what the false albacore eat. After casting at a swirl, let the rig sink for a five-count, then retrieve in jerky, staccato manner. TIP: When false albacore won't eat your cast metal jig, try rigging a weightless Fin-S fish, a five-inch model, pearl or white, on a 2/0 offset worm hook. Cast it out and twitch it in the surface.

The light spin gear allows me to present a lure to these speedy phantoms from a greater distance.

That last bit can be important. Besides their keen eyes and preference for miniscule offerings, the other challenge false albacore present to prospective anglers is their ghost-like ability to move from one place to the other. If you've had frustrating days running and gunning to cast for bluefish, only to have the fish sound or break up once you got to where they were, multiply that by a factor of 10 for false albacore. These fish are very boat shy and you really have to use instinct and observation to "pattern" their movements and attempt to show up where they do, when they do, ready to cast. Profiling may be politically incorrect on land but it is an essential skill for the successful fisherman.

How do you find them? In Late August and September, all along the Ocean Beaches, In Gardiners Bay, up into Plum Gut and the Sound as far West as the Norwalk Islands, these fish will give their presence away in one of two ways.

Birds are a tell-tale, and will follow and dive above a feeding school. But don't think bluefish or schoolie bass tearing up bait, sloshing the surface and drawing a cloud of terns and gulls. Albacore make the most delicate surface ripples when feeding near the surface. A little slurp or swirl is all you might see. And instead of a big cloud, the birds following these fish will be small knots, dropping into funnels when Fat Albert chases his prey to the top. Mostly, the birds will just be picking and pecking away, so be aware of birds acting this way. They are doing what you are, waiting for school to surface. Of course they do it for a living, giving them an advantage.

Grey Triggerfish
(Balistes capriscus)

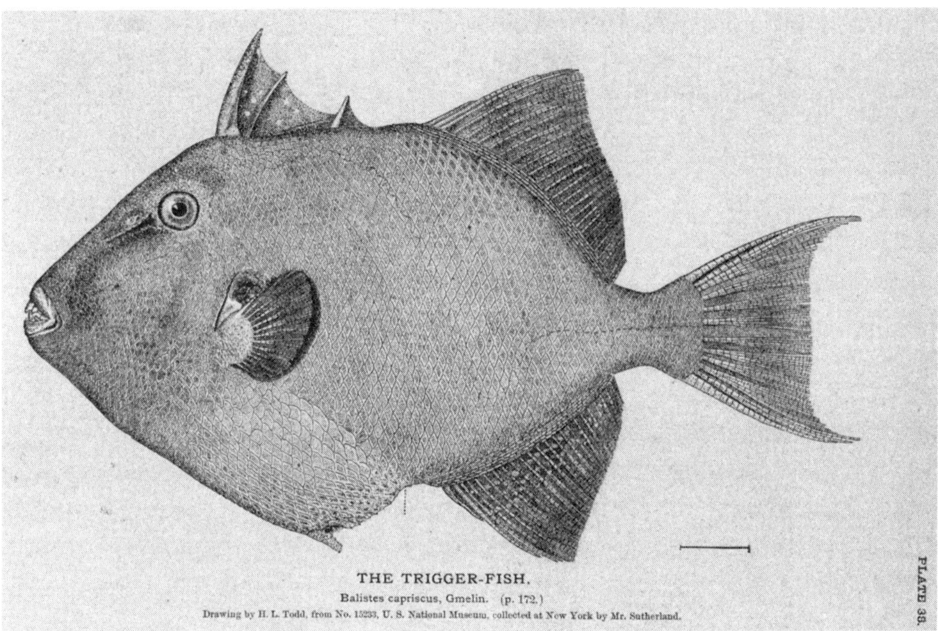

THE TRIGGER-FISH.
Balistes capriscus, Gmelin. (p. 172.)
Drawing by H. L. Todd, from No. 15233, U. S. National Museum, collected at New York by Mr. Sutherland.
PLATE 38.

Triggerfish are adroit bait stealers, so I think many fishermen just write them off as a weird stray when they catch one while bottom fishing. They do thrive on coral reefs in Florida, the Bahamas, the Gulf of Mexico and the Caribbean. But the fact is, gray triggerfish range as far north as Nova Scotia, and across the Atlantic to Ireland. They are in our waters in August and September, caught regularly in the Chesapeake, and off Virginia October and November; are pursued off Georgia and Jacksonville, FL, in mid-winter; and are available further south year-round. They have a much greater tolerance for cooler water temperature than “truly tropical” triggers, like the queen triggerfish and clown triggerfish. So in summer, it ranges North, before returning South again in late September. Lucky for us.

You won’t mistake a triggerfish for any other species. It’s a flat and short, nearly as long as they are deep. They are narrow-bodied with a tall, spiny dorsal fin. When a triggerfish is threatened, they back into a crevice in the rocks and then use the big, forward spine on their dorsal to wedge themselves in. The second spine is then erected. This locks the first spine, which cannot be folded until this second, trigger spine is folded flat—hence their name.

So ensconced, the triggerfish presents it's heavily armored head and a beak full of razor sharp exposed teeth to any potential predator. Good luck! Those teeth can put a hurt on. I've been bitten by sharks, bluefish, a fluke with both sides filleted off, and have been eye-pecked by a shearwater bird I snagged while casting diamond jigs for tuna. I escaped all of these with more damage to my pride than my body. But the one time I let down my guard while unhooking a two pound triggerfish, I ended up on my knees in pain, the fish clamped to my profusely bleeding left hand. I still have the scar.

The skin of a triggerfish is also part of its defense system. You will find no tougher-skinned fish in our waters. The family "ballisitidae" to

Triggerfish have bear-trap mouths and tough skin.

which triggerfish belong, stands for ballistic, as in ballistic-cloth and has earned them the nickname, “leather jacket.” While skinning them, you will find that even black-backed gulls will not swallow the skins you chuck overboard. That speaks to the toughness of the triggerfish’s skin more than anything else.

Most triggerfish we catch will measure 12 to15 inches long, and weigh between two and three pounds, though there’s always a few three-pound, 18-inchers, in the mix. The IGFA All-Tackle World Record weighed 13 pounds, 9 ounces, and was caught at Murrells Inlet, South Carolina in 1989. The New York State Record gray triggerfish was captured in 1999, and weighed five pounds, three ounces. That fish was 21 inches long. Remember, triggers are “square” nearly as deep as they are long.

Offshore, triggerfish can be found at the surface, under sargassum, flotsam and buoys. They are very curious. In fact, during one offshore trip, my good friend Capt. Scott Horowitz caught triggerfish by tying a line to a bucket and hanging it over the side. They swam right in!

Inshore, triggerfish inhabit the shell beds, wrecks, rocky bottoms, and reefs that Long Island is blessed with. The South Shore inlets, right along the rocks, are ideal habitat, though these require some thought to fish properly, as I’ll explain below. In the Sound, I only have experience catching them on deep, offshore reefs, out east, but am aware of their capture further west. But any spot that’s holding black sea bass in August and September should be holding triggers, especially if it’s relatively high profile—open shell bottom isn’t the ideal habitat. Bridges, jetties , lighthouse and other navaid rip-rap, and the higher sections of the artificial reefs are ideal.

Triggerfish eat crabs, barnacles, bivalves and starfish. Those killer teeth just grind up and chew this tough assortment of prey. Those same teeth drive your tackle selection.

The triggerfish’s beak-like mouth is small. Big baits are not required. With this in mind, you might be tempted to use a small, fine wire hook like the Beak or Sproat that you use for porgy or sea bass. Big mistake. The trigger’s vise-like jaws and razor teeth can cut through such light wire hooks. Remember, these fish crush clams and barnacles. TIP: You need a forged hook. Select either a 1/0 O’Shaugnessy or Virginia instead.

Triggers are lightening-quick and very aggressive. If they are present, you won’t have to soak your bait like you might for other bottom species. For that reason, I like an in-line terminal rig that minimizes my get-

Mixed bag of triggerfish, sea bass, and porgy from an artificial reef.

ting snagged in the structure. Clinch Knot or Snell your hook to a two foot length of 20 pound mono leader and tie an overhand knot in the leader's middle. This makes the leader easy to break if you hang-up—you're not likely to "bend-out" a forged hook, like a Virginia or O'Shaugnessy. Tie a perfection loop at the leaders top and snap it onto a drail, of enough weight to reach bottom, tied to your main line. Make several of these leaders in advance, particularly if inlet-fishing. With spares at the ready, if you hang the rocks you can break off at the overhand knot, reel-up, snap on a new leader, and be back in the action in little more time than it takes to re-bait. As an aside, this is an excellent wreck/rocks drifting rig for numerous species, for its resistance to snagging and ease of re-rigging.

Rod and reel for triggerfish can be any medium-weight conventional outfit. Whatever you use for porgies or sea bass will be fine. I don't bottom-fish with spinning gear, but if you must, use a stout-tipped rod.

Bait your hook with care. I like clams and restrict myself to using only the tough foot when triggerfishing. Using the belly usually results in a stolen bait, and unlike other species, Triggerfish don't seem to relish the belly any more than any other part. Use a small piece, just enough so that you can wind it over the point a few times. Leave no dangling tail. Make sure the point is exposed and that your hooks are sharp.

Now, my favorite place to fish triggers is at slack tide in one of the South Shore Inlets. The inner bar of our inlets—the high spots just inside the jetties—such as at the end of Shinnecock's west jetty, are usually covered in shell. This plus the proximity to the jetty itself, makes these bars ideal trigger habitat.

Remember that slack water occurs after the time of high or low tide. Depending upon location, the current will continue to roll in/out for as long as two hours after the tide time. This is your window to get in and wind-drift as slow as possible, and as close as possible, to the rock jetties. Those jetties are pyramidal in section, so the base is further into the inlet than the exposed part. Visualize your drift to place the boat along this wider base. You cannot legally anchor in an inlet, so slack water allows easy fishing, (boat traffic notwithstanding—AGGHHH!—weekdays are better) and if the triggers are there, the 30 minutes to an hour's worth of slack will be all you need. When triggerfish are present, the bite is furious.

Drop your baited hook down to the bottom as quickly as possible. TIP: Triggerfish will often hit on the drop, and you won't feel a thing. You'll catch more if you use an oversized weight that gets you down faster and more vertically. Then bring it up slowly—as in working a jig for weakfish slow. Count the turns. Remember the count when you get a fish. Do so and you'll be able to precisely place your bait in the strike zone on the next drop.

Blackfisherman are good at catching triggers. The technique is different, but the attitude is the same. Zone-in and pay attention. Triggers are so quick that you have to be ready. Do not set the hook like Curt Gowdy. Rather, keeping the line tight, a slight bend in your tip, the rod angled down, and your hand on the reel handle. At the first peck, lift and reel simultaneously. Got 'im!

Triggerfish pull like nobody's business. A two pounder will double a bay rod and pull some drag in short, zip-zip-zip, runs. They circle and use their slab sided aspect to very good advantage. I'm tempted to say that if you don't get them off the bottom immediately following a strike, that they are going to use that spine fin to lock themselves inextricably into a crevice. Fact is, if you are asleep at the strike, your bait is going to be gone. So don't worry about techniques for rock removal.

Finally, carry a serrated knife when targeting triggerfish. Use this to make the first diagonal cut behind the head. Then use a fillet knife to finish filleting them. A regular fillet knife will not cut through a triggerfish's tough skin. It's worth the effort—the flesh of the triggerfish is as delectably flaky and flavored as you will find.

Herring
(Alosa aestivallis; Clupea harengus)

I can remember sneaking out of my house and riding my bicycle down Loop Parkway enroute to Long Beach's Magnolia Pier on a cold, December night. My quarry? Herring! I loaded up, filling the cooler in my bike's paper route basket. The bug has never left me.

Herring, both Atlantic and Blue Back, are what I'm talking about here, though Menhaden (bunker) and a several shads are other herrings that live locally. Atlantics are thinner, more entirely silver and make up the bulk of our winter herring fishery. Blue Backs are a bit deeper-bodied, and have a blue-to-green tinge on their backs. These school up in the Sound and near-shore ocean waters around Thanksgiving and invade the bays an harbors though early spring.

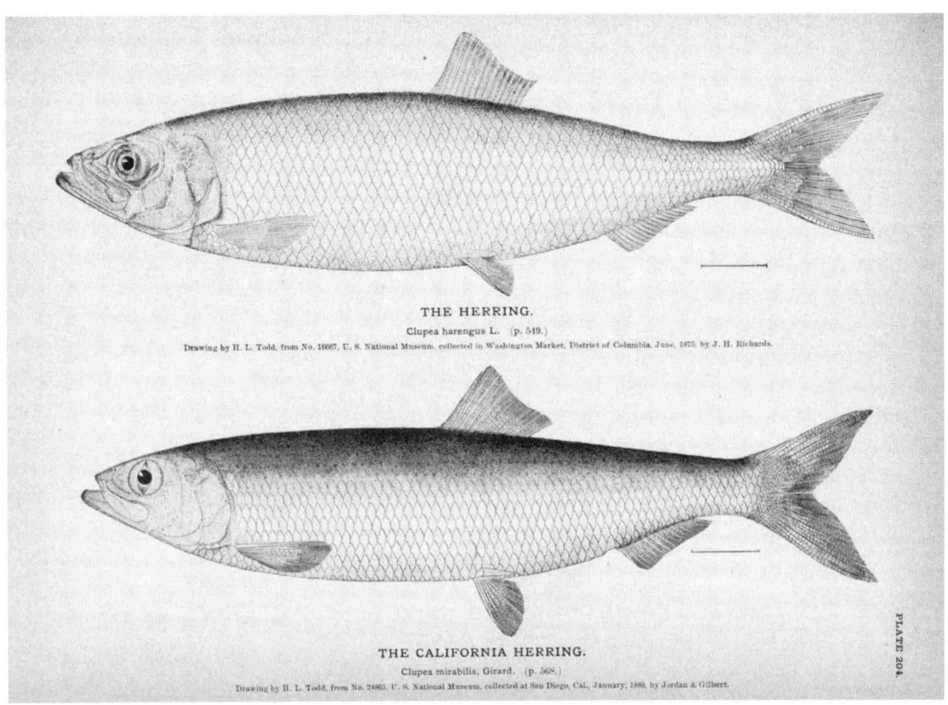

One thing that herald's their arrival is the presence of dive-bombing gannets. Gannets are big seabirds that follow the herring schools. Another harbinger of the herring run is your local tackle shop running out of Sabiki rigs. Striped bass anglers look forward to the herring run with great anticipation, especially at Montauk, where live-lining herring is a specialty.

But when the herring come inside the bays and harbors, anglers in the know pound the planks of docks projecting into moving, ice-free, water to jig up a mess of these fish for bait, for pickling and mostly, or just to be fishing. The Magnolia Pier, Jones Beach Field 10, Port Washington Town Dock… on out to Orient, around The Point, and back to Long Beach, herring can be caught day or night. The run lasts from about Thanksgiving through January. When herring are running, the word gets out. Keeping in touch with your local tackle purveyor is probably the best way to get in on the run. It's a great shore-based trip for kids, despite the cold, as a lot of fish can often be caught in a short time.

A light 10 or 12 pound spinning outfit is ideal for herring. Rig up using a Sabiki rig purchased at the tackle shop. These are "tree" rigs, consisting of three to six tiny feathered hooks, dropper-looped on a leader complete with a snap at both ends—one for your line one for a weight. They are not the same as Mackerel Trees, which have bigger, usually tubed, hooks. You can catch macks on a Sabiki, but you won't catch many herring on a mackerel tree.

Snap the Sabiki onto your line, and attach enough weight to reach bottom or cast efficiently. I'll sometimes use a diamond jig as a weight. Its adds some flash to the rig and I have caught a few stripers by "accident" this way.

If you are fishing from shore, select a pier where some current is available. If you are fishing at night, it helps if the pier is lit, which attracts herring. You can attach a chemical light stick for added attractiveness. I do this by sliding a short piece of clear plastic tubing, the diameter of which is a snug fit for the light stick, on my main line above the leader. Than I gently jam the light stick into the tube for a snug fit. TIP: Be advised that an illuminated rig is not a substitute for an illuminated pier. Lots of light draws a school of fish. Your individual lightstick only helps members of a school already present target your rig. If boat fishing, either get close to illuminated shoreline or use spreader lights near inlets and harbor entrances.

Now, ready? Drop your Sabiki to the bottom and retrieve it in slow, jerky fashion. Count the number of turns you make of the reel handle. When you hook up remember the number of turns so you can consistently fish the same depth. Also, vary your retrieve. Sometimes static jigging works; at other times, a fast retrieve brings the hits. Experiment. TIP: Once you feel a herring on, don't swing him up. Wait a beat. Often, several more will jump on, and you'll feel them if you are attentive. Multi-headers are common. Pass the Ball jars and crackers.

Squid
(Loligo pellaili; Ilex illecebrosus)

There are two squids frequenting Long Island's waters. The long-finned Loligo and the short finned Ilex. Fin-length of Loligo is about half the body length. Ilex fin length is about one-quarter of body length. Loligo are further distinguished from Ilex by a pair of extra-long tentacles. The tentacles of Ilex squid are all about the same length.

Squid fishermen, a.k.a., the Brotherhood of the Inked, are a dedicated bunch. Many are the same guys on top of the herring runs. You can tell one of these boys as he will arrive at the dock with a cart or wagon. In the wagon will be an electrical supply (batteries) and some kind of big, personal light apparatus. This is usually comprised of a big Hydro Glow submersible fluorescent light, or a home built facsimile which is tied off at the dock and sent over board at the guy's fishing spot. They may also have a clamp-on, tie-on, nail-on, or otherwise home-made rig of light fixtures designed to shine into the water from above. Sometimes it's just a Coleman lantern. In all cases, supplanting the light from the dock will up your chances at your particular spot. These are the guys who fill a freezer with bait for the season as well as enough to make as much calamari as the family can eat. Invariably, these squid-sharpies—who number among the best shore fishermen on Long Island, by the way—arrive well before dark to select a good spot on the dock, usually near the seaward end. Yes, squid fishing is a night game, and if you show up at a hot dock at the height of the run, and it's already after dark, you may find yourself waiting for someone to leave before you can wet a line. I've seen families fishing three deep when squid fishing. Mom is sitting on the dock, dangling her legs over; Junior is standing up and fishing over her shoulder; Dad is behind Junior, fishing over his shoulder. Needless to say, wearing foul weather gear is essential when squid fishing. Not only will it stave off the weather, but squid squirt ink when they come up. You can be careful when the bite is slow. But when it's quick, and you're fishing elbow to elbow, you will get inked. So, how do you get them?

Squid are present in our waters year round. But in early spring they school en-masse inshore for spawing. This usually occurs the last week in

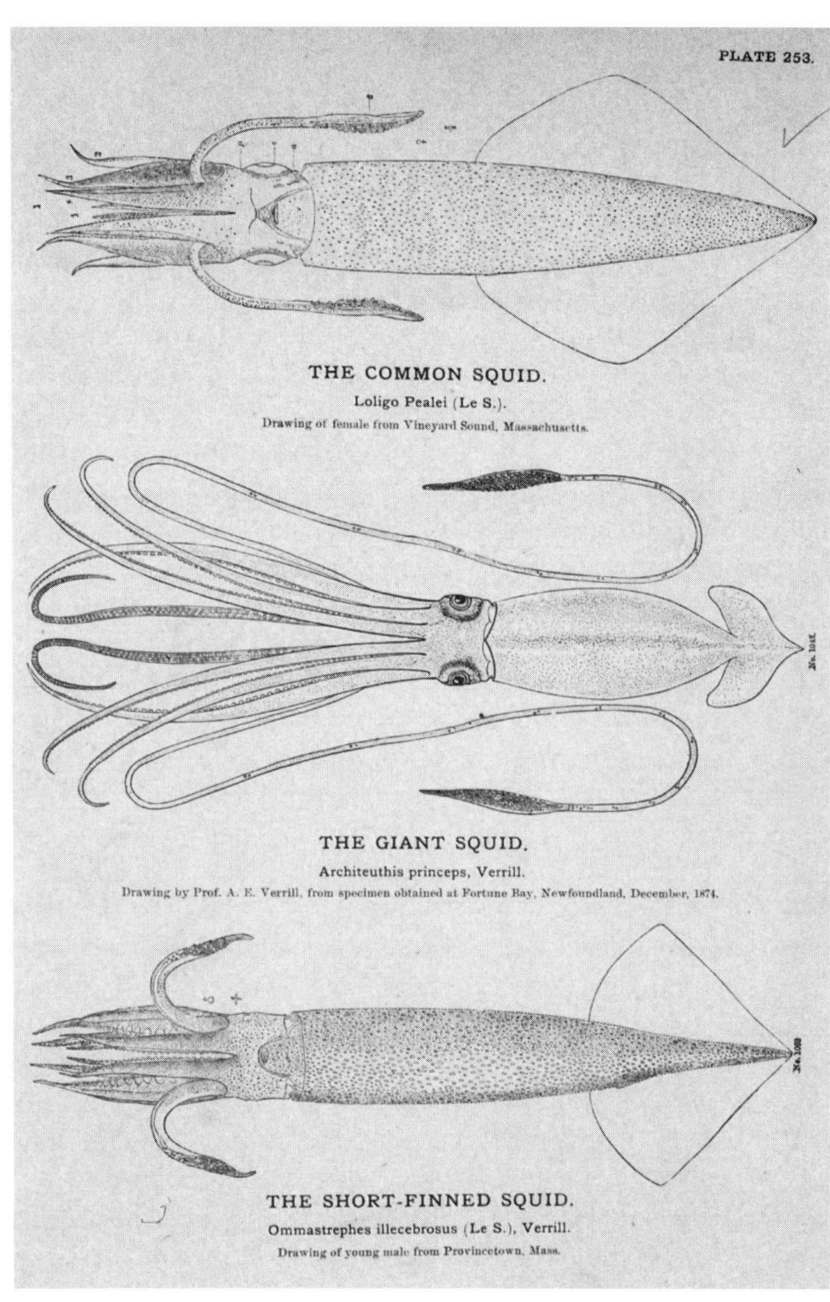
PLATE 253.
THE COMMON SQUID.
Loligo Pealei (Le S.).
Drawing of female from Vineyard Sound, Massachusetts.
THE GIANT SQUID.
Architeuthis princeps, Verrill.
Drawing by Prof. A. E. Verrill, from specimen obtained at Fortune Bay, Newfoundland, December, 1874.
THE SHORT-FINNED SQUID.
Ommastrephes illecebrosus (Le S.), Verrill.
Drawing of young male from Provincetown, Mass.

April or the first week in May. That's when inshore fishing for them, from illuminated docks and piers, is a viable proposition. The run is best on the East End, with numerous Greenport area piers being hot. Most of these are private, or not talked about by those that fish them. But anyone can fish at the Railroad Pier. I've met anglers from as far away as Westchester while squidding at the Railroad Pier. Other spots have less consistent fishing than Greenport. But I have caught squid at the Ponquogue Bridge, Wantagh Park, and from a private dock in Mt. Sinai. Pay your dues, try out some spots, you may well score.

What to use? Squid jigs. The old style ones were simple, colored plastic cylinders, usually green. The newer generation are fished-shaped plastic with feathers and embedded sparkle. In either case, the jig consists of this plastic body, an eye at the top to tie to your line, and at the bottom, a series of small, inverted pins. Think pincushion. Squid don't get "hooked," they attack the jig and get their tentacles tangled in the pins. Squid jigs come in weighted and unweighted styles —get a few of both. I like green or pink.

To rig the jigs, take a two foot, 20 pound fluorocarbon leader and tie two dropper loops in it. Tie a perfection loop at either end. Attach a weighted squid jig to the bottom loop, and one un-weighted jig to each Dropper Loops. Use a snap to connect the top loop the main line, or splice leader to line with a blood knot, nail knot, surgeon's knot, whatever. I have seen nights where guys with less hardware scored higher—a word to the wise.

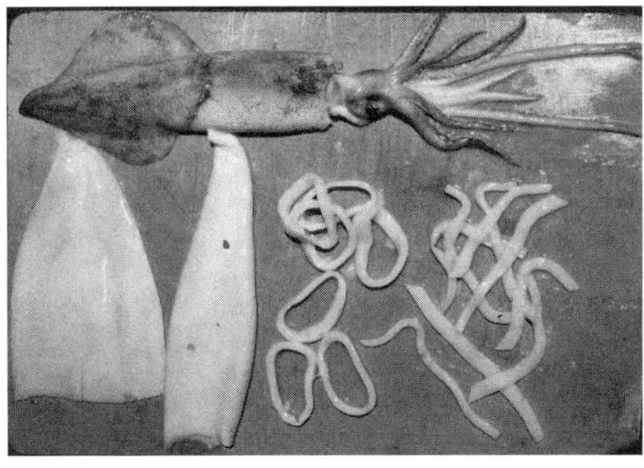

Here squid is prepared as calamari!

To fish, get under a light and fire up your personal light if you brought it. Drop the jig and slowly work it at various depths until you get a hit. Sometimes, no action at all is required—just suspend the jig at depth. Other times, picking it up off the bottom draws the strikes. Experiment, as the squid will alter their habits from night to night and even tide to tide. TIP: Squid Jigs glow in the dark. Store yours in a bag with a lit flashlight enroute to the dock and while fishing. Swap out the lures occasionally, to keep the luminescence "charged."

Capt. Scott Horowitz with squid caught at Greenport. Note the jig.

Atlantic Mackerel

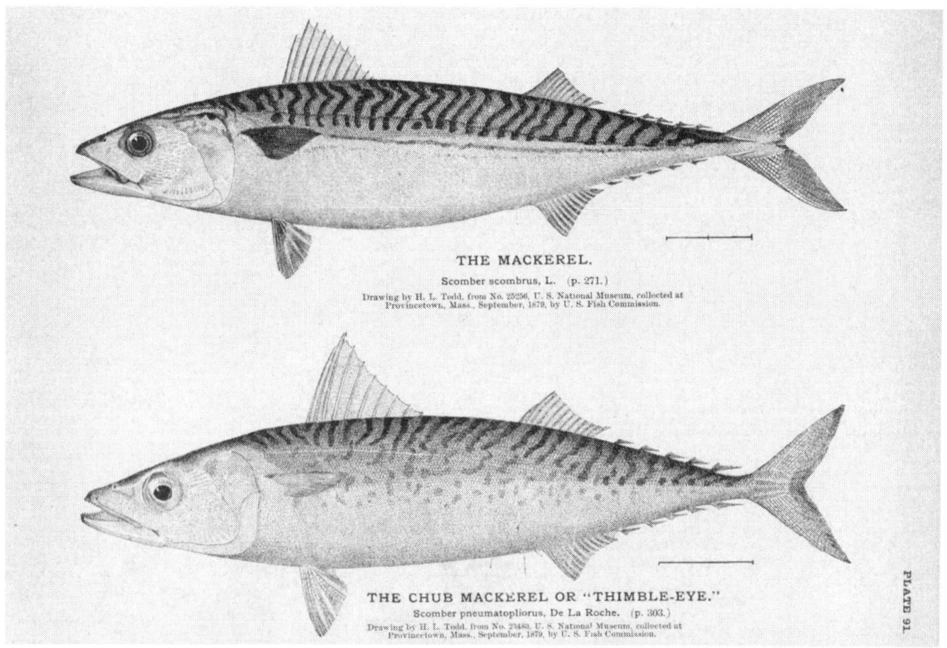

(Scomber scombrus)

Mackerel are voracious feeders, school densely and can provide non-stop action that sees the boat and anglers literally coated in scales. When you're on them, it's a blast. Though not an inshore fish, they are included here because many inshore fishermen, both boat and shore based, love to catch mackerel. So whether you take your own boat, or jump on a party boat, try mackerel for fast action and a great time.

Atlantic mackerel, also know as Boston mackerel, range both sides of the Atlantic Ocean; here between Nova Scotia and North Carolina. They are torpedo-shaped fish, green to blue along the back and fading to silvery white along the belly. These small members of the tuna clan are marked with very dark, distinct, wavy vertical bars. They have big mouths and rows of small, canine teeth. They have small finlets, like tuna, between the dorsal fin and tail. These "heat exchangers" allow mackerel to sustain swimming speed for long periods of time. It shows: These fish are fast and real sporty on ultralight tackle, provided conditions permit its use.

Mackerel grow to about two feet long and four pounds. Most will be about 15 inches long, or one to two pounds. The largest recorded Atlantic mackerel was a six pound monster caught in Sweden in 1995. Hot-damn! I bet that one fought like a little tunny.

Mackerel are very opportunistic feeders, eating everything from krill and shrimp to squids (Ilex, Loligo,) sandeels, whiting and more. In turn, mackerel are fed upon by most every predator imaginable, from squids (when the macks are small) to large tuna, sharks, and of course, you and me.

Macks over-winter well offshore and near the bottom, between Maine and Virginia. They return inshore in late April or early May to spawn, and all then move north into the Gulf of Maine and Bay of Fundy to spend the summer. Our April/May run consists of fish that over-wintered directly east of us, offshore, and mixes with fish that spent the winter offshore further south and have migrated north.

These fish are on the move. They will often remain in Long Island inshore waters for less than week or two. When the run starts you have to be ready to go.

You can find mackerel along the Ocean Beaches, anywhere from 60' of water out to 20 fathoms during the spring spawn run. Most of my own private boat mackerel excursions take place in water less than 100' deep, say up to three miles off Shinnecock and about six or eight miles off of Debs. Mackerel do not like brackish water. As such, on the North Shore, mackerel are mostly confined to mid-Sound, East of Centerport.

Mackerel are open-water fish. The best bet is to go out and look for them. Signs such as slicks, "nervous water" and bird activity will often point the way. They don't need structure, at least not to live in, like so many other species. But bottom contour, wrecks, and reefs can provide the current changes and eddies that congregate bait. These areas are worth a look if you have no other sign.

Mackerel are also easy to spot with a fish finder because they school so densely, but you have to run over them. You can hunt around and try "blind fishing" mackerel when reports that they have solidly arrived are in. However, you burn a lot of fuel doing this, and a quick tally of my mackerel logs shows that I'm successful less than 50 percent of the time when fishing for them without seeing a slick, ripples or birds. That's a good case to hop a party boat, let someone else drive, someone whose fished every day, and

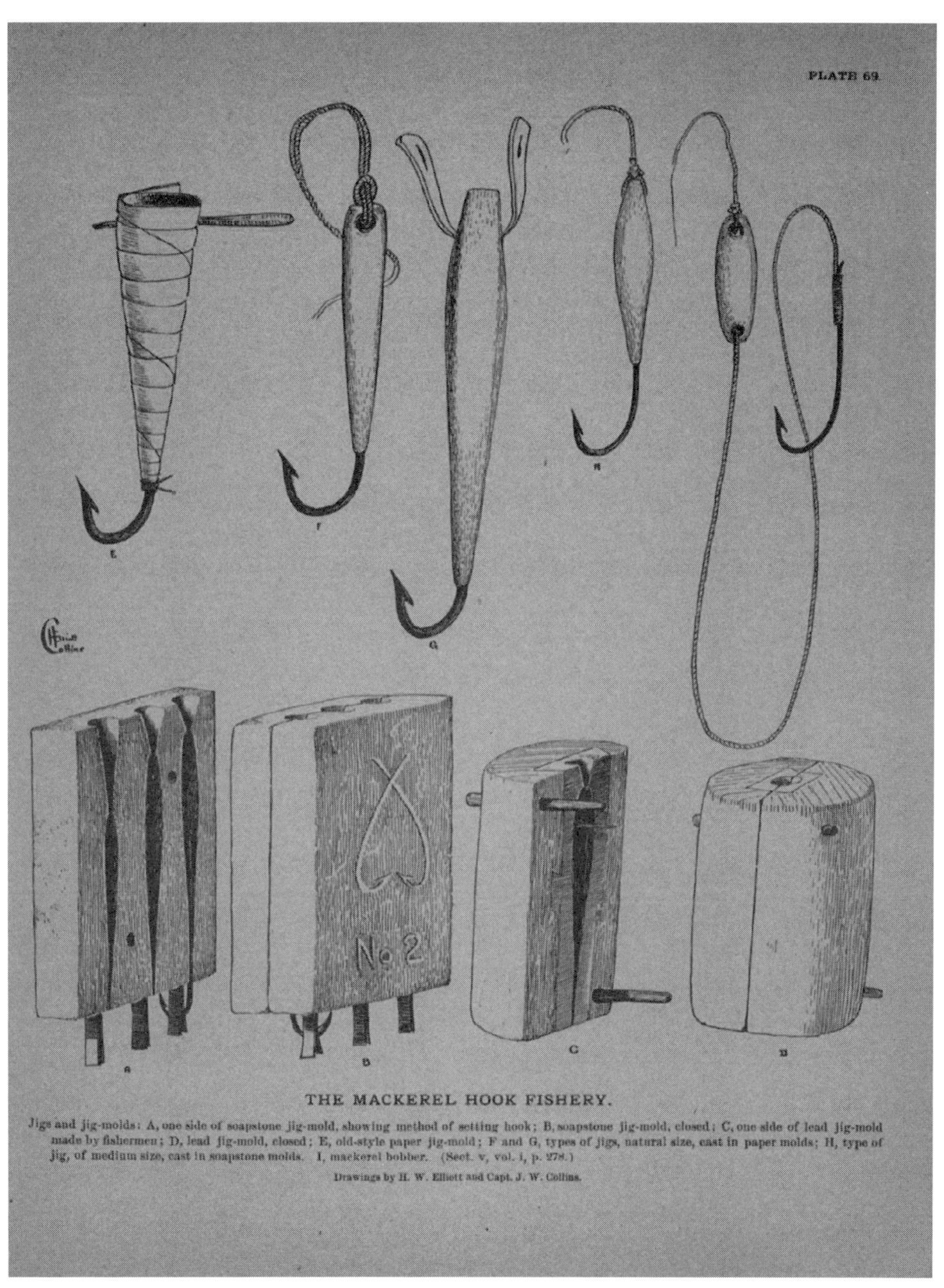

Look familiar? This plate is from 1876.

who probably has a better line on the fish. Plus, you won't have to clean your boat. Mackerel fishing is fun—but as messy as chunking for tuna. When you find the fish, you can hold them by putting a bag of bunker chum overboard. You can also just drift and chum and hope they come along, but I wouldn't. It's better to actively seek them, find them, and then use chum.

Traditional mackerel tackle consists of a medium-heavy conventional rod with a tip capable of handling eight to 10 ounces. This is for getting a heavy jig down if currents are strong in deep water. Plus if you are party-boat fishing, it's only polite to use such tackle. Being heavy, it ensures you can control four or five macks at a time with less chance of tangling your rail mates. When the run is on, plan on getting to the boat early to get a spot, and expect elbow-to-elbow fishing. Leave the light stuff home.

If you are on your own boat however, break out light, 10 pound spin or casting tackle and have a ball. Mackerel are excellent light tackle sport. My good friend Dave Falkner, an avid flyrodder, has enjoyed several innings with me using a single epoxy fly on sinking line. Spin and baitcasters can use small Hopkins, Sidewinders, even little popping plugs, if the macks show on top.

Typically, though, you'll be using the heavier stuff. Terminal rigging is easy: buy some mackerel trees. These consist of up to four tubed or feathered hooks, 1/0 O'Shaugnessy, usually. The tubed hooks are spread along the leader on dropper loops. A snap at the bottom allows you to attach a diamond, or other flashy, metal jig. TIP: Look for mackerel trees that have snap swivels, not just snaps, to prevent line twist. If they just have snaps, add swivels yourself.

To fish, snap on a jig heavy enough to allow vertical fishing right to the bottom. Let the jig drop to the sea floor and then retrieve it in sweeping arcs, counting each turn of the reel handle. I usually make three bottom bounces, then reel up 10 turns, make three sweeps at that depth, and then reel up another 10 turns. On and on, counting the turns, until I get bit. At that point I note the number of turns off the bottom and reel in my fish. Subsequently, I go right to that depth on the next drop. A twist on this method works well if you have more than one crewmember aboard. Have everyone fish at a different depth until someone gets in. Then, everybody moves to that depth. Fishing is often best played as a team sport.

You'll often catch more than one mackerel at a time, and my memory banks are full of scenes in which mackerel seemed to be filling the air, sea, and boat deck around me. But sometimes, despite the competitive nature of these (and most all) tightly schooling fish, it takes a knack to fill up your tree. Here's how I do it.

After a hit, I set the hook with a gentle lift and leave the rig at depth and jig a little. Usually, I can feel one or more hits on the other "open" hooks. If I'm attentive, and keep track of how many hooks I have overboard, I can often fill most of the hooks before reeling up.

Mackerel should be iced to preserve the flesh best, even if all you want them for is bait. In truth, if I blast out for a two–hour trip in my own boat, I might not bring ice. However, for an all day affair, a cooler and some cubes will go along way towards netting you superior baits. Mackerel is excellent bait for sharks. Cut into chunks, stripers and blues love it. And for fluke, mackerel belly is a prime strip bait. They're even not bad as food. If kept on ice, with the dark meat removed from the fillet, bled, and eaten fresh, or smoked, mackerel make pretty darn good table fare.

The mid-winter offshore fishery aside, the New Millenium has not provided mackerel runs the size or duration that were experienced in de-

A pile of fresh-caught macks

cades prior. But this is just a small slice of the mackerel's history. Yes, foreign fleets hammered these fish in the 60's and 70's. But Colonial records show that mackerel underwent wide swings in availability as far back as 1673 to 1689, when they suddenly became non-existent. Maybe they just chose another route for awhile. Sixteen years isn't long in the life of a species. The Ocean is vast.

CHAPTER 10
Fishing Knots
(Tangledupus frustratem)

Knots can drive anglers crazy. They come with weird names, most can be tied in several variations, and if you don't practice over the off-season, chances are fair you'll have to re-learn them once you start fishing again. In truth, and given the fact that rigs that were once "custom" can now be pretty much bought at any tackle store, you could get by with just one or two knots. The improved clinch knot is easy, strong, and can be made to serve for everything from hook attachment and, with the help of a swivel, leader attachment. If you use braided line, the Albright knot is helpful for connecting to your backing line and your leader.

For all of that, knowing how to tie knots properly and making your own rigs in advance of a trip, or over the winter, serves a purpose above and beyond economy and expertise. It keeps our heads in the game. When I'm tying rigs, I visualize its deployment in the water. If I move a dropper loop, will that present the bait better? Is a longer leader going to up my chances of success or just be a pain to stow? What's the relationship between the size and shape of the hook and the size and shape of the fish's mouth? Am I going to try a different bait or spot that requires a different approach to the rig? Whether any of these questions actually need answering is debatable. Posing them is what's important. You can bet that the guys who limit consistently ponder then all the time. So: lubricate every knot with saliva. Pull-em down in tight, neat, coils. And, if after tying it you think something's amiss, cut it off and tie it anew.

Here are the knots I use most frequently for inshore fishing around Long Island.

THE ALBRIGHT KNOT

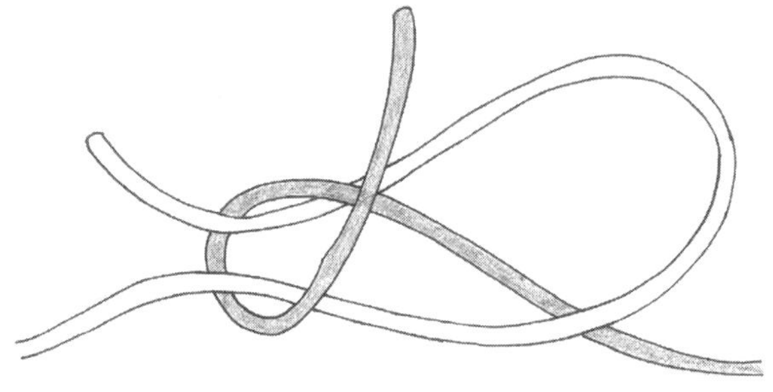

Form a loop on the end of the main line, run the second line through it, and around it.

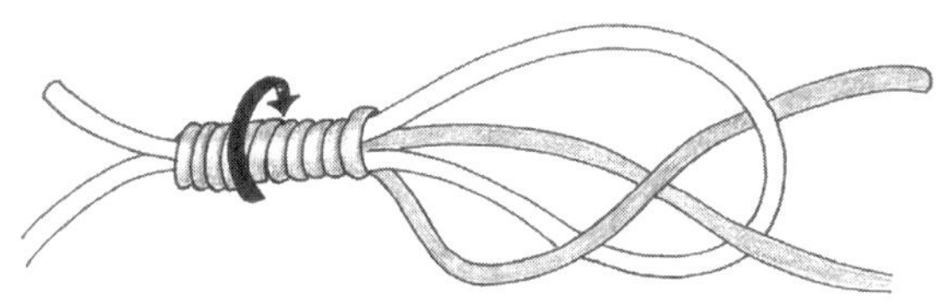

Make six wraps around the doubled main line and second line, with the tag end of the second line.

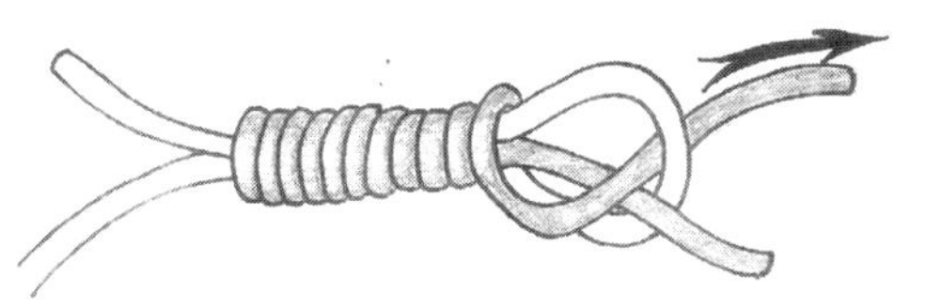

Bring the tag end out through the loop, and pull the lines tight.

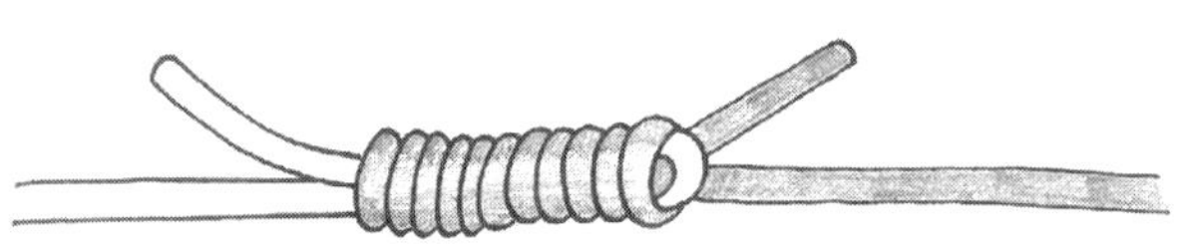

Clip off the excess.

THE DROPPER LOOP

Make a loop in the line.

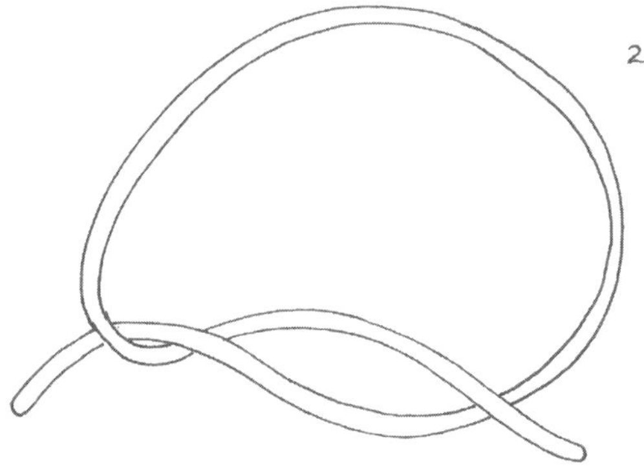

Pass the line around it four times.

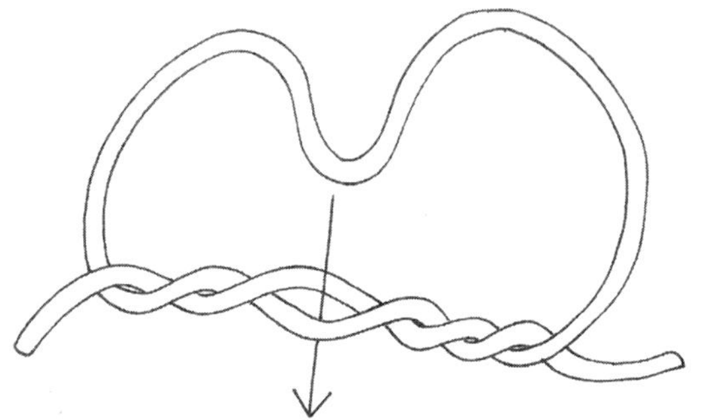

Separate the lines in the middle of the turns.

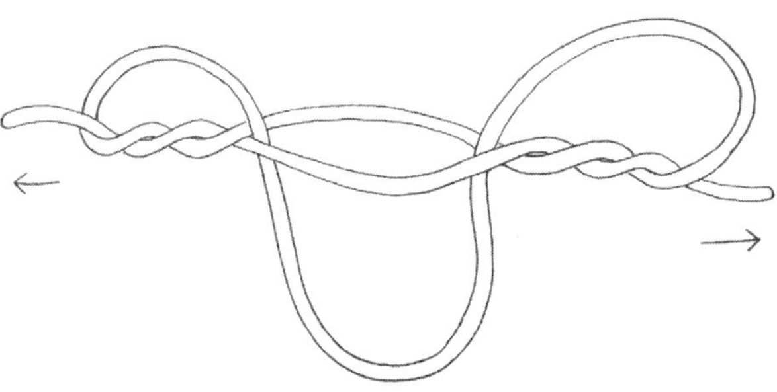

Bring the head of the loop back between the two lines, where you separated them.

Pull the loop tight.

SNELLING A HOOK

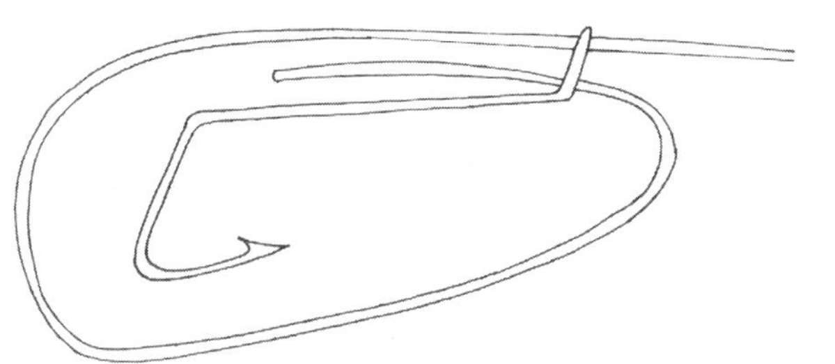

Pass the line through the eye of the hook, around the hook, and through again.

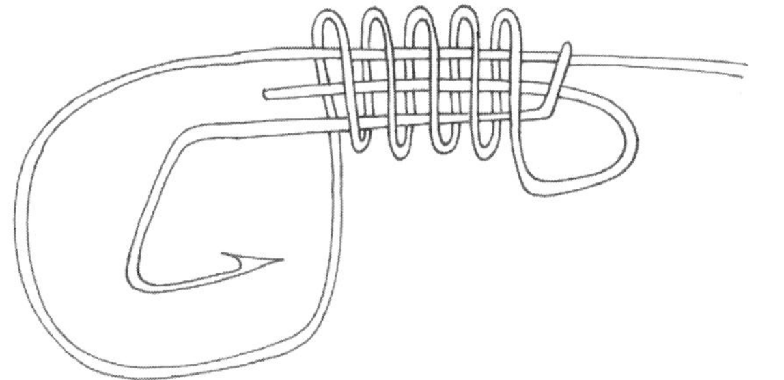

Make five wraps around both line and hook.

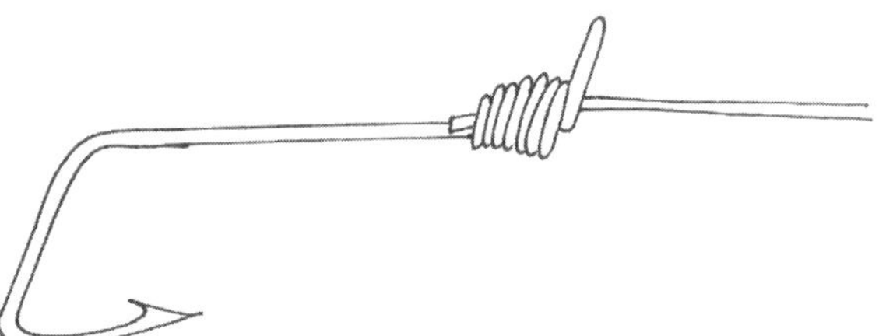

Pull it tight, and clip off any excess line.

THE IMPROVED CLINCH

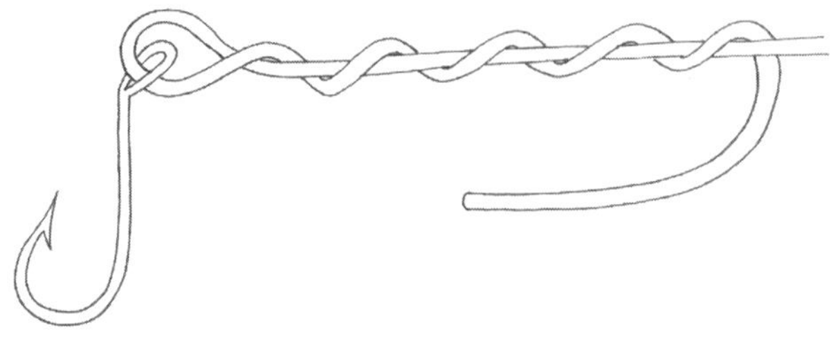

Pass the line through the eye of the hook, and wrap it back around the main line five or six times.

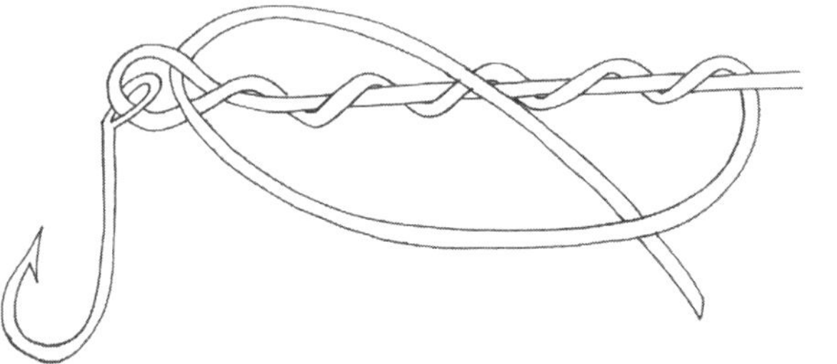

Pass the tag end through the loop at the hook's eye, and back through the loop you made, while doing so.

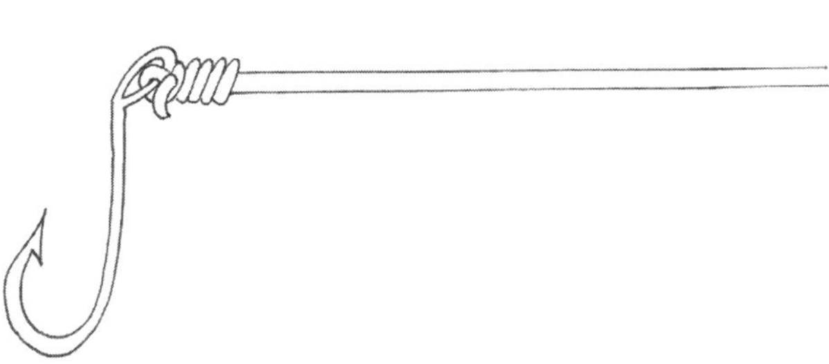

Pull it tight, and clip off any excess line.

THE PALOMAR

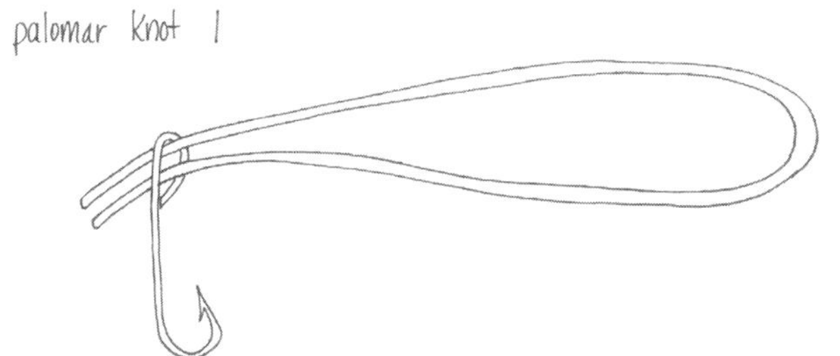

Double the end of your line, and pass it through the eye.

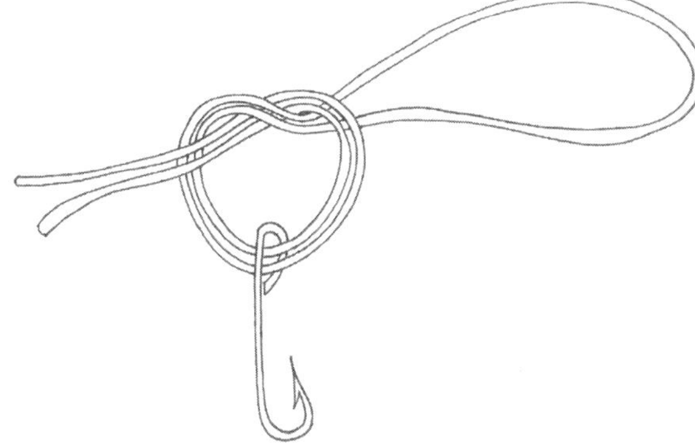

Tie an overhand knot in the doubled line.

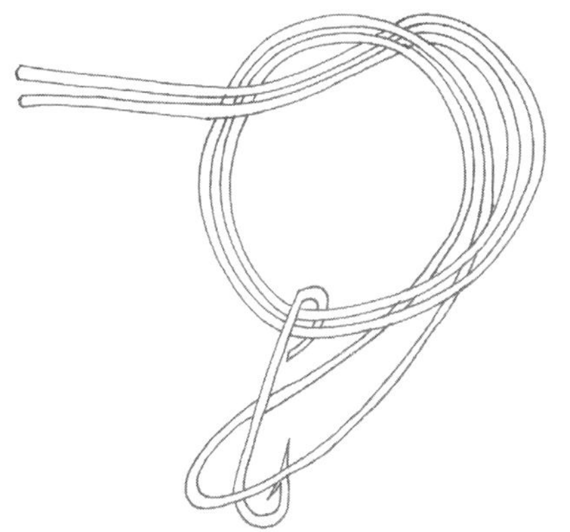

Pass the hook or eye through the loop in the end.

Kevin Falvey has spent his life fishing Long Island, from Throg's Neck to Montauk. He's caught fish in four oceans and won or placed in tournaments from Maine to Florida. He is the Senior Technical Editor at BOATING magazine and a long-time contributor to The Fisherman. He has made numerous appearances on TV and radio, at boat show seminars, and, more recently, Internet pod casts. He lives in East Quogue, NY, with his daughters, Keira and Margaret.

Boat Launch Ramp Locator

Location	Address	City	Phone	Access
WESTERN LONG ISLAND SOUND				
World's Fair Marina (1)	122-01 Northern Blvd.	Flushing, Queens	718- 478-0480	Flushing Bay, East River, Long Island Sound Huntington Harbor, Northport Harbor
Mill Dam Marina (2)	Mill Dam Road	Huntington	631-351-3089	Long Island Sound
CENTRAL LONG ISLAND SOUND				
Note: Facilities in Smithtown are for residents, only. Brookhaven Town facilities may be used by non-residents for a higher fee. Contact Brookhaven Town (631) 451-6100 and Smithtown (631) 360-7643 for information.				
Mount Sinai Marina (3)	Harbor Beach Road	Mt. Sinai	631- 928-0199	Mt. Sinai Harbor, Long Island Sound
EASTERN LONG ISLAND SOUND				
Mattituck Creek Boat Ramp	County Road 48	Mattituck	(631) 765-1801	Mattituck Creek, Great Peconic Bay
DEC Oysterponds Boat Ramp (4)	Main Road	East Marion	(631) 444-0439	Block Island Sound, Long Island Sound
PECONIC ESTUARY/NORTH FORK				
Orient-by-the-Sea (5)	Main Road	Orient	(631) 324-2424	Plum Gut
Strong's Marine (6)	Camp Mineola Road	Mattituck	(631) 298-4470	Great Peconic Bay
Cutchogue Harbor Marina Inc.	West Creek Avenue	Cutchogue	(631) 734-6993	Wickham Creek, Cutchogue Harbor, Great Peconic Bay
Port of Egypt Marine	Main Road	Southold	(631) 765-2445	Great Peconic Bay
New Suffolk Boat Ramp	First Avenue	New Suffolk	(631) 765-1800	Southold Bay
South Jamesport Boat Ramp (7)	Peconic Boulevard	South Jamesport	(631) 727-3200	Great Peconic Bay
PECONIC ESTUARY/SHELTER ISLAND				
Daniel Lord Road Ramp (8)	Daniel Lord Road	Shelter Island	(631) 749-0291	Shelter Island Sound, Block Island Sound
PECONIC ESTUARY/SOUTH FORK				
Note: Many facilities in this area are provided for residents of Southampton and Quogue, only. Contact Southampton Town (631) 283-6000 and Quogue Village (631) 653-4498 for information.				
Gone Fishing Marina (9)	East Lake Drive	Montauk	(631) 668-3232	Lake Montauk, Block Island Sound, Atlantic Ocean
Montauk Yatch Club	Star Island Road	Montauk	(631) 668-3100	Lake Montauk, Block Island Sound, Atlantic Ocean
GREAT SOUTH BAY & MORICHES BAY				
Moriches Bay Waterway Access (10)	Moriches Island Road	East Moriches	(631)444-0439	Moriches Bay
Smith Point Marina (11)	Smith Point	Shirley	(613) 281-7788	Great South Bay, Narrow Bay, Moriches Bay
Hecksher State Park (12)	Hecksher Parkway	East Islip	(631) 581-2100	Great South Bay
Captree State Park (13)	Robert Moses Cuaseway	Babylon	(631) 581-2100	Great South Bay
Frost Boat Yard	Shore Road	Babylon	(631) 669-1645	Moriches Bay
Charlie's Marina	910 South Broadway	Lindenhurst	(631) 226-6250	Great South Bay
MECOX BAY, SHINNECOCK BAY & QUANTUCK CANAL				
Note: Many facilities in this area are provided for residents of Southampton and Quogue, only. Contact Southampton Town (631) 283-6000 and Quogue Village (631) 653-4498 for information.				
Edward Warner 'Old Ponquogue Bridge' Marine Park (14)	Dune Road	Hampton Bays	(631) 283-6000	Shinnecock Bay
SOUTH OYSTER BAY/JAMAICA BAY				
Hempstead Town Marina (15)	Lido Boulevard	Point Lookout	(516) 431-9200	Reynolds Channel, Jones Inlet
Albany Avenue Boat Ramp (16)	Albany Avenue	Freeport	(516) 377-2314	Merrick River, Freeport Creek, Jones Inlet
Old Harbor Marina	Alder Place	Seaford	(516) 758-0358	Oyster Bay, Jones Inlet
Treasure Island Marine Basin	Ocean Avenue	Seaford	(516) 758-0358	Oyster Bay, Jones Inlet
Inwood Marina (17)	Bayswater Boulevard	Inwood	(516) 239-0945	Jamaica Bay
FRESHWATER BOAT LAUNCH RAMPS				
Lake Ronkonkoma Fishing Access Site (18)	Victory Drive	Ronkonkoma	(631) 444-0280	Lake Ronkonkoma
Lower Peconic River	Route 25	Riverhead	(631) 444-0280	Peconic River
Lower Yaphank Lake	Exit 67, off LIE, north on Route 21	Yaphank	(631) 444-0280	Yaphank Lake
Forge Pond/Peconic Lake	South River Rd., 1/2 mile east of Edwards Ave.	Calverton	(631) 444-0280	Peconic River/Forge Pond
Fort Pond	South Erie Street, off Edgemer Street	Montauk	(631) 444-0280	Fort Pond

This abbreviated directory was compiled from the NYS DEC publication, Boat Launch Ramps Long Island Region. Visit www.dec.state.ny.us/website/dfwmr/marine/access/mrfacces.html and www.dec.state.ny.us/website/dfwmr/fish/foe4cbl1.html to download the complete list. See page 7-8 for the site locations in parentheses.

Fishing Access

Authority[a]	Phone
NYS DEC Freshwater Unit	
General Information, Access & Stocking	(631) 444-0280
Fishing & Hunting License	(631) 444-0273
NYS DEC Marine Bureau	
General Information	(631) 444-0435
Marine Permits	(631) 444-0470
Fishing Access	(631) 444-0439
NYS Office of Parks	
Long Island Region(b)	(631) 669-1000
Belmont Lake State Park(f)	(631) 667-5055
Caleb Smith State Park(e)	(631) 265-1054
Captree State Park(b)	(631) 669-0449
Caumsett State Park(b)	(631) 423-1770
Connetquot State Park(e)	(631) 581-1005
Hecksher State Park(b)	(631) 581-2100
Hither Hiller State Park(b)	(631) 668-2461
Jones Beach State Park(b)	(631) 785-1600
Montauk State Park(b)	(631) 668-2461
Robert Moses State Park(b)	(631) 669-0470
Sunken Meadow State Park(b)	(631) 269-4333
Wildwood State Park(b)	(631) 929-4314
Nassau County Parks, Recreation & Museums	
General Information	(516) 575-0200
Bay Park(d)	(516) 593-5855
Inwood Park(d)	(516) 571-7894
Wantagh Park(d)	(516) 785-7777
Suffolk County Parks, Recreation & Cons.	
General Information	(631) 854-4949
Blydenburgh County Park(e)	(631) 369-4966
Southaven County Park(e)	(631) 854-1415
Town Municipalities	
Babylon(d)	(631) 369-4966
Brookhaven(d)	(631) 854-1415
East Hampton(b)	(631) 329-3078
Hempstead(d)	(516) 292-9000 (516) 431-9200
Huntington(d)	(631) 351-3089
Islip(c)	(631) 224-5648
North Hempstead(d)	(631) 288-1654
Oyster Bay(d)	
Harry Tappen Beach	(516) 671-0484
Theodore Roosevelt Beach	(516) 922-5812
Tobay Beach & Boat Basin	(516) 679-0720
John J. Burns Park	(516) 797-5010
Riverhead(b)	(631) 727-5744
Shelter Island(d)	(631) 749-1166
Smithtown(d)	(631) 269-1122
Southampton(b)	(631) 283-6011 or (631) 287-5717
Southold(d)	(631) 765-5182 or (631) 765-1801
Cities & Villages	
Amityville(c)	(631) 264-6000
Babylon(c)	(631) 669-1500
Bellport(c)	(631) 854-1415
Freeport(c)	(516) 377-2314
Quogue(c)	(631) 653-4498
Sag Harbor(c)	(631) 725-2368
Westhampton Beach(c)	(631) 288-1654
Other	
Gateway National Recreation Area (Ranger Station)	(718) 474-4600

[a]Key to codes:- (b) fishing access, including boat launch ramp and four wheel drive permit; (c) boat launch ramp/permit; (d) beach fishing/boat launching; (e) fishing access; and (f) row boat rental

The publishers would like to thank NYFTTA, United Boatmen of New York, The Bob Sweeney Sportfishing Education Center, North Fork Captains Association, Montauk Boatmen's & Captain's Association, Captree Boatmen's Association, the NYS DEC, and the sportfishing community for their support and contributions to this publication.

Site Name		Northwest	Northeast	Southeast	Southwest
Rockaway Reef	Latitude Longitude	40°32.730 73°51.210	40°32.730 73°49.920	40°32.200 73°49.920	40°32.200 73°51.210
	Loran C	26935.6 43753.5	26925.5 43752.1	26924.1 43746.9	26934.1 43748.2
Atlantic Beach Reef	Latitude Longitude	40°32.020 73°43.700	40°32.020 73°42.400	40°31.530 73°42.400	40°31.530 73°43.700
	Loran C	26874.4 43737.6	26864.0 43736.2	26862.7 43731.5	26873.1 43732.9
Fishing Line (McAllister Grounds)	Latitude Longitude	40°32.300 73°39.700	40°32.300 73°39.200	40°32.100 73°39.200	40°32.100 73°39.700
	Loran C	26843.2 43735.6	26839.3 43735.1	26838.8 43733.2	26842.7 43733.7
Hempstead Town Reef	Latitude Longitude	40°31.250 73°33.350	40°31.500 73°31.370	40°30.920 73°31.550	40°30.670 73°33.520
	Loran C	26790.0 43719.0	26775.0 43719.0	26775.0 43713.0	26790.0 43713.0
Fire Island Reef	Latitude Longitude	40°36.100 73°13.500	40°36.100 73°11.500	40°35.600 73°11.500	40°35.600 73°13.500
	Loran C	26640.9 43739.8	26624.4 43737.7	26623.2 43733.1	26639.7 43735.2
Moriches Anglers Reef	Latitude Longitude	40°43.470 72°46.640	40°43.540 72°46.360	40°43.470 72°46.330	40°43.400 72°46.615
	Loran C	26432.9 43771.9	26430.7 43772.1	26430.5 43771.4	26432.5 43771.2

Site Name		Northwest	Northeast	Southeast	Southwest
Shinnecock Reef	Latitude Longitude	40°48.167 72°28.667	40°48.217 72°28.300	40°48.083 72°28.333	40°48.033 72°28.717
	Loran C	26289.0 43788.0	26286.0 43788.0	26286.0 43787.0	26289.0 43787.0
Fisherman (Yellowbar) Reef	Latitude Longitude	40°37.954 73°14.595	40°38.051 73°14.354	40°38.016 73°14.327	40°37.918 73°14.569
	Loran C	26652.1 43757.2	26651.8 43756.9	26653.7 43756.1	26654.0 43756.5
Kismet Reef	Latitude Longitude	40°38.140 73°12.938	40°38.310 73°12.329	40°38.285 73°12.317	40°38.115 73°12.926
	Loran C	26636.7 43757.0	26636.5 43756.7	26641.2 43755.9	26641.3 43756.1
Smithtown Reef	Latitude Longitude	40°55.975 73°11.170	40°56.005 73°11.070	40°55.955 73°11.035	40°55.920 73°11.140
	Loran C	26671.9 43916.3	26671.4 43916.5	26671.0 43916.1	26671.6 43915.8
Matinecock Reef	Latitude Longitude	40°54.579 73°37.741	40°54.689 73°37.250	40°54.581 73°37.210	40°54.479 73°37.701
	Loran C	26891.4 43943.7	26887.6 43944.0	26887.0 43943.0	26890.8 43942.7

Rockaway Reef
Location: Atlantic Ocean, 1.6 nautical miles south of Rockaway Beach
Size: 413 acres (2000 yards X 1000 yards)
Depth: 32 to 40 feet
Materials: 6,000 tires in 3-tire units; 60 steel buoys; rock; concrete slabs, pipes, culvert, decking and rubble.
Comments: Rock rubble is scattered throughout the reef site.
* Fish pots banned by State Law *

Atlantic Beach Reef
Location: Atlantic Ocean, 3.0 nautical miles south of Atlantic Beach
Size: 413 acres (2000 yards by 1000 yards)
Depth: 55 to 64 feet
Materials: 30,000 tires in 3-tire units; 404 auto bodies; 10 Good Humor trucks; 9 barges; the tug Fran S; a steel lifeboat; steel crane and boom; surplus armored vehicles; rock; concrete slabs, pipes, culvert, decking and rubble; 530,000 cubic yards of rock from a U.S. Army Corps of Engineers dredging project.
Comments: Auto and truck bodies have disintegrated. Rock drop along north boundary of site.

Fishing Line (McAllister Grounds)
Location: Atlantic Ocean, 2.8 nautical miles south of Long Beach
Size: 115 acres (925 yards X 600 yards)
Depth: 50 to 53 feet
Materials: Concrete bridge rubble; 4 steel barges; 2 steel workboats; sailboat; 8,900 cubic yards of rock.
* Fish pots banned by State Law *

Hempstead Town Reef
Location: Atlantic Ocean, 3.3 nautical miles south of Jones Beach State Park
Size: 744 acres (3000 yards X 1200 yards)
Depth: 50 to 72 feet
Materials: 11 vessels; a drydock; surplus armored vehicles; concrete rubble; 2 steel barges.

Fire Island Reef
Location: Atlantic Ocean, 2.0 nautical miles south of the Fire Island Lighthouse
Size: 744 acres (3000 yards by 1200 yards)
Depth: 62 to 73 feet
Materials: 1500 tires; 10 barges; 2 boat hulls; 2 steel clam dredges; 2 drydocks; sailboat; surplus armored vehicles; coal ash blocks (experimental); rock; concrete cesspool rings, slabs and rubble.
* Fish pots banned by State Law *

Moriches Anglers Reef
Location: Atlantic Ocean, 2.4 nautical miles south of Moriches Inlet
Size: 14 acres (450 yards by 150 yards)
Depth: 70 to 75 feet
Materials: 2 small boats; 4 steel barges; 5 steel trawlers; 2 steel vessels; 90 foot steel tugboat; surplus armored vehicles; 600 tires; 112 foot steel clam dredge; concrete pipes.
* Fish pots banned by State Law *

Shinnecock Reef
Location: Atlantic Ocean, 2.0 Nautical miles south of Shinnecock Inlet
Size: 35 acres (680 by 250 yards)
Depth: 79 to 84 feet
Materials: 3,000 tires in 3-tire units; 3 barges; a tug; a wood drydock; 2 wood boats; a steel cruiser; a steel and concrete tower; 2 steel trawlers; surplus armored vehicles; steel and concrete bridge rubble; 2,400 tons of jetty stone.
Comments: Charted dimensions and location are different from permitted ones.
Fish pots banned by State Law

Fisherman (Yellowbar) Reef
Location: Great South Bay, 900 yards east of the Robert Moses Fixed Bridge
Size: 7 acres (400 yards by 85 yards)
Depth: 25 to 40 feet
Materials: 100 concrete Reef Ball units; concrete pipes; 2 wooden vessels; steel cruiser; steel barge.
* Fish pots banned by State Law *

Kismet Reef
Location: Great South Bay, 120 yards north of the South Beach, between Kismet and the National Seashore dock
Size: 10 acres; (1000 yards by 50 yards)
Depth: 16 to 25 feet
Materials: 4000 tires in 3-tire units; 2 barges; 24,000 cement blocks; concrete slabs, culvert and rubble.
Comments: Charted dimensions are different from permitted ones.
* Fish pots banned by State Law *

Smithtown Reef
Location: Long Island Sound, 1.6 nautical miles northwest of Stony Brook Harbor entrance
Size: 3 acres (150 yards by 100 yards)
Depth: 38 to 40 feet
Materials: 22,000 tires; 5 barges; 6 concrete-filled steel cylinders.
Comments: Tires are scattered around site.
* Fish pots banned by State Law *

Matinecock Reef
Location: Long Island Sound, 0.5 nautical miles north of Peacock Point
Size: 41 acres (800 yards by 250 yards)
Depth: 30 to 40 feet
Materials: unknown
Comments: Undeveloped. Charted dimensions are different from permitted ones.
* Fish pots banned by State Law *

Do You Want to Catch More Fish? Then Get Geared Up!

All of Geared Up's fishing books—covering sharking, offshore fishing, fluke fishing, stripers, and more—are written by professional saltwater anglers who are dedicated to producing books that are jam-packed with information instead of fluff. We started the fishing division because we were tired of reading books written by people who don't know the difference between a buzz bait and a ballyhoo. But our authors are professional captains, mates, and tournament anglers. You'll find their bylines in magazines such as *Saltwater Sportsman, Sport Fishing, Coastal Fisherman, The Fisherman,* and *Big Game Fishing Journal.* If you want poignant fishing stories, get Hemingway. But if you want to become a more effective saltwater angler, get Geared Up.

Our guarantee: If these books don't help you catch more fish, we'll eat our bait!

Geared Up Publications is a Division of Schiffer Publishing, Ltd.
www.schifferbooks.com